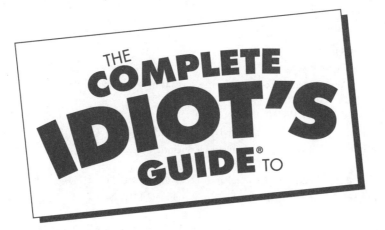

THE
COMPLETE
IDIOT'S
GUIDE® TO

Oracles

D1607258

*by Gary R. McClain, Ph.D.,
and Carolyn Flynn*

ALPHA

A member of Penguin Group (USA) Inc.

ALPHA BOOKS

Published by the Penguin Group

Penguin Group (USA) Inc., 375 Hudson Street, New York, New York 10014, U.S.A.

Penguin Group (Canada), 10 Alcorn Avenue, Toronto, Ontario, Canada M4V 3B2 (a division of Pearson Penguin Canada Inc.)

Penguin Books Ltd., 80 Strand, London WC2R 0RL, England

Penguin Ireland, 25 St Stephen's Green, Dublin 2, Ireland (a division of Penguin Books Ltd.)

Penguin Group (Australia), 250 Camberwell Road, Camberwell, Victoria 3124, Australia (a division of Pearson Australia Group Pty. Ltd.)

Penguin Books India Pvt. Ltd., 11 Community Centre, Panchsheel Park, New Delhi—110 017, India

Penguin Group (NZ), cnr Airborne and Rosedale Roads, Albany, Auckland 1310, New Zealand (a division of Pearson New Zealand Ltd.)

Penguin Books (South Africa) (Pty.) Ltd., 24 Sturdee Avenue, Rosebank, Johannesburg 2196, South Africa

Penguin Books Ltd., Registered Offices: 80 Strand, London WC2R 0RL, England

International Standard Book Number: 1-59257-497-1
Library of Congress Catalog Card Number: 2005937490

08   07   06   8   7   6   5   4   3   2   1

Interpretation of the printing code: The rightmost number of the first series of numbers is the year of the book's printing; the rightmost number of the second series of numbers is the number of the book's printing. For example, a printing code of 06-1 shows that the first printing occurred in 2006.

Printed in the United States of America

Note: This publication contains the opinions and ideas of its authors. It is intended to provide helpful and informative material on the subject matter covered. It is sold with the understanding that the authors, book producer, and publisher are not engaged in rendering professional services in the book. If the reader requires personal assistance or advice, a competent professional should be consulted.

The authors, book producer, and publisher specifically disclaim any responsibility for any liability, loss, or risk, personal or otherwise, which is incurred as a consequence, directly or indirectly, of the use and application of any of the contents of this book.

Most Alpha books are available at special quantity discounts for bulk purchases for sales promotions, premiums, fundraising, or educational use. Special books, or book excerpts, can also be created to fit specific needs.

For details, write: Special Markets, Alpha Books, 375 Hudson Street, New York, NY 10014.

Publisher: *Marie Butler-Knight*
Editorial Director: *Mike Sanders*
Senior Managing Editor: *Jennifer Bowles*
Senior Acquisitions Editor: *Randy Ladenheim-Gil*
Book Producer: *Lee Ann Chearney/Amaranth Illuminare*
Development Editor: *Lynn Northrup*
Production Editor: *Megan Douglass*

Copy Editor: *Keith Cline*
Cover Designer: *Becky Harmon*
Book Designer: *Trina Wurst*
Indexer: *Brad Herriman*
Layout: *Becky Harmon*
Proofreading: *John Etchison*

Contents at a Glance

Appendixes

Contents

Appendixes

Introduction

It's not health, and surprisingly, it's not wealth. Like the Hebrew King Solomon, we want wisdom. Wisdom is the key that opens the door to health, wealth, and the pursuit of happiness.

Ancient peoples knew this. They had elaborate enterprises devoted to the delivery of oracles—the Oracle of Delphi in Greece chief among them.

This book is about how to use oracles to access the wisdom that will help you live your fullest life. Oracles are divine messages that come in the form of people—in the visionaries and emissaries that shaped our worlds. They also are in places, the sacred places that the hearts and souls of our ancestors sought out to receive wisdom. Or oracles can be the messages themselves, written in inscriptions or echoed in the pronouncements of a conduit of wisdom.

Oracles have their root in mythology and archetypes, the stories and figures that humans share, that transcend time or distance. What we share is this: we all want to live our best lives. We all want to be assured that happiness is ours. We just want to know the right path.

Oracles take us on a journey. You, too, are about to go on a journey of self-discovery in this book. We promise you, it will be a magical, mystical journey.

How to Use This Book

This book is divided into a five-part exploration of how to use oracles to gain insight about living your fullest life.

Part 1, "We Want Answers!" introduces you to oracles in their many shapes and forms, ancient and contemporary.

Part 2, "Wise Oracle Sees All," delves into a further understanding of the people who serve as oracles, the places that speak to us as oracles, and the messages themselves.

Part 3, "Wise Oracle Knows All," takes a deeper look at what we want to know when we consult oracles. It will help you compose your questions, prepare your heart, and prepare gifts to your oracles—and maybe even become one yourself.

Part 4, "Wise Oracle Tells All," examines various styles of oracles, from Egyptian yes-or-no oracles and the I Ching, to nature and poetry, from the ancient Mayan calendar to your own dreams and visions.

Part 5, "Everyday Oracles," puts your knowledge to practical application, where you can improve your loving relationships. You'll find a guide to oracle decks, as well as tips for drawing on oracle wisdom on-the-fly.

Following these parts you'll find three useful appendixes: an oracle finder that will guide you to websites, sacred places, and oracle decks; a list of resources if you want to delve deeper into this topic; and a glossary of terms.

Extras

Throughout each chapter of this book, we've added four types of extra information in boxes, to help you learn even more about manifesting your vision:

Tell It Like It Is

These stories and related information about oracle wisdom serve to deepen your understanding of how they might apply to your life.

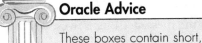

Oracle Advice

These boxes contain short, practical tips that help develop your oracle wisdom techniques.

At Your Peril

These cautionary tidbits help steer you clear of less-than-reliable oracles and otherwise take the wisdom with a discerning eye.

Wise Words

These definitions provide more illumination to a specific aspect of oracles.

Acknowledgments

From Gary:

I would like to acknowledge friends and clients who both challenge and teach me, often at the same time, and Carolyn Flynn for being a patient and insightful co-author.

From Carolyn:

I would like to acknowledge the clear, calm, steady hand of my co-author, Gary R. McClain. Many thanks go to book producer Lee Ann Chearney for sending me work that expands my imagination and takes me into the deeper realm of the soul. Thanks, also, for keeping me on track. Thanks to Alpha Books for its commitment to publishing books like this that enrich people's lives. Mostly, though, I would like to thank you, the reader, and encourage you to believe that you can live your best life.

Finally, I'd like to thank my twins, who bring me joy every day as they turn their wise eyes on the world. And I would like to thank my Creator and Source, who continues to bless me with wisdom, strength, and grace amid the chaos, shedding light on my path so that I may see the way.

Trademarks

All terms mentioned in this book that are known to be or are suspected of being trademarks or service marks have been appropriately capitalized. Alpha Books and Penguin Group (USA) Inc. cannot attest to the accuracy of this information. Use of a term in this book should not be regarded as affecting the validity of any trademark or service mark.

Part 1

We Want Answers!

No matter the time or place, no matter the culture, oracles have been present. That's because—call it what you want, animal, vegetable, or mineral—oracles represent timeless wisdom that people of all cultures have recognized, no matter the form. Wisdom transcends the trappings of culture, whether the oracle is the mysterious mutterings from a cave in ancient Greece or stock-market advice spewed in electronic bits and bytes. In this part, we define oracles, help you recognize them, help you cultivate them, and put you at ease with any skepticism you might have. Along the way, we give you a walking tour of oracles, from ancient Greece to now.

Chapter 1

What, Where, or Who Is an Oracle?

In This Chapter

◆ Identifying oracles

◆ The oracle of oracles: Delphi

◆ Starting the journey: Nine Wise Ways

◆ Introducing the Goddess Oracle Deck

◆ Getting to know oracles

An oracle is a message of divine wisdom, but what is it, really? Is it a person, place, or thing? Is it animal, vegetable, mineral? Is it bigger than a breadbox? Will it fit in your laptop case? Just how many megabytes is this message?

For some people, the word *oracle* conjures up images of white marble ruins of ancient Greece. Others think of the database software company Oracle. For still others, it may summon dark visions of the occult, whereas others are reminded of biblical oracles such as Samuel or Ezekiel. Whether any of those or none of those came to mind, it's time to deepen your knowledge of what, where, and who oracles are. There are as many ways to use oracles to enrich your understanding of your life as there are stars in the sky.

Divine Announcements

A good place to start is the dictionary. *Webster's New World Dictionary* defines an *oracle* as a divine announcement. The definition breaks down into three meanings. An oracle can take the form of a person, a place, *and* a thing. Among the Greeks and Romans, an oracle was the *place* where people consulted deities. It also was the medium—or the person—who relayed the message from the deities. It could also refer to the revelation itself. The English word derives from the Latin word *oraculum*, which came from the root word *orare*, which means "to speak, pray, or beseech." (And there is some beseeching involved, as we will get to in Chapter 10.) Of course, the Latin word comes from the family of words that produces words such as *oral*. Oracles were generally spoken, though they can many times be written.

Wise Words

Are **oracles** a who, a what, or a where? Oracles are traditionally defined as divine messages requiring interpretation, sacred places of prophecy, or priests/priestesses who embody the divine message. So the answer is, yes, they can be a who, a what, *and* a where.

Although most of us think of the Oracle of Delphi from Greek mythology, oracles are not limited to the Greek tradition. Nor are they limited to any one belief system. Oracles turn up in every written religious text from Christianity to Buddhism to Judaism and beyond. Before oracles became all the rage in Greece, there was already an oracle underground, as it were, with accounts of sacred trees, rivers, or caves. Many of the places of oracular prophecy that the Greeks set aside were sacred long before the rise of Greek culture. So it's clear that oracles have been around since the beginning of time—since the first inquiring minds wanted to know.

So an oracle can be the message itself, the place where the message was received, or the person interpreting the message. An oracle can have one, two, or all three of these aspects. Many oracle traditions begin with a divine message, and the place at which the message was received is deemed sacred. In this act, the culture announced its intention to receive further wisdom. Contact had been made. Out of that creation of a sacred place often came a priest, priestess, or prophet, who continued to receive and interpret divine messages. So, as you see, oracles can become more "organized" as thriving entities over time. That is pretty much what happened at Delphi. It was the ancient Greek equivalent of a modern-day corporation.

To delve into what oracles really are, let's start right there at the beginning, with the Oracle of Delphi at the Temple of Apollo in Greece. Let's remember that Apollo was the sun god, the son of Zeus, and the symbol of youthful masculine beauty, often taken to represent the Greek ideal. As with many myths, it all started with a serpent, in this case a python. A cave at Delphi was the abode of a great serpent, Python. Apollo climbed up the side of Mount Parnassus and engaged the serpent in combat. After a protracted battle, he slew the serpent and threw him down a fissure, into the cave that became the oracle. From that day forward, Apollo gave oracles from the vent of the cave.

From the fissure, fumes rose that were supposed to have come from the dead body of the serpent. The legend grew, and many pilgrims flocked to the site, all with the same result: religious ecstasy, wild dancing, unintelligible muttering. Some, delirious, threw themselves into the fissure. To protect the surge of wisdom-seeking tourists from this fate, a priestess was designated to act as a mediator between the oracle and the wisdom seekers. A female hierophant of the oracle was named Pythoness, or Pythia, which quite literally means "one who has been thrown into a state of religious ecstasy by inhaling fumes rising from decomposing matter." With that dramatic event, a tradition was born.

> ### Tell It Like It Is
>
> One legend says the Oracle of Delphi was discovered by shepherds who were tending their flocks near Mount Parnassus. They noticed that goats who had wandered near the fissure in the rock danced and cried out and acted quite silly. A shepherd approached to check it out, and when he inhaled the fumes, he was seized with a prophetic ecstasy. He danced, he sang, he jabbered unintelligibly—and he foretold the future.

Meet Gary, Meet Carolyn

Gary's work life is on two tracks. He is a counselor, with a focus on stress management, life transitions, and catastrophic illness. He is also a researcher, working mainly in health care, for companies and hospitals. In both sides of his work, Gary has clients who are looking for oracle wisdom. His counseling clients are looking for someone who can give them answers, who can be wise and discerning and tell them what they need to do in their lives. With clients who have a devastating illness, they are not just looking for answers, but also some kind of hope. Gary's business clients are looking for that singular insight that will get their communications spinning in the right direction.

Carolyn is a journalist, literary fiction writer, and editor of a women's magazine. It's appropriate that her magazine's name is *SAGE*, which means wise person, because the sensibility of the magazine is that of empowering women to live their best lives. As a journalist, Carolyn's career orientation is to gather information for people so they can be resourceful and make life decisions. As a fiction writer who also teaches writing, her orientation is gaining insight into the human experience through literature.

Both Gary and Carolyn are in life roles where they can serve as conduits of wisdom, although they embrace that role quite humbly. But they also have their own sources of wisdom to which they turn, people who are in the public realm as well as in their personal lives. Among the people Gary has cultivated in his life to be oracles is a friend who is very wise and knows him very well. Sometimes he asks her for advice because she knows his talents and she can see where he is being shortsighted. He trusts her to give him a second opinion when he is not totally comfortable with his instincts.

There are oracles in Gary's field of psychology, too. But an oracle goes beyond being an expert in a specialized field of knowledge. When Gary went to the conference of the American Counseling Association, the keynote speaker was a psychiatrist who is a pioneer in treatment for mental illness. Gary wanted to hear not only what he had to say about treating people, but also about where we are as a society and where he thinks we are going. In other words, the expert had a vision and had a message beyond his specialized field. Gary would call this person an oracle.

The Qualities of Oracles

Oracles fit with our need for quick answers in a fast-food, fast-everything society, but that desire for a clear, definitive answer is the same for oracles throughout history.

Often the oracle was the beginning of a journey. In Greek mythology, the Oracle at Delphi often precipitated a journey that the seeker had not intended. Often, as in biblical oracles, the seeker was dissuaded from going forward—sometimes he did so anyway, as did the pharaoh of Egypt despite Moses' warning of the 10 plagues or King Saul despite the advice from Samuel. Sometimes an oracle transforms a life, as it did with Jacob in the Old Testament or the apostle Paul in the New Testament. The same is true of Buddha at the bodhi tree, or St. Teresa de Avila and her visions of the soul as "a castle made of a single diamond or of very clear crystal, in which there are many rooms, just as in heaven there are many mansions." Many times, an oracle foretells the future, sometimes laying it out in vivid detail that rings remarkably true despite the great distance of time, as with Nostradamus or the revelation of the apostle John.

Not all oracles are about religious matters, however. Many oracles throughout history are about the issues that hit closest to home. Some are about love, and some are about business. Should I sail my boat today? Is this a good day to start a battle? How long will this famine last? So the questions through the ages have ranged from "does he love me?" to "will there be a storm?"

So, as you can see, oracles accomplish many things. They …

- Start the process of self-discovery.

- Test the seeker.

- Warn you.

- Reassure you.

- Enlighten you.

- Open you to new possibilities.

- Get you in line with your truth.

- Reveal the future.

Always, though, oracles point to self-discovery, and the journey that an oracle precipitates leads to the getting of wisdom. Sometimes the journey seems to be off course—as in the Buddhist tale of the search for a mustard seed. A woman who was grieving the death of her child was instructed by a Buddhist master that if she could return with a mustard seed from a home that has not known grief, the master would restore her child to life. The woman knocked door after door, searching through village after village. She heard incredible stories of grief, and through them, others' courage to work through it. She felt compassion for the others whose lives were touched by grief. That journey in and of itself was the grief process for that woman. In advising her to take it, the master mapped out her grief passage, and she learned to increase her capacity for compassion.

Oracles most often require interpretation. They are often mystical in that they cannot be immediately explained in scientific terms. They are often puzzles that need to be deciphered. At best, they are ambiguous. "Why?" you might ask. Seeking and receiving the message of an oracle is a two-way street. The act of interpretation requires both the effort

At Your Peril

"What if I find this all kind of spooky?" you might ask. After all, oracles are pretty mysterious, and here we are talking about snakes and fumes. Our aim is not to steer you toward inscrutable mysteries nor New Age woo-woo divination. Instead, learning how to use oracles is about tapping into your intuition, accessing the Source in your belief system, and developing your capacity for self-knowledge.

to further understand the deity relaying the message as well as to understand yourself. Ultimately, then, we return to the oracle's message on the threshold of the Temple of Apollo: Know thyself.

Putting Oracles to Good Use

An oracle is used to connect with the divine and with natural, universal truths. But practically speaking, what the Greeks used them for was to get answers for their lives. Questions of the Greeks of nearly 3,000 years ago are much like the questions we have now: "Will I have children with this man/woman?" or "Should I go on this journey?"

To get started on using oracles, let's examine the areas of your life where you might have questions. Look at where you want to live your fullest, brightest life, and ask how it might look if you sought answers from the Divine. We have broken down areas of life where most of us have many hopes, dreams, and desires—and where we function day in and day out. We call them the Nine Wise Ways.

By the way, it might be helpful to record your answers to these questions in a journal—an Oracle Journal—that you can use throughout this book. Your journal can be plain and simple, a spiral-bound notebook with blue-lined paper, or it can be elaborate, with a beautiful beaded cover or a Monet painting or Asian calligraphy—something that inspires you. Choose the style of journal that reflects your intention for what you hope to get out of using this book. As we go along, there will be exercises for which you can keep notes.

Looking at each of the areas in the Nine Wise Ways, answer these questions:

- ◆ What are your basic needs for this area?
- ◆ What do you want but don't quite have?
- ◆ What do you desire fully?
- ◆ What would bring you bliss?
- ◆ What are the challenges you face?
- ◆ What do you wish the most often that you could change?

Before you go through the list, we want to broaden your perspective on the Ways. Notice that we did not list money, but instead listed prosperity, which is beyond the day-in, day-out flow of paycheck and bills. Notice that on career, we included calling. We make a distinction between your job and your niche in the world, your unique and personal gift to the world. If you are one of the fortunate ones, your job and your calling are one and the same. But for many of us, calling is only a sliver of career or separate from career. Whether your desire is to merge career and calling or simply to give more energy to calling outside of your day job, this is the place to start the journey.

On family, don't limit your consideration of this area to your immediate family or your family of origin. Include what we call the "family of the heart," those people who are an integral part of your life through shared values and shared experiences. For home, we called it home and hearth, because this area is about more than home decorating; it's about creating a place where you can be comfortable with who you are, a place where you invite others to share your magnificent life. Likewise, well-being is about more than physical health. Learning/self-actualization is about gaining the skills and knowledge to manifest your desires in the other Wise Ways. And when we say spirituality, we want you to know there are many ways to be spiritual that are not necessarily religious.

Nine Wise Ways

Love _____

_____

Prosperity _____

_____

Career/Calling _____

_____

Family and Community _____

_____

Home and Hearth _____

_____

Well-Being _____

_____

Creativity _____

_____

Learning/Self-Actualization _____

_____

Spirituality _____

_____

How did doing this exercise make you feel? Undoubtedly, it felt good. It always feels good to get clearer on what you *really* want in life. Probably, the excitement was mingled with some anxiety, too. Gary finds that the biggest barrier people need to overcome is being willing to admit that they want more in their lives. Admitting that opens up a whole Pandora's box of doubts and what-ifs, and also gives voice to that fear that we all have—what if I admit that I want more and figure out what I really want and then don't get it? Is my life going to be a failure? Isn't it better to try to relax and stay where I am? There may be things on your list that you hope to do but don't know whether they will happen. Even amid the excitement, there may be a doubt working like an undertow, about whether it's worth starting the journey. Never fear, that's what oracles are for—to ask the hard questions and get answers that point you on the way with confidence.

Gary works to help clients listen to their own inner wisdom, to be their own oracles in a sense. When Gary is working with a client, he tries to get the client to visualize the worst thing that could happen. In the *Harry Potter* books and movies, this is known as "name your fear." When you name something, you take its power away because you make it rational. You give it flesh and blood, and then you can deal with it. You can figure out a tactic for taking its power away, just as Harry did when he faced the Boggart in *Harry Potter and the Prisoner of Azkaban*. Oracles through ancient history played this sort of role when they told kings about their enemies and gave them advice about vanquishing them. We can face our own demons if we are willing to face down our fears. This is certainly true with the transition issues that Gary sees in his clients, whether it's going back to school, changing a career, or leaving an abusive relationship.

Fifty-Two Ways to Be Wise

Throughout this book, we use the Goddess Oracle Deck, one of the many oracle decks out there. Oracle decks are decks of cards that depict oracle figures—in this case, the feminine goddesses from many traditions. The cards are convenient, easy, and fun to use for quick guidance. We like them because the myths about these goddesses can represent strength and wisdom that you want to bring into your life. In getting to know their stories, you may find surprising insights and open yourself up to your intuition. *The Goddess Oracle Deck*, written by Amy Sophia Marashinsky and illustrated by Hrana Janto, was published originally by Element Books (2004) and is available from U.S. Games Systems, Inc. The Goddess Oracle Deck features 52 goddesses you can use as archetypal oracles of divine wisdom. We encourage you to experiment with other oracle decks as they speak to you, too. We offer a guided tour of oracle decks in Chapter 19.

Sophia: Goddess of Wisdom

SOPHIA
WISDOM

To get started, let's examine the story of the Greek goddess of wisdom, Sophia. Many believe Sophia is the representation of the Judeo-Christian god's female soul. She has many faces: the divine feminine, the mother of God, mother of creation. In this depiction, she is immersed in her symbol, the dove, which represents spirit. (In the Bible, there are several instances in which the Holy Spirit is represented by a dove.)

Contemplating on this card, imagine Sophia holding out a cup of wisdom to you. Though you are turning to oracles for guidance, Sophia is a reminder that you possess a deep wisdom within.

Isis: Mother of All

ISIS
MOTHERING

Isis, the Egyptian goddess of all life, was a mother and wife on Earth. She was worshipped as the immortal goddess, one who brings the many into being. The depth of the Egyptian people's love for her—their need for her and their trust in her—is seemingly endless, for Isis's story about undying devotion is quite touching.

Isis was the sister and the wife of Osiris. They had a brother, Seth, who was jealous of Osiris and twice arranged his murder. Seth held a banquet in honor of Osiris, and he invited Osiris to climb into a casket he had made specially to fit him. When Osiris did, Seth clamped down the lid, trapping Osiris inside it, and threw the casket into the Nile. Isis set out for her husband and found his casket. Taking the form of a large bird, she fanned him with her wings, breathing life into him. But Seth found Osiris and hacked his body into 14 pieces, scattering them throughout Egypt. Isis set out once again to find them, finding all but his penis. In its stead, she gave him one of gold, and in this form, she conceived their son, Horus.

Let Isis's story of love and devotion be inspiring to you as you set out to use oracles in your Nine Wise Ways. Your devotion to your deepest desires is what will breathe life into them.

Getting to Know the Oracles

Gaining wisdom is a way of lifting yourself out of the anxiety and doubt that might shadow your desire, want, or need. Wisdom is rock-hard certainty that keeps you from holding back. It's quite possible you don't have all the information you need just yet, but wisdom allows you to proceed anyway. That is what oracles can do.

To understand that, let's take a look at the qualities that all oracles have—no matter the tradition, no matter whether they are ancient or modern:

- **Oracles are timeless.** Even though an oracle may have existed thousands of years ago, the lesson to be learned can be just as pertinent now.

- **Oracles are mystical.** The mystical quality of an oracle requires the receiver to work to uncover the hidden truth.

- **Oracles are catalysts for action and change.** Oracles provoke us to think and act, as they did for Odysseus on his journey, and as modern-day oracle Bill Gates does, in his own way.

- **Oracles expose what was hidden and bring it to the light.** Oracles may expose your shortcomings or test your values. Oracles may demand a higher level of integrity on the part of the seeker—on the part of someone whose actions are influencing the seeker's life. Oracles deliver the truth of who you are.

- **Oracles are omniscient.** Oracles see all. They see beyond the boundaries we set for our lives. They see all factors coming together to work for the good.

Tell It Like It Is

Contemporary oracles include business entrepreneurs such as Bill Gates and Warren Buffett (called the Oracle of Omaha); the oracle in the movie *The Matrix*; the writings of mythologist Joseph Campbell or the Dalai Lama; the lyrics of rock stars such as the Irish group U2 in "Dismantling an Atomic Bomb"; and the ideas of healers such as Caroline Myss and Deepak Chopra.

♦ **Oracles are ever-present.** The oracles of ancient times, no matter the tradition, showed up in caves, trees, rivers, scarabs, music. In the ancient cultures, they didn't have a body of knowledge just a World Wide Web address away. They learned to listen for wisdom from any and every source imaginable, from the movements of the sun in the Mayan and Egyptian cultures to the rustling of the trees that sent Alexander the Great on his quest.

♦ **Oracles are both ancient and modern.** Though we think of oracles as ancient, they are just as alive in our time, showing up in writings or lyrics. The late Pope John Paul II drew flocks to him like a rock star, both in life and in his passing, because people—Catholic or not—sensed his powerful message, and believed the Holy Father to be connected to a timeless source of divine wisdom. Even the visionaries in your field of work, whether it be psychology or computer science or ecology or nuclear physics, could be considered oracles.

Opening the Door

It's just human nature to want to find some person, place, or thing in possession of the answers, a conduit to the source with the ability to unlock the wisdom of the ages for us, to tell us where we have been and where we are going. Or if this conduit can't unlock all of the wisdom, perhaps it can create the opening through which we can access a big chunk of it. Consulting oracles is a little bit like that. In beginning the quest for answers, you create the opening for oracle wisdom to find you.

The Least You Need to Know

♦ An oracle can be a person, place, or thing.

♦ Oracles turn up in many belief systems, but their truths transcend those times and places and can have meaning for us now.

♦ Using oracles is a journey of self-discovery.

♦ Oracles can provide practical answers for big-picture questions in our lives.

♦ Oracles can give you confidence in your own wisdom.

Ancient Oracles

In This Chapter

- ◆ A tour of ancient oracles
- ◆ Science, poetry, and oracles
- ◆ Oracle pilgrimages
- ◆ The inner journey

Throughout the ages, spanning many cultures, oracles have been central to obtaining wisdom. The history of oracles is rich and enduring, from the Egyptian scarab to the Mayan calendar. They are rife with mysteries, and that only makes them more alluring.

In ancient times, people looked for and found wisdom anywhere and everywhere—the Egyptians in the industriousness and foresight of ants, the Babylonians in mapping the night sky into 32 sections, Plato in his cave of shadows, and even more recently, Sir Isaac Newton in an apple. Many people, ancient or contemporary, have made long journeys to find wisdom, making pilgrimages to sacred sites such as Lourdes, Fatima, or Medjugorge, Stonehenge, the Aztec site at Teotihuacan, Chartres Cathedral in France, or Angor Wat in Cambodia. The search for wisdom is universal, common to all cultures, all times.

Beyond Delphi

First, let's get acquainted with some of the most famous oracles of ancient history. Here's a quick tour of some of the other well-known oracles besides Delphi.

Ancient Egyptians

The ancient Egyptians used prophecy for just about every decision, from life to the afterlife. The mythical Sphinx, with the body of a winged lion and the head of a woman, was the essential mystery of nature and the embodiment of a secret doctrine. To all who approached, she posed a riddle.

In the scarab beetle, the Egyptians found the embodiment of strength; they equated the scarab with the sun and the resurrection of the soul. Scarabs were considered the emissary of the sun, and the sun god, Ra, was symbolized by the head of a scarab. Egyptians adorned mummy cases with scarabs. Men and women who were initiated into the Egyptian mysteries were the oracles of their time, and they were often called scarabs.

Tell It Like It Is

One modern cultural reference to the oracles of ancient Egypt is in Steven Spielberg's movie *The Prince of Egypt,* in which Moses must outdo the two oracles of the pharaoh's court with magical effects to free his people, the Hebrews, from captivity. Both characters—one tall and knife-thin, the other short and round—are "played" by the voice of comedian, actor, and author Steve Martin (you may remember his hilarious King Tut sketch on TV's *Saturday Night Live*). Moses turns a staff into a cobra, and the two prophets must equal or better *that.*

Pythagoras

Although you may remember him from ninth-grade geometry class—Pythagorean theory, A squared plus B squared equals C squared and all that—Pythagoras was born of an oracle itself. It is told that his father was in Delphi on business and his mother urged her husband to stop by Delphi and consult the oracle about whether the weather would be good for their journey home to Syria. Instead, the oracle told Pythagoras's father that a son would be born to him who would surpass all men in beauty and wisdom. Indeed, a son was born, and the happy couple named him Pythagoras, after the Pythoness oracle.

Though he is mostly known for mathematical theory and astronomy, Pythagoras could almost be called the oracle of everything. His writings reveal he was conversant in oriental and occidental esoteric knowledge. He was initiated into the Egyptian, Babylonian, and Chaldean mysteries, possibly also the Eleusinian mysteries, as well as the mysteries of the Egyptian goddess Isis and the mysteries of Adonis. Some scholars also think he received instruction from the Jewish rabbis in the secret traditions of Moses.

Many of the symbols of Pythagoras have been interpreted as oracles, such as the "Y," said to symbolize the forking of ways, a symbol that you now can find alive and well in a deck of tarot cards—another form of oracle. The symbol signifies the moral dilemmas one must overcome when being initiated into the ways of wisdom.

Mayan Calendar

The Mayans used a sophisticated calendar to track the rhythms of the earth and guide their decisions. To this day, many find wisdom in the accuracy and complexity of their predictions. We look at this in more depth in Chapter 17.

Stargazing

Seeking wisdom by watching the movements of the stars is a tradition that derives from many cultures from the beginning of recorded time, from the Babylonians to the Egyptians, from the Mayans to the Native Americans. Of course, one of the most memorable examples of using the stars as a guide is that of the wise men who came from afar to see the Christ child. The stories of the constellations are infused with the tales of Greek mythology, all lessons to be learned, from Orion to Cassiopeia.

Pythagoras believed that the celestial bodies of the planets and stars encased souls, minds, and spirits. Some cultures in the ancient world believed that all life was evolving to a higher level of consciousness: a grain of sand was evolving to human consciousness, and humans were becoming planets, planets were becoming solar systems, and solar systems were becoming the cosmos.

Taken in that respect, the stars were more than oracles of wisdom about the way we are, the way we are with others, and the way a day may go. The stars were the stories of self-actualization—a spiritual journey of what we are becoming.

Buddha

In Buddhism, the life of the Buddha was set into motion by an oracle. The Buddha was born a prince, and a prophet told his father that he would grow up to become a great world leader or teacher. The king, not wanting him to follow that path, decided he did not want Gautama Buddha to see any of the pain and misery in the world. So the king kept him cloistered within the palace grounds, where beautiful women tended to his every need and he was surrounded by beautiful music and gardens with lotus flowers and sparkling ponds. But three times Buddha left the palace, and despite the father's edict that the kingdom be sparkling clean, with any sign of suffering erased, Buddha encountered what could be considered four oracles, in the form of men. The first three: age, frailty, and death. The last: holiness. This set him on his journey to seek release from life's sorrows and to his revelation under the bodhi tree—another oracle.

Tibetans

Oracles have long played an important role in Tibetan religion and government. Tibetans use the word *oracle* to refer to the spirit that unifies the physical and spiritual realms. The men and women who act as mediums are called *kuten*, which literally means "the physical basis," or the vessel through which the spirit is received. Today, the Tibetan Buddhist leader, the Dalai Lama, consults an oracle called *Nechung Oracle*, a process he describes in his book *Freedom in Exile* (see Appendix B).

Mohammad

Mohammad was leading a caravan of camels, working hard and living an ordinary life. He would retreat to a cave during the heat of the day to meditate. One day, he heard the voice of Allah say, "Write." From this emerged the Koran.

Black Elk

This Sioux tale is one of many Native American myths that describes shamans, or people who relay divine messages through mystical experiences. Black Elk was a young Sioux boy about 9 years old who had a prophetic vision of the intersecting hoops of his tribe with all the other tribes, joining all the nations in a grand procession. He had a vision of the central mountain, a mythological place where all the wisdom of the ages converged.

Zoroaster

Zoroaster, or Zarathustra, was a religious mystic who lived in Persia (now Iran) in about 1000 B.C.E. (though other sources say it could have been 600 B.C.E.). It is believed he was created by a ray of light that entered his mother's bosom, and so he was born of a virgin birth. It is also believed that he died, at the hands of his enemies, and three days later ascended into heaven. Zoroaster is said to have received the spirit of glory (Khva-renanh) from Yima, an Iranian deity. The religion was founded when the supreme god, Ahura Mazda, appeared to Zoroaster on Mount Elburz. Zoroaster created a new system of faith, one that requires communal daily prayers. Central to Zorastrianism are good thought, good word, and good action. In Zoroastrianism, the priesthood—those who can receive divine wisdom and perform miracles as Zoroaster did—is hereditary.

Chaldean Oracles

Many attribute the writings in the Chaldean oracles to Zoroaster, though some schol-ars believe the author was Julian the Theurgist, a soldier in the Roman army. One legend has it that Julian began uttering the wisdom of the oracles while in a trance. The Chaldeans held these oracles in high esteem, much as the Greeks did with Delphi. Their culture thrived in what we now know as northern Iraq, southeastern Turkey, and northwestern Iran, centered on the Tigris and Euphrates. The Chaldeans ruled Babylonia from about 606 to 525 B.C.E. The ascendance of their culture coin-cides with the time described in the Old Testament when Daniel served as a prophet to King Darius. Along with Egypt, Chaldea had the greatest influence on the Greek thinkers.

Kabbalah

These ancient Hebrew teachings are an inter-pretation key to the soul of the Torah, the Hebrew Bible. The writings of the Kabbalah contain the esoteric knowledge of the divine nature of God. The Kabbalah explains the unique, universal, mystical nature of God and the universe, the laws of nature, and the laws of light.

At Your Peril

Ancient oracles are a win-dow into another culture and another time, but as fascinating as they are, it's important to remain cognizant of the context. Ancient oracles were recognized for their wisdom precisely because they were the right message at the right time and place. When studying ancient oracles, stay true to your modern-day context.

More Greek Oracles

Of course, there were many Greek oracles apart from Delphi. Two of the most famous are the Oracle at Dodona and the Cave of Trophinius.

The dove was the most famous symbol of the Oracle of Dodona, where Zeus presided, although the oracle also spoke through the oak trees and vases of brass. The dove would alight on the branches of sacred oak trees and then discourse at length on religion and philosophy, answering questions from wisdom seekers. (The image of a dove also appears in both the Old and New Testaments, relaying divine messages. A dove returns to Noah's ark, bearing an olive branch that indicates dry land. A dove also descends from the clouds as John the Baptist baptizes Jesus Christ.)

At Trophinius, there was a cave that was barely visible in the side of a hill. To seek wisdom from this oracle required much preparation and gifts and offerings, something we delve into further in Chapter 10. Once prepared, the seeker would lower his feet into the cavern, and he would be drawn into the cave. When the oracle was done, it forcibly ejected him, feet first, from the cave. (Oracles, apparently, have a sense of humor!)

Biblical Oracles

The Roman Christians largely were the force that led to the end of the oracle era in Greece, shutting down the thriving business at Delphi. But paradoxically, the Judeo-Christian tradition is studded with examples of oracles throughout the Old and New Testaments. Many of the great leaders of the Bible, such as Moses, were trained as oracles, some scholars believe, and of course, there is a long tradition of prophesying the coming of the Messiah (as in the writings of Isaiah, Ezekiel, Jeremiah, and others). But there are others: after Joseph was sold into slavery, he became an oracle in the Egyptian court, prophesying a famine that the pharaoh was therefore able to prepare for and save his people from starvation. Daniel was the prophet to King Darius in Babylonia, and he was so beloved for his accurate predictions that Darius agonized over being tricked into passing a law that sentenced Daniel to the lion's den.

In the New Testament, many of the great leaders of the early Christian communities formed some of the basic tenets of the faith after receiving visions. Saul, who was persecuting the fledgling Christians, was hit by a blinding light on the road to Damascus. As a result, he made a big life change, renamed himself Paul, and established many early Christian communities. The letters of encouragement he wrote to the early Christian communities became much of the New Testament (Corinthians I and II, Thessalonians, and so on). Peter, one of Jesus' disciples, received a vision of a white sheet descending from heaven. The sheet contained a mix of every animal, four-footed mammals, beasts of prey, birds, and reptiles. From this vision, he received God's instruction to take the message of Christianity to all nations. The apostle John received visions while in exile on the Greek island of Patmos, in which he glimpsed heaven and the end times.

Then there are countless examples of angel visitations, the most notable and most artfully rendered being the annunciation, when Gabriel came to Mary to let her know she would give birth to the Christ child.

Why Oracles Still Fascinate Us

Caves that swallow you, stars that guide you, trees that speak to you, mythical creatures such as the Sphinx—no wonder oracles are utterly fascinating. They puzzle us, they tease our minds, and they spark our imaginations. Their mysteries live on, thousands of years later. But just why are they so beguiling and so enduring?

- Oracles provoke us to fresh endeavors and new encounters.

- Oracles, quite simply, make you think. They exercise mind muscle that you ordinarily don't use.

- Oracles contain timeless wisdom. Some truths transcend time, as in the teachings of Confucius or Lao-Tzu (founder of Taoism), two other oracles. They remind us we are part of something bigger than what we can immediately see.

- Oracles have changed lives dramatically. It's inspiring to see how others changed after receiving an oracle, particularly when they are ordinary people. Jesus was a carpenter; Buddha, a prince; and Mohammad, a camel herder and a merchant. Oracle stories show that we can change, too.

- Oracles open us to eternal truths. Looking to oracles, we can find a context for our lives and where we fit into history. Oracles can give us insight into our place in the world.

- Oracles provide perspective. In our uncertain times, it is comforting to know there have been other times that were equally uncertain—yet the human race persevered and prevailed.

- Oracles deepen our self-knowledge. Remember, the inscription above the door to the Temple of Apollo at Delphi read "Know thyself."

Tell It Like It Is

Many tales of oracles are more about the journey of self-knowledge than reaching a goal. An example of this is Moses, who was Hebrew but raised in the Egyptian pharaoh's court. It wasn't until he truly understood his identity as a Hebrew that he could receive the message of the oracle (Yahweh in the burning bush) exhorting him to lead his people. Once convinced of the truth of who he was, Moses was able to stand tall before the pharaoh and say, "Let my people go!" Moses' internal process is what mythologist Joseph Campbell calls "the hero's journey."

At their most basic level, oracles are about making wise decisions for our lives. If we could know the future, we could prepare for it. But why not just turn to science for the answer? Science does that for us in many ways. It's logical and clear cut.

The people of ancient times were no different from us. In consulting oracles, they were looking for a certain kind of science, or at least what passed for science in their day. Astrology, the study of the stars, was considered a science in ancient times. Psychology, Gary's profession, was not established as a science until the early twentieth century, though Freud's work in the nineteenth century helped to move the field in that direction. So when you look at it that way, we have not really changed all that much. We have a different language for oracles and twenty-first century techniques, but that's all.

The Sphinx: Challenging Your Knowledge

SPHINX
CHALLENGE

The Sphinx card from the Goddess Oracle Deck depicts a woman with the body of a lion, the wings of an eagle, and the tail of a serpent. In Greek mythology, she posed a riddle to all who sought passage between two mountains. The riddle, which Oedipus solved, was "What animal is it that in the morning goes on four feet, at noon on two feet, and in the evening on three feet?" The person who could answer the riddle could go forward. The Sphinx in Egypt also served as a guardian of a passage, observing the rising and the setting of the sun. (The answer: man, who as a baby, crawls; as a man, walks; as an old man, walks with a cane.)

This card represents the idea that you must unlock the gate to the realm of wisdom through your own wits. You will be tested to look within and examine the knowledge you already possess.

Two Oracle Sciences

Modern-day scientists, such as Sanjay Gupta, senior medical correspondent for CNN, are oracles, too. A neurosurgeon, he speaks on a wide variety of medical issues as an über-authority. He can stand outside his profession and look at the broader issues. He can speak to the day-to-day issues of medicine and how it is practiced, but he can also talk about cultural and spiritual issues as they relate to health care. He is a spokesperson for our times in that way.

Psychology has established scientific credibility, putting mental-health professionals on par with physicians. But despite that, Gary believes that psychologists are more oracle than science. Psychologists ask their clients to have faith that they have the answers, and they set themselves up as having the ultimate wisdom. That is, they are part shaman, part mystic. Gary believes it's vital for a client to have a somewhat mystical view of his or her psychologist in order for them to open up and be guided in making changes. Psychologists need some of that aura of an oracle.

Oracle Advice

In your Oracle Journal, start a list of well-known figures, contemporary and historical, who are oracles to you. What larger message does the person convey to you? What values do you share with this oracle? Also recall books you have read that have changed your way of thinking, and conversations you have had or interviews you have heard that created a shift in how you live your life.

Poetry: The Oracle Tradition

The oracle tradition is closely related in many cultures to the oral storytelling tradition, in which the storyteller relays wisdom through metaphor and image. Usually storytellers were in the employ of the king, to make him a smarter, better king.

But in any culture, at any time, when people sense the presence of a great wisdom, they want to tap into it. Lebanese poet Kahlil Gibran begins the unfolding wisdom of *The Prophet* (see Appendix B) with Almustafa, whom he identifies as "the chosen and the beloved," about to return to his homeland after dwelling 12 years among the people of Orphalese. As the ship arrives that will take him home, the people of Orphalese gather around him, and a woman emerges from them to speak for the group, saying, "Yet we ask you ere you leave us, that you would speak to us and give us of your truth."

In that respect, poetry and literature work as oracles, too. The romantic troubadours of medieval times were the ones who carried stories of wisdom from place to place. Poet and playwright William Shakespeare is another example of an oracle. To quote *Hamlet*, "To thine own self be true," echoing the words at Delphi. It is said that Buddha's last words to his disciples were, "be a lamp unto yourselves," meaning to be your own light, your own authority, your own Buddha.

BRIGID
INSPIRATION

Brigid: Source of Inspiration

The Celtic goddess Brigid, from the Goddess Oracle Deck, is the first of many triple goddesses we introduce in this book. A triple goddess represents the three aspects of the divine feminine: maiden, mother, and crone. This trinity represents the three phases of the natural world: growth, maturity, and decay. It is represented in many ancient mythologies in the sun deities: rising, midday, and setting. In these representations, the trinity is the cycle of life.

Brigid is the goddess of fire. She represents inspiration, the spark that fires new ideas. This card depicts her as many legends depict her: with flames reaching from the top of her head.

Use this card to direct your meditation to invite inspiration into your life. Nurture your creative spirit. Appreciate your imagination. Let yourself dream. Let no dream be impossible. Bring in the energy of inspiration, and find yourself clearer, with a sharper vision, and full of vitality.

Many Travels

From the dawn of time, humans have known that there are places where there is a wisdom so profound and so illuminating that it is worth the travails of many travels to receive it. Still today, people flock to some of these ancient sacred spots.

We delve more deeply into sacred places in Chapter 7, but here is a quick guide to some of the most popular *pilgrimage* destinations in the world:

Wise Words

A **pilgrimage** is a journey made to a shrine or holy place. The journey to the holy place is for the purpose of deepening your wisdom. Generally, the pilgrim sets out with a specific question. The journey is made with reverence and usually in and of itself provides lasting insight.

- **Lourdes, France.** This village at the foothills of the Pyrenees in southern France is famous for the appearance of the Virgin Mary. The spring is believed to have healing properties, drawing thousands of visitors each year. Medjugorge in Bosnia and Herzegovina and Fatima in Portugal are other places where the Virgin Mary has allegedly appeared.

- **Chartres Cathedral, France.** This Gothic cathedral built in the twelfth century is dedicated to the Virgin Mary but is believed to have goddess origins predating Christianity.

- **Stonehenge, England.** These circles of massive stones arranged on a plain in England are believed to have spiritual or astronomical applications, or both. The site is estimated to have been built between 2800 and 1400 B.C.E.

- **The pyramids, Egypt.** The pyramids were burial vaults for the great pharaohs of Egypt, built about 2700 B.C.E. Amid them is the Great Sphinx.

- **Ganges River, India.** This river, in the Himalayas, is considered to have great healing powers. It is the most sacred river in Hinduism.

- **Chimayó, New Mexico.** On Good Friday each year, thousands reenact the journey of Christ carrying the cross. In the sanctuario, pilgrims may receive healing holy dirt.

- **Teotihuacan, Mexico.** These Aztec pyramids are sometimes called the "place where men become gods." The word *Teotihuacan* translates from the ancient Nahuatl language as the "City of the Gods."

- **Angor Wat, Cambodia.** This temple, built from 879 to 1191, honors the Hindu god Vishnu. Pilgrims say to stand in its midst is to be inspired by angelic grandeur and infinite possibility.

Destination Not Yet Known

Of course, there are other famous journeys that amount to pilgrimages. Perhaps the pilgrim himself or herself did not even know he (or she) was about to begin such a journey. This is what mythologist Joseph Campbell calls the hero's journey, and we discuss more examples in subsequent chapters. Examples of these journeys are the quest for the holy grail, Homer's *The Odyssey, 2001: A Space Odyssey*, Luke Skywalker in the *Star Wars* movies, or the *Harry Potter* books and movies. But they also could be the journeys of explorers such as Lewis and Clark, who traversed the western United States, forging the Oregon Trail in search of the Northwest Passage. These journeys often begin with "the calling," in which the hero receives the call but does not yet know the full purpose of the journey. He or she may not yet know the destination.

Pilgrimages Without a Map

You don't have to travel to the wild jungle of Cambodia or the fertile Nile Valley to have a pilgrimage. You just have to be willing to travel through mind and soul. The oracle journey can take place right in your own home.

To set the stage for an oracle journey, set aside a place in your home that can be held sacred. By this we mean quiet, free from distractions, and held with great intention. Writing and yoga teacher Jeff Davis (*Journey to the Center of the Page*; see Appendix B) defines *intention* as "a conscious gesture to align your heart, mind, imagination, and body with whatever act you're about to begin." Create a place where you can cultivate peace of mind. Create a place where you may readily get in touch with the present moment, forgoing all thoughts of the past and the future, setting them aside, just for now. In Chapter 7, we delve further into ways you can create your own sacred space.

Timeless Wisdom

There you have it. Oracles are everywhere, and they are timeless. Even if you do not consider yourself a spiritual person, oracles can just bring good things to your life. Using oracles is about teaching yourself a wider array of ways to obtain wisdom. There are many different kinds of oracles, and each has a different source and different truth. Remember always to seek out the essence of oracle wisdom for your unique self.

The Least You Need to Know

- The oracle tradition shows up in many cultures and many times, from ancient Egypt to Mayan culture to stargazing to Buddhism.

- Because oracles are often puzzles, they challenge us.

- Some modern-day professions such as medicine and psychology, although the thrust of them is scientific, have many qualities of an oracle. Doctors and counselors, for instance, are part scientist, part shaman, part mystic.

- Literature, poetry, and music, too, have a long tradition of being a conduit for oracle wisdom.

- The profound wisdom that can be found in sacred places draws thousands of visitors each year to sites such as Lourdes, Chartres Cathedral, Stonehenge, and the pyramids.

- Creating your own sacred space—where no one can interrupt you or judge you—is a way of inviting oracles into your life.

Are You Looking and Listening?

In This Chapter

- ◆ Activate your awareness
- ◆ Finding stillness and simplicity
- ◆ Oracle rituals
- ◆ Success breeds more success

We know now that oracles transcend time, distance, and culture. We know they are a current that runs through religion, philosophy, and many disciplines of knowledge, from medicine to psychology to business to technology. If that's the case, then oracles surround us. If they are everywhere, the secret to seeking an oracle may be just a matter of just tuning in.

An oracle, then, is wisdom you invite into your life. The number and quality you receive are determined solely by you. The wisdom is in how you interpret the oracle and apply it to your life. In short, an oracle is what you make of it.

Stop, Look, and Listen

When you start opening yourself to the idea of oracles in your life, you will suddenly become aware of them in everyday life. So the first step is to ask to know more about oracles and how they might benefit you. The first question, the one that likely caused you to pick up this book, is the beginning of opening up: "What's this all about, anyway?" And if then you asked, "Is there more to it than this Greek mythology stuff?" or "Is there more to it than this New Age stuff?" the answer is yes.

Learning to cultivate oracles in your life is a matter of raising your awareness. Train yourself to sharpen your senses—and trust the information you receive through your senses. *Clairsentience* is the big word for it, but it means "clear feeling"—a full, activated awareness using all five senses. Think about it: when you take the time to slow down and taste every bite, you *really, really taste it!* Many people realize when they do savor the subtle tastes of their foods, they connect the sensation to a person or a memory. It awakens something anew in them. This heightened sensory awareness stirs the imagination and activates creativity.

> **Wise Words**
>
> **Clairsentience** is the state of heightened awareness in which all five senses are operating at their optimum. In a state of clairsentience, all senses are clear and alert, at their full powers. Clairsentience is a fully experienced moment.

Train yourself to observe your everyday world, to take note of the details that surround you. Practice it in the course of your regular day. It may be as simple as noticing five new things on your commute to work. Or you may meet someone new, and study that person as though you had to write about him, observing gestures, tone of voice, and facial expressions, taking note of his posture, diction, and fashion sense.

Being more mindful of the present can also cultivate the skills that open you to receiving oracle wisdom. The present moment can bring you into mindfulness, a high state of consciousness. Meditation, prayers, and affirmations are devices that can return you to mindfulness, an antidote for when you allow yourself to do too much thinking. Most of the time, we let the past and future dominate our thoughts. The past has an uncanny way of replaying itself without our conscious permission. It's the ego's misguided way of protecting us from painful mistakes and little failings. In our busy lives, the future can have a tremendous hold on our thoughts. When life is frenzied, our thoughts must keep pace with *where do I go next?* We are always planning our next move, forgetting to savor the gifts of the present moment.

Begin to create blocks of uncommitted time for yourself. It can start with 10 minutes here or an hour there. Even in our busy lives, we can find ways to block tasks into certain times, leaving other times completely free, with no commitment to anyone but yourself.

It's important that the time have no preconceptions. This allows the imagination and spirit to flourish. As an example, Carolyn often leads writing workshops in which participants write solidly for 10 minutes without stopping. There is no other task but this: keep the pen moving. (For more about this writing practice, consult Natalie Goldberg's books, including *Writing Down the Bones;* see Appendix B.) People come into the workshops with their minds crammed with the incessant details of life, feeling their creativity is lost on the other side of a vast ocean. In just 10 minutes, they are able to calm their minds, push through the chatter, and find the well of inspiration. It's like a freshwater spring just below the surface, always renewing and refreshing. It's like finding your soul again.

The same is true of a simple relaxation meditation. Just returning to the breath and anchoring yourself in your deep center is a way to free your mind from rational, critical thinking mode to that place where your imagination runs free, the "place of elsewhere," as the French philosopher Charles Baudelaire named it. Baudelaire described imagination as "an almost divine faculty which perceives immediately and without philosophical methods the inner and secret relations of things, the correspondences and the analogies."

"Elsewhere" is where the wisdom of oracles lies. We turn to them because the rational, scientific world cannot explain everything we need to know to make decisions that will bring us our best and brightest lives. "Elsewhere" takes you beyond your ego, your self, your old rules and outdated paradigms, and transports you across the limitless sea to the clear blue horizon.

Your Five Senses: Activation for Relaxation

Use this meditation to activate your five senses. It's helpful to do it at the beginning of the day, creating the intention to continue practicing high sensory awareness throughout the day.

Find a quiet place in your home. Make sure you are seated comfortably. Close your eyes and take in a deep breath, filling up your lungs with air. Exhale fully. Take in two more deep breaths, inhaling and exhaling fully.

When you open your eyes, notice one thing you *see*.

Notice one thing you *hear*.

Notice one thing you *taste*.

Notice one thing you *smell*.

Notice one thing you *touch*.

Repeat the rotation. You may find that on the first round, you chose the most obvious objects or sounds. Then as you go through a round, you must sharpen your awareness to notice new things. Many people find this particularly true with smell and taste, the two senses that we use in the most limited ways. Listen more deeply to the sounds beneath the sounds. Find the stillness. Suddenly, as the radius of your awareness expands, you notice that stillness has a sound. In the stillness, you find the essence of the present moment and all of its sweetness.

Goddess Guidance: Tara's Stillness

TARA
CENTERING

You may use the Goddess Oracle Deck card of Tara to find your own stillness within. Tara is a major goddess in the Tibetan tradition, and she is celebrated in India, too. Her name means star. She is an oracle to call upon when you are seeking star clarity. She guides you in finding your own stillness beneath the sound of life. Choose one of the items from your list of Nine Wise Ways. Invite her to show you the path.

Full-Sensory Living

Carry the sharp sensory awareness of the previous exercise into the rest of your day. Bring it to mind as you encounter people, even people you see each day. Notice new details about them. Bring it to mind as you take a walk. Time your breath with each step, being conscious of the inhale and exhale with each stride. Walking can be very meditative, even on the busy streets of New York City. Even doing the dishes can be an experience of mindfulness. Focus on the soapy water, the scrubbing of the pans, the warm water rinsing over your hand, the scent of the lemony soap, the sparkle of the porcelain dishes. Working with the hands, with mindfulness, often frees the subconscious.

Simplicity

A message of wisdom will not come to you if your life is too full to receive it. When we live cluttered lives, we can't let new ideas and teachings in. Although cultivating mindfulness creates the space in our psyches for fresh ideas, simplifying our personal space serves the same purpose.

While you are working on the inside, work on the outside, too. Get rid of the stacks of papers, the overflowing bookshelves, the cluttered closet. As you simplify the world you take in, you simplify the stimuli you take in, which cultivates more awareness of your surroundings. You are retraining your mind to notice the deeper dimensions of life. As you create simplicity in your environment, you will notice you are more serene.

Unclutter your life in other ways. List your commitments and examine which are vital and which are obligations. Which activities promote your health and well-being? Which activities fit the person you are now? Which promote your best self? Which activities are about who you used to be? Which activities could wait for another time in your life? You are looking for activities that you can replace with quiet, mindful time.

Likewise, make every object you purchase pass the simplicity test. Will that Palm Pilot really make your life easier, or is it just another gadget that means you have to upgrade to new software, buy a memory stick, or manage the compatibility of peripherals?

Does your car really need the GPS (global positioning system) navigation feature, or could you just use a map from Triple A? Zen teaches that every possession in your home is an attachment. Look around you: you are attached to that many things!

Oracle Advice

A Zen garden is the ultimate in serenity and simplicity. It is a dry landscape garden created with stones and sand. In Zen gardens, the sand is raked to evoke the flow of water, or in the larger sense, the life force energy of chi. The raking in and of itself is a daily meditation, and some famous Zen gardens require six to eight hours of raking daily. A Zen garden is stillness (stones) and flow (raked sand) at the same time, a metaphor for being in alignment with the present moment.

Rituals

We can draw upon the rich history of oracles in learning how to use ritual to invite oracle wisdom in.

HESTIA
HEARTH/HOME

Hestia: Inviting the Light

Hestia, the Greek goddess of the state, home, and hearth, kept the fires of the temples burning. In tending to the flames, she is credited with perpetuating the ideals of fledgling democracy in Greece. These were the temples where the debates were held. The flame is the symbol of wisdom, a reminder of all that the Greeks aspired to become.

The early Egyptians, Greeks, and Romans often sealed lighted lamps in the sepulchers of the dead. Some of these lamps were found still burning when the vaults were opened hundreds of years later. Scholars have tried to figure out the mystery of the ever-burning lamps but cannot. There are also accounts in India, Tibet, China, and South America of lamps that burned continuously without fuel.

Flames, lamps, and candles are used in rituals to summon us to mindfulness. They keep the ideals of who we are and what we stand for in the forefront of our minds. They remind us to be watchful, hopeful, and serene.

You, too, can use the ritual of candle lighting to invite the wisdom of oracles such as Hestia into your life. Use the lighting of a candle to announce your intention to be more receptive to the undercurrents of wisdom in your life that come in nontraditional ways.

Maya: Extending the Invitation

MAYA
ILLUSION

Maya is a virgin maiden goddess who figures in Buddhist and Hindu Indian traditions. She is the goddess of intelligence, creativity, water, and magic. In the Buddhist tradition, she was chosen as the virgin mother of Gautama Buddha. In Hinduism, she is the wife of Brahma. In this set of cards, she is depicted lifting the veil between the realm of earthly knowledge and opening to the true light of the universe. She represents intelligent enlightenment.

Visualize Maya leading you past your own illusions, the ones that keep you from seeing your true nature and the light of the universe. Even if you have no inclination toward Hinduism or Buddhism, you may benefit from meditating on this card. Gary often encourages clients to create an inner sanctuary or sacred space that they can hop into when they are feeling out of control or in the dark. The image of Maya may help you imagine a guide leading you to that inner sanctuary. Imagining her as a loving presence, as a guide or counselor, can be even more powerful.

If you could meet Maya, what would you ask her? What would you discuss? Extend the invitation for her to be your guide.

Synchronicity: Oracles in the Intersection of Time

As defined by psychologist Carl Jung, a synchronicity is when two unrelated, disconnected events occur at the same time, creating a transcendent truth. No doubt examples abound in your life, but you may not have always paid attention to them. An example might be the young woman who senses the presence of her grandmother seated next to her in the passenger seat as she is driving at night. Later, she learns that that was the moment at which her grandmother died.

Tell It Like It Is

Synchronicity suggests that two unrelated events, precipitated by separate causes, are interconnected. Jung's famous example was the clock that stopped at the same moment of its owner's death. In that connected moment, a source of wisdom that you would not otherwise have been able to access is apparent. Even if there is no causal relationship between your inner psychic work and an external event, you may still be able to see the significance of the event and choose to act upon the insight you receive. That makes a synchronicity a form of oracle wisdom!

Gary and Carolyn really believe in synchronicity. "When we have a need, or a readiness, then the universe itself presents an opportunity," is the way Gary puts it. Synchronicity was at work when Carolyn returned to her senior management position at the newspaper after a week of vacation, and she just knew her work was complete in that position. A lot of desire for change was swirling around her: she had just had a miscarriage, she was hoping to sell her house, and she was wanting to devote more of her career to writing. She couldn't see how the opportunities were going to come to her, but she knew she was in alignment and had done the inner work to prepare. She told a friend at lunch that she believed the answers would come to her in the sequence of events. How she knew this, she did not know. When she returned to the office, the managing editor told her the editor position of *SAGE*, the women's magazine, was open. The managing editor asked her whether she knew of someone in the newsroom who would want the job. Carolyn thought two seconds about whether she was ready to leap, leaving senior management, and said, "*I* want that job!" and the other editor, caught by surprise, said, "Why, you'd be great at that job!" That night, Carolyn took a pregnancy test, thinking it might be good to know all possible factors because she was applying for a new job. It was positive. And a few weeks later, she learned she was carrying twins. Applying for the job was a leap she was ready for—but one she might have hesitated to make if she had known ahead of time that she was pregnant.

When we are open and ready, we vibrate differently. When we believe that the best is coming, we are like magnets. The universe responds to that. Every synchronicity is an opportunity, a test. Are we ready to learn and grow?

Focus your meditations on being open and in harmony with the world. Visualize yourself being more accepting. Visualize yourself standing with your hands open and up-turned, your heart lifting from your chest, wide open. You are defenseless. You no longer need to protect. You are open to greater compassion and wisdom.

Built for Success

Streams of oracle wisdom surround us daily, but how are we to glean the truth? Still, you may hesitate to derive wisdom from messages that are ancient, synchronistic, subtle, or downright cryptic. You may wonder whether it's wise to base your hopes and dreams on such messages. Surely there is some risk involved.

The success of an oracle depends on you. Your biggest protection from false wisdom is a strong sense of self, a clear-minded purpose and a life-affirming intent. By life-affirming, we mean you must use oracles for the highest good, for the good of all, seeking the best life for yourself and for all beings. You must do no harm.

Take a few minutes to write in your Oracle Journal about your purpose. What are your values around it? What kind of person would you be if you achieved this purpose and lived it? How might your values be put to the test? What kind of people would you share your life with if you attained this goal? What kind of person would they say you are? What would you give up to reach your goal? What belief could you never relinquish, even when tested? Do you believe you must always tell the truth? Put your children first? Be true to your word? Honor those who are absent? Look for the good in everyone? If someone made *It's a Wonderful Life* with you as the main character, what would be missing if you had not walked this earth?

Then again, there is no substitute for good old-fashioned hard work and commitment. The idea of using resources such as oracles is to enhance our well-being and to promote spiritual and psychological development—not to avoid looking at ourselves honestly or turning over our authority to someone else. We caution you not to let oracles become a crutch. In this age of highly specialized knowledge, we are trained to hand over our authority to experts. Usually our experts have high-level university degrees and lots of initials following their names—or perhaps lots of money or celebrity. But whether you turn to a Ph.D. or an ancient oracle, you must never lose sight of the wisdom you hold within. Don't transfer the responsibility for your fulfillment in life to someone else—not even a psychologist and a writer of *Complete Idiot's Guides*.

True personal power derives from gaining a sense of your own truth. Listen to your own truth. Apply your own truth test to the messages you receive from oracles:

- What feels scary to you—not what feels scary to most people—but what feels scary to *you?*

- What about the oracle message felt true? Why did it feel true? (You may not always be able to answer the second question right away, not until you practice the truth test for a while.)

- What part of this message felt familiar—like someone you already knew or information you already had? On some level, could you already see it coming?

- What part of the message feels exciting?

- What part of it made you expand? By expand, we mean open up to myriad possibilities where previously you only saw one or two.

- What part of the message felt odd? What didn't square up?

- What part of the message did you not want to tell anyone or write about in your Oracle Journal? What would you not even want to tell your therapist?

You may notice the feelings of expansion or excitement or fear in your body. Excitement may feel like the thrill in your belly when you rush down the slope of a roller coaster. Expansion may feel like suddenly there is space between all of your internal organs or like your spine is lengthening. Fear may feel like a stab of queasiness in your stomach, doubling-over cramps in your abdominals, or ringing in your ears. For every person, it is different, but increasing your body awareness is a good way to boost your intuition and trust your sense of truth.

Using counseling in conjunction with practicing with oracles can be an excellent way to gain the self-understanding that will equip you to use them in the wisest way.

Successes and Failures

Another way to increase your success and trust with oracles is to study the way others have used them. We can learn from the Lydian king Croesus, who asked the Oracle of Delphi whether he should attack the Persian king Cyrus. The Oracle said if he crossed the River Halys, a great empire would fall. Eager to conquer Persia, Croesus rushed to battle, crossing the river, assuming that the empire that would fall would be that of Cyrus. Instead, it was his own. It was a crushing defeat.

The Roman emperor Nero also let pride get in the way. The Oracle of Delphi told him, "Let him fear the 73 years." Thinking this meant he had many more years to live and rule, Nero partied on. Meanwhile, in Spain, Galba, a man of 73, assembled an army that would challenge Nero. After Nero's death, Galba ascended to power to become emperor.

Contrast that with the way Socrates used the Oracle of Delphi, which proclaimed him the wisest man of all. Socrates, doubting this was possible, set about to find a man wiser. He went to politicians, to poets, to artisans. In all he found great knowledge, and with it, great pride in their knowledge. But he was sharply aware of the limits of their knowledge, whereas they themselves were not. Socrates concluded that "real wisdom is the property of God." He realized that the oracle did not mean Socrates literally was the wisest man, but that the wisest man is he who has realized, as Socrates had, that "in respect of wisdom, he is worthless."

Delphi itself flourished for 3,000 years. It became in and of itself far more than a tourist attraction. Scholars congregated at Delphi, and it became a focal point for intellectual inquiry and debate. It also came to be a showcase for art treasures. It became a high point of the Greek culture—success breeding success.

> **Oracle Advice**
>
> A Spanish tongue twister aptly describes the brand of wisdom the Oracle of Delphi recognized in Socrates. It goes like this: "El que sabe no es el que sabe, pero el que sabe es el que sabe que el no sabe." It means: "He who knows is not the one who knows, but the one who knows what it is he doesn't know." The proverb's message: humble yourself, and seek wisdom from outside of yourself.

The Role of the Soul

"It is the soul that translates incident into experience, knowledge into wisdom," says Jane Hope in *The Secrets of the Soul* (see Appendix B). It is the soul that breathes into existence our awareness of the interconnectedness of all living things. The soul is the bridge to higher spiritual knowledge. The soul poses the questions we ask of oracles. The soul translates the answers. In deepening our knowledge of the soul, we can learn to trust the way we process answers from oracles.

Hope says the soul ...

◆ Helps define what is invisible. How do you believe in something you cannot see? How do you trust? How do you begin to know the qualities of your God/Creator/Source?

◆ Is the vital essence of life.

◆ Is creative. It breathes humanity into existence.

◆ Recognizes synchronicities.

◆ Translates symbols, gives them meaning.

◆ Understands the ecology of the spirit of all living things. We are interdependent. We need oxygen to breathe. Plants produce it. Plants need carbon dioxide. We exhale it. We sustain the plants; the plants sustain us, giving us air to breathe and food to eat.

◆ Trains us in compassion for self and others.

◆ Suffuses the mundane with the sense of the sacred.

Harmonious Wisdom

Apollo, the god who originated the pronouncements from Delphi, was the god of harmony. Through many of the stories about Apollo, the common thread defining his divine powers is harmonious order. He is often depicted with a lyre, for instance.

Knowledge of self restores order. Knowledge integrated into a strong, still, centered self creates a harmonious experience. Use oracles to tune yourself into this kind of wisdom, and you will learn to make the most of them.

The Least You Need to Know

- ◆ Raise your awareness to oracles by creating relaxation and meditation rituals that heighten your senses.

- ◆ Unclutter your life and cultivate the mindfulness that creates the space for oracles to flourish in your life.

- ◆ When you are open and ready for wisdom, you vibrate differently. Like a magnet, you attract the best and brightest wisdom into your life.

- ◆ To glean the truth from an oracle, do a values check. Make sure your motives are clear and life-affirming.

- ◆ The soul is the bridge to higher spiritual knowledge, and soul is what brings oracles to life—in your life.

Chapter 4

A Message for Skeptics

In This Chapter

- Calling it into question
- Reality versus imagination
- From chaos to order
- Moving from intuition to proof

Maybe you pride yourself on your critical thinking. You are logical and discerning, and you rely on science to prove your beliefs. So oracles, quite frankly, leave you a little skeptical. Maybe some of this rings true for you, but until you can explain it in scientific terms, you would not act upon it for your life.

Yet so many times in our lives, the most significant choices we make come from pure gut instinct. In an instant, our values are put to the test and our desires materialize before us, and we act. We're guessing you have already experienced and know the beauty of that kind of truth, and in this chapter we show you how to use oracles in the wisest of all ways.

The Skeptic in Us All

The word *skepticism* originates from the ancient Greek Skeptics, and it is defined as the philosophical doctrine that the truth of all knowledge must always be in question. A skeptic is someone who doubts everything and is constantly engaged in a state of inquiry. The doubts give rise to a constant stream of questions.

It's a healthy survival mechanism to be skeptical. Journalists such as Carolyn need a healthy dose of skepticism as they test facts and question sources. Every fact must be corroborated, and every source must be deemed reliable and credible.

But here we want to make a distinction between skepticism and discernment. Discernment is the process by which you apply skepticism to a purported truth, test it, and act on it. Skeptics often avidly take on the task of disproving a belief, but neglect to carry it forward to a conclusion upon which they might act. It's too easy to stay in the role of doubting observer, dismissing any truth. Skeptics can be too comfortable staying in the state of doubt. The questions are easy; the answers, and the actions—well, that's another story.

> **Wise Words**
>
> **Skepticism** is defined in *Webster's New World Dictionary* as a philosophy that one must always question the truth of all knowledge. A skeptic must be in a constant state of inquiry. A skeptic must know how we know what we know. A skeptic questions all assumptions.

Skeptics say, "I'll believe it when I see it," and wait to act. Psychologists such as Gary know that our wants and needs have a strong effect on what we see. In the case of the skeptic, the skeptic's world is framed by doubt, and a skeptic sees doubt everywhere he or she turns. But, as Albert Einstein said, "The true sign of intelligence is not knowledge but imagination." So free your inner skeptic, and let yourself imagine the answers to the questions you seek.

Selective Thinking

The other side of believing only what you see is *selective thinking*. In selective thinking, you select favorable evidence, and you remember that and only that. Like the Lydian king Croesus, when you hear that an empire will fall, you want to believe it will be that of your enemy and not your own. So, to bolster a belief you have already decided you'd like to have, you ignore unfavorable evidence.

Your best antidote against selective thinking is self-knowledge. The Greek oracles were famous for their inscrutability. As Richard Buxton put it in *The Complete World of*

Greek Mythology (see Appendix B), "one of the most insistent themes in the whole world of Greek mythology … is the impossibility for humans to anticipate the future with accuracy." Perhaps the words *Know thyself* engraved above the entrance to the Temple of Apollo at Delphi were a warning to us as well as those hapless Greeks who sought to know the future.

Gary has had clients who have agonized about decisions in their lives—whether to take a new job, whether to end a relationship. They became obsessed with signs, and everything around them became a potential message. They would even analyze casual comments from strangers. We want to believe, and we want to see what we want, so we can turn any coincidence to a sign or message. Obviously this can be dangerous, as it sometimes was for the Greeks.

Objectivity vs. Subjectivity

But although subjectivity can color your thinking, objectivity can also shut you out from the truths that will expand your life. Objectivity is not always useful. Objectivity is another way of saying "cut yourself out of the picture." Objectivity teaches us to observe the world we see without recognizing that we influence that world.

Objectivity, of course, is the highest goal of any journalist reporting on a public issue, and for that reason, the prevailing wisdom in journalism is that you create a wall between you and the community on which you report. So journalists must know their sources and work their beats but not become involved in the stories. They must not voice their own personal and political opinions in print (except in the editorial pages) or even privately; they must always protect the appearance of objectivity. Typically, that means journalists reporting on their communities have been dissuaded from volunteer community service, but over the past two decades, newspapers have realized that the fallout from that is journalists who don't *care* about their communities and don't know them that well, so that is changing.

At Your Peril

Be careful as you collect information from oracles that you don't sway too far into absolute objectivity. The truth of the matter is that you *do* care whether the oracle message is favorable to you—or not. Part of being objective is knowing the areas where you are subjective. In other words, know your blind spots.

Absolute objectivity, however, is not possible, and we must recognize that to achieve the ideal state of objectivity. The scientific experiment of Schrödinger's cat is a telling example. In that experiment Austrian scientist Erwin Schrödinger placed a cat in a steel chamber. He placed a radioactive substance into the chamber, which if it decayed would trip a hammer, break a vial of acid, and kill the cat. But if the chamber were to be opened, the radioactive substance would be activated, and it would kill the cat. However, there was no way to know whether the radioactive substance decayed and killed the cat *before* the chamber was opened or *because* the chamber was opened. This is called the quantum theory of superposition, which means that in quantum law, the cat is both dead and alive. Sometimes this is called quantum indeterminancy or the observer's paradox.

Schrödinger's experiment illustrates that the observer can change the outcome of an event simply by observing it. It can never be known what the outcome would have been if the event had not been observed. There are countless examples in recent times of ways the media, simply by its presence as observer, influences the outcome of an event, from the Michael Jackson trial to the embedded journalists in the Iraq war.

When we realize we cannot be wholly objective, we can accept that we are subjective, and that it influences what we choose to see. So go ahead, get in touch with what you desire the outcome to be. And don't wait for a definitively proved truth to know your own truth and your own desires.

What's Real, What's Not

We all want to see beyond the limitations of our perceptions. We know there is something beyond what we can immediately see and hear. The ancient Greek philosophers were among the first to explore the line between illusion and reality. Plato argued that true reality existed not through the world of our senses but in the realm of "ideas" or "forms" that we understand through reason. Plato used the cave of shadows to illustrate this idea. He described an underground cave in which prisoners were chained facing a wall on which they saw dancing shadows. The prisoners had never seen any other reality, so they believed that the shadows were the real world.

In her literary short story *Blood*, Carolyn played with this idea of reality and sanity. The character, who is a schizophrenic resident in a psychiatric hospital, wakes from a dream, remembers walking along a tropical beach, entering a hut, hearing the faint music of a ukulele, and drinking coconut milk. The images from the dream were so striking that he wonders, "This, this room that smells of Pine Sol, this room with the stainless steel tray just removed from the refrigerator, water forming in beads along the rim. You and the nurse and the one brown shoe and the unknown. This is the life that is not real. Could it be the other way around? Could you be in the tropics wearing a necklace of bear teeth and feathers lying in a cool, dim hut—and could you be dreaming instead about being here in a hospital room, lying on sheets tinged yellow with sweat?"

Some of the brilliant thinkers of modern times, such as physicist Albert Einstein, have used dreams in their work. Einstein paid attention to the metaphorical images in his dreams, using them for insight into his scientific experiments. "The intuitive mind is a sacred gift and the rational mind is a faithful servant. We have created a society that honors the servant and has forgotten the gift," Einstein said.

> **Tell It Like It Is**
>
> Daoist philosopher Zhuang Zhou wrote about how beguiling the soul's search for true identity can be. Zhuang Zhou awakens from a dream in which he was a butterfly. "… although he was awake, he did not know if he was Zhuang Zhou dreaming that he was a butterfly, or a butterfly dreaming he was Zhuang Zhou."

Einstein was aware that human perceptions were limited, that there were other dimensions that we do not necessarily experience. This is a theme through the movie *What the (Bleep) Do We Know?* The film uses part documentary, part narrative to illustrate other dimensions of reality beyond our normal, waking reality.

So why do we turn to oracles when we have science? Because science can't explain everything.

Guarding Against Deception

Yet the reason skeptics hold on to their skepticism is they know all too well the trap of deception. More than 100 years ago, French poet and philosopher Paul Valery wrote: "The folly of mistaking a paradox for discovery, a metaphor for a proof, a torrent of verbiage for a spring of capital truths, and oneself for an oracle is inborn in us."

Creating Order from Chaos

In his book *How We Know What Isn't So* (see Appendix B), Cornell psychologist Thomas Gilovich cites the example of sports fans who believe that basketball players have "hot streaks" and nurses who insist that more babies are born when there is a full moon. We all know these little modern folk wisdoms: the infertile couple who decides to adopt and—presto!—conceive a child of their own. If an athlete makes the cover of *Sports Illustrated*, he will have a disastrous game (known as the *Sports Illustrated* curse). If you wash your car, it will rain. Bad events come in threes. Somehow, we just can't help but see patterns where none exist.

We all want to sort out order from the chaos of the messages we receive. Our minds seek patterns. We want to see order in the randomness. It is useful to become more aware of the way your mind works to put patterns together. That was the thinking behind the now-outdated Rorschach inkblot test that some psychiatrists used to evaluate the personalities of their subjects.

Being more aware of the way you make sense of order can inform you about the ways in which you deceive yourself. It can point you to your own biases and wishful thinking.

So the real question is what we can learn about our heightened awareness of patterns. For instance, take the folk wisdom that people are a little crazy during a full moon. Emergency room nurses and doctors will tell you all the crazies show up then. But what this common folk wisdom might be telling us is that when the moon is full, we are all looking to create more openings in our lives—maybe noticing the full moon and noticing the people who are "a little crazy" is to acknowledge that every so often, we ourselves need to loosen up, let go, and be a little crazy. Maybe we notice the people who are doing what we would like to do for ourselves: speak the truth, get rid of something old, try something new.

KALI
FEAR

Goddess Oracle: Kali

Kali is a Hindu goddess who personifies the opposing forces of destruction and death. Her keyword, *fear*, illustrates how much we fear the destruction of the world we know, though what Kali is all about is regenerating—letting go of the old to embrace the new. She is also the goddess of fertility and time. In this depiction, she wears a necklace of heads and a girdle of severed hands. In some tantric depictions, she holds the sword and scissors of death in her two right hands and a bowl of food and the lotus of generation in her two left hands.

Kali is one of the triple goddesses of creation, preservation, and destruction, and so she represents the cycle of life. She is fearsome, because her hunger is insatiable: she births, then she devours what she has birthed. She is nearly unstoppable.

Kali represents that crazy full-moon feeling of being out of control. She is the goddess oracle that shows up and announces, "Going to be some changes around here." She bids us to look at what we have been needing to dump from our lives. She gives us permission to be ruthless and rather unceremonious about it. She gives us courage to embrace the new stuff with gusto.

What is holding you back? What are you holding on to that you think you absolutely can't live without? Kali forces you to loosen the grip. She forces you to do the inner work that you fear you'd have to do if you let go—and she equips you with the vigor to pursue that work and progress to the next level.

The Big Picture

Focusing on the minutiae and trying to detect a pattern is to lose sight of the big picture. The big picture lies in the Nine Wise Ways you outlined in Chapter 1. This is where you really want to go. This is the path of the heart.

Gary finds that when he focuses on the big picture, he opens himself up to new growth and new directions. It helps him realize he doesn't even know what the questions are. At times he has been intensely focused on what he wanted and interpreted everything as a sign, positive or negative. The result was that he seesawed between feeling elated and feeling disappointed.

Gary encourages his clients to look up from the minutiae and see the big picture. When they take their eyes off their own navel and look outward, they begin to see more opportunities and more guidance. Sometimes we close ourselves off from guidance from certain people because we assume they are too remote from the situation or too different in their frame of reference. But that, of course, is the point. Oracles come to us, but we don't always do such a good job of seeing them and trusting them because our viewpoints are colored by what we think they ought to be.

Beginner Mind

In Buddhism, there is the concept of beginner mind, in which you rid yourself of any preconceptions. With beginner mind, you don't shut yourself off to any avenue of information. A baby doesn't know of any harm. A baby doesn't retreat from the world, because a baby doesn't know that the world can hurt. This happens to us over time— we stop giving to the world because we form ideas about what will give back to us and what will not. We form preconceptions about whether it's worth it to "go there." Will seeking this goal or this knowledge pay off? As adults, we can quickly assess whether it's worth investing our energy.

Oracle Advice

Focus simply on being awake and aware—not to be awake and aware with a goal, but the goal itself is to be awake and aware. Focus on giving to life rather than getting. Give your life and your world your awareness. Create the best in your life and those around you, regardless of the outcome. When you do this, prepare for many surprises—you will find you are quite surprised at the oracles that reach out to you from unexpected places.

The point is we don't know what we don't know. If we stay focused on what we think we should know, we risk missing out on a whole lot of important knowledge.

Free Your Mind

So you see, using oracles wisely is a proactive approach. "There are many, many gates to the sacred, and they are as wide as we need them to be," say Sherry Ruth Anderson and Patricia Hopkins in their book *The Feminine Face of God* (see Appendix B).

Being open to accepting oracles from sources outside of yourself and outside of your normal realm of thinking and deciding is a big first step. Automatically, it gets you out of the box. If you are left-brained (logical), oracles can spur you to push your logic aside and ask yourself what you feel in your gut. Becoming more subjective and more intuitive are the first steps. If you are right-brained, like Gary, you may be all about intuition but get bored with logic. When Gary makes a decision, he has to force himself to exercise the left-brained, logical side.

When he was deciding about becoming self-employed, he had to look beyond his dreams and visions, sit down, and create a budget. Gary was getting a lot of advice from people who were acting as oracles, but it was in the vein of, "Only believe." He was reading books that were saying the same thing.

But he knew he didn't need that piece of it, so he decided to listen to oracles from the other side of the coin. He decided he was even willing to listen to the ones who didn't tell him what he wanted to hear. After he did this, though, he felt a whole new sense of confidence. He was able to bring the nagging concerns at the back of his mind to the forefront. He faced the fears he had about being self-employed and responded with emotion and logic. This made him feel complete, and he was able to go forward with his decision.

How did he know he was not deceiving himself? Because he didn't have the question anymore. He had looked at the problem from all angles, and he knew that self-deception was no longer a factor.

If you have a nagging doubt about an oracular wisdom you have received, define it. Open yourself up to options that will guide you to answer that doubt. Nagging voices are our intuition trying to wake up.

Science Meets Intuition

We have talked about science and logic as though they are opposed to intuitive wisdom, but the truth is, they work hand in hand. The scientific journey begins with intuition, as it did when scientists in the 1930s just had a hunch that there might be water on Mars. The scientific journey begins with a mix of curiosity and an intuition that there just may be something to this. That leads to gearing up a space explorer to collect evidence that might support the hunch. If there had been water at one time on Mars, what would the evidence be? Where would we look? And how would we get there? In early 2004, when the Mars rovers Spirit and Opportunity explored the surface of the red planet, NASA scientists announced that they had found evidence that the water that could sustain life had once flooded the site where Opportunity landed.

Science alternates between curiosity, doubt, intuition, skepticism, truth, and discernment. Science is often the product of serendipity, hard work, and imagination. The scientific research about the origin of the Oracle of Delphi itself is an example. In the August 2001 issue of *Geology*, a team of scientists reported that the explanation that the Greeks had traditionally given for the oracle's inspiration was indeed true.

For years, scientists could find no geological proof that vapors rising from a fissure could have emitted a chemical that induced prophetic trances. But a team of an archaeologist, a geologist, a chemist, and a toxicologist have produced a wealth of evidence that suggests it is exactly so.

Serendipity brought geologist Jelle Zeilinga de Boer to Delphi. He was there by invitation of the Greek government to assess whether the area around Delphi had any hidden faults that would preclude the development of a nuclear reactor there. He noticed a fault in the hills east of Delphi where his tour bus turned around, and he decided to investigate. Tracing his steps for days, he discovered a fault that appeared to be right underneath the temple.

De Boer knew of the writings of the Greek philosopher Plutarch and others about the Oracle at Delphi, but what he didn't know was that archaeologists had largely dismissed

Isabella Herb, an early twentieth-century anesthesiologist, found that ethylene induced a trance in which people could hear questions and answer them. Sometimes their voice and speech patterns were altered. They felt no pain and were not aware of their own extremities. Scientists now believe a geological fault at Delphi produced ethylene, which produced the utterances of truth and wisdom that became known as the Oracle of Delphi.

the possibility that a fracture existed in the earth from which the prophetic fumes arose. He is an excellent example of "we don't know what we don't know."

But the knowledge stayed with him—just a hunch, just a curiosity—so years later, when he was sharing a bottle of Dao, a Portuguese red wine, with an archaeologist colleague, the story came out. That scientist, Dr. John R. Hale, from the University of Louisville, played the role of doubter. "There is no such fault," he said, knowing about the conclusive research of early twentieth-century French archaeologists.

So the two men decided to find out. They organized expeditions, bringing in a chemist and a toxicologist, and discovered two intersecting faults and evidence of ethylene, a narcotic gas that produces a feeling of disembodied euphoria. They had their answer to an ancient mystery.

Being in the Flow

Gary has found that some of our greatest inspirations come to us when we are living in the moment. In the present moment, we forget the trappings of the past or the future. A terrific example is the flow state, when we become so engrossed in an activity that we lose track of time. This is sometimes called "cathecting," in which we almost become one with the activity itself. Not only do we lose track of time, we lose track of our bodies. We might be so engrossed in writing or bike riding or whatever that we fail to notice the rumble of hunger in our bellies. In the flow state, we are performing at optimum, and we have relinquished any boundaries between ourselves and the activity. We set aside for the moment any doubts or preconceptions. The "can't" voice in our heads is silenced.

In the flow state, we forget our day-to-day concerns and insecurities. We completely accept the present moment as it is. We accept ourselves as we are. We don't worry about how we look or what people think of us. We don't think about whether we are getting anything back or whether we are giving too much or not enough. We set aside our personal agendas.

To free your mind of skepticism and doubt, cultivate your imagination. The writer Julia Cameron encourages artists of all kinds in getting in touch with their imagination and creativity in her book *The Artist's Way* (see Appendix B). Central to her method are two techniques, the morning pages and the artist's date. The morning pages are three pages you write every morning, fresh out of bed, without stopping. These aren't your official writing, if you are a writer. And they aren't anything you will show to anyone else, if you're just a regular person. You don't judge these pages. You don't evaluate while you are writing them. You simply get them out of your system.

Cameron's morning-pages technique is similar to that of Natalie Goldberg's (*Writing Down the Bones* and others; see Appendix B), who emphasizes writing practice in the same way that an athlete or musician practices before performing. Writing practice is something you do to train your mind—and know your mind. At her workshops in Taos, New Mexico, she blends a little of her Zen Buddhism philosophy into the practice. In Zen, you don't evaluate. Nothing is positive; nothing is negative; it just is. The goal is to always return to an equilibrium of peace, to return to living in the moment and all the peace it offers to us.

Cameron's artist date is about freeing your imagination. Get out of the box. Change the scenery. The artist's date amounts to taking yourself on a date to a place that is visually stimulating. This could be an art gallery, a card shop, a park in a part of town you rarely go to, a hike in the mountains, a play at the community theater, folk music at a house concert. Just trying something new, just getting out of your routine, is likely to get the creative juices flowing. If you are visual, or even if you aren't, walking through an art museum or gift shop will fill your imagination with fresh images. Nature, music, new faces—all of these have a way of getting us out of the rut.

Eurynome: Free-Spirited Creativity

In Greek mythology, Eurynome is the goddess of all things. She is the epitome of creativity. Her keyword in the Goddess Oracle Deck is *ecstasy*, and she is depicted dancing in the clouds with abandon. She represents that surge of ecstasy we feel when we free our minds to all the possibilities that exist.

EURYNOME
ECSTASY

Eurynome emerged from chaos. To stand, she had to divide the sea from the sky. She grasped the North Wind between her hands, and the serpent Ophion emerged and coiled himself around her legs. She represents that to create what we want our lives to be, we must create order from chaos. In dividing the sea from the sky,

Eurynome shows us that we need to listen to oracles on both sides—those who support our wishes and desires, as well as those that challenge and confound us. The serpent coiled around her legs is symbolic of our need to be proactive with oracles, to looking at all aspects of the truth, to be aware of our own ways of imprisoning ourselves.

In the legend of Eurynome, the North Wind fertilized her, impregnating her. She changed forms and became a dove, laying the universal egg. Again Ophion showed up, coiling around the egg seven times until it hatched. From this egg, it is believed, came all things.

Eurynome shows us how to be fertile in our imaginations, in what is possible. But she also shows us what we must tame so as to create. What needs to be divided in your life? What needs to be sorted through? What coils itself around you, challenging you to reiterate your desire to create what you want in your life?

Human Tools, Divine Message

Much of what we know about the Oracle of Delphi comes from Plutarch. Two thousand years ago, Plutarch was fascinated with reconciling religion and science. He was a priest of Apollo, and he was called to answer the challenge to the idea that the Divine might use the capricious fluctuations of a gas emitted from a crack in the earth to perform miracles and dispense wisdom. But Plutarch argued that the gods had to rely on the materials of the natural world, however noxious, mysterious, or transitory they might be.

So free your mind, and let the mysteries unfold.

The Least You Need to Know

- It's good to be skeptical, but don't let your doubting hold you back from arriving at a conclusion and acting.

- Allow yourself to see beyond the limitations of your perceptions.

- Our minds naturally want to see patterns in the chaos. Becoming aware of the way your mind seeks patterns can help you better understand how your own biases and wishful thinking color your wisdom.

- Be open to accepting oracles from sources outside of yourself and outside of your normal realm of thinking and deciding.

- Some of our best ideas occur when we are living in the moment, when we have suspended the need to evaluate and judge.

Part 2

Wise Oracle Sees All

In this part, we get up close and personal with oracles. If we understand their sources, we just might understand them better. We say oracles are divine messages, but just who or what is the source? And what role does the highest level of human knowledge play in accessing and understanding oracles? Oracle wisdom can be found in messages, places, or people themselves. What kinds of messages do they have for us? Where can we find them? Who is conduit for the message? We take our search for wisdom further by breaking it down. Let's take a closer look.

Chapter 5

Collective Conscious ... or Big, Fat Database?

In This Chapter

- The thinking layer of human knowledge
- Translators of wisdom
- Collaborating and synthesizing knowledge
- The spiritual side

Just what exactly is the source of oracle wisdom? Is it divine? Is it supernatural? Is it the occult? Is it the best wisdom in all of us?

We would suggest that it is divine—and no, nothing dark and scary like the occult. But we would also suggest that it draws strength from the highest layer of thinking knowledge. The highest layer of thinking knowledge is not the collective *unconscious*, the source of archetypes and dreams as psychologist Carl Jung conceptualized, but rather the collective *conscious*.

In this chapter, we explore the source of oracle wisdom so that you might better access it, trust it, and understand it.

Right to the Source

One of the best "getting to know you" questions we can think of is to ask someone to name three famous people, living or dead, whom she would invite to dinner. People like to list the most impressive names they can think of: Jesus Christ, Allah, the Buddha, if they are really trying to appear holy. Or if they want to appear noble, they might say Mahatma Gandhi, Abraham Lincoln, Martin Luther King Jr., or Thomas Jefferson. Or, if they are pop-culture-oriented, they might name entertainers such as John Lennon; Bruce Springsteen; Sarah Bernhardt, the famous twentieth-century actress; or Bono, lead singer of the Irish rock group U2. Or perhaps if their focus is on personal growth, relationships, or healing, they might name Oprah or Dr. Phil or Deepak Chopra or Caroline Myss. And if they just want stock tips, they might invite billionaire extraordinaire Warren Buffett, the Oracle of Omaha, called the world's greatest stock market investor.

Still, the common thread in this group is that they are all visionaries, people who have great wisdom to share with us. By and large, their knowledge exceeds their particular area of expertise. (Well, that's kind of an understatement for the Christ, Buddha, Allah group!) In the case of the rest of the crew, we turn to them because they are at the forefront of the highest layer of thinking knowledge in our culture. They are leading the charge, breaking new ground, charting new territory. They are advancing the outer edge of our collective knowledge.

We have already said we believe oracle wisdom comes from the Divine, but as Plutarch suggested, the Divine uses human tools to advance our knowledge of the divine. That's what modern-day oracles do. They serve as instruments of greater knowledge.

French philosopher Pierre Teilhard de Chardin wrote in the early twentieth century about the evolution of human knowledge, saying that our concern for our fate as individual nations will fade away, that we will evolve to a shared passionate concern for a common destiny. This "global village" concept would pull the thinking layer of human knowledge ever onward, he wrote. He called this highest layer of human thinking the "noosphere," a term that sounds decidedly computer geeklike. The "noosphere" is an interlinked consciousness—something that the Internet explosion of the millennium has made possible.

And speaking of computer geeks, they may be the ones who have made this collective human knowledge most apparent to us. Oracle, of course, is the name a bunch of visionary computer geeks chose some 20 years ago to name their database software. More and more computer scientists have designed huge databases of questions and answers about any subject you could name. And now, the powerful and all-pervasive search engine Google, the one whose stock everyone wished they had bought, plans to put the great libraries of the world on the Internet.

The information age allows us increasingly to share vast amounts of knowledge quickly. The database model is going to be the wave of the twenty-first century as computer scientists develop more sophisticated ways to use databases to share knowledge within working groups. Two major computer operating systems, Apple's Tiger and Microsoft's Longhorn shift away from a folder file-management orientation to a database orientation.

So we like to think of oracles as the interpreters of the big, fat database of humankind, the ones who point the way to the greatest knowledge we have.

How and What Is the Collective Consciousness?

The *collective consciousness* represents the innate wisdom that is in all of us. Gary finds evidence of this innate wisdom in the similarity of some of our highest concepts of human virtue from belief system to belief system. For instance, when he reads about mindfulness in Buddhism, he finds his experience of it similar to that of the concept of grace in Christianity. Likewise, the Buddhism tenet of lovingkindness is parallel to the Jesus Christ's teaching about turning the other cheek.

Mythologist Joseph Campbell highlights this current of innate wisdom that runs through so many cultures and times. Again and again, in the mythology, from culture to culture, we find the retelling of significant parts of the Christ story (a deity born of a virgin, for instance).

Wise Words

The **collective conscious-ness**, contrasted with Jung's concept of the collective *un*consciousness, is the vastness of the highest human knowledge. It represents the highest and best thinking of all humans.

Evolving Consciousness

The collective consciousness represents the evolution of thought. On the most basic level, this means we don't have to reinvent the wheel. Each generation that comes along doesn't have to go to great lengths to prove that the earth is round, not flat, and that the earth revolves around the sun, and not the other way around. Copernicus proved it, so we don't have to.

But we also benefit because Benjamin Franklin discovered electricity, and Thomas Alva Edison invented the light bulb. From those two discoveries, a wealth of knowledge unfolded, with myriad uses for electricity. Knowing already that there was such a thing as a light particle, someone could invent an LED display so that Carolyn and Gary could write this book on a lighted screen that's easy on the eyes.

Our collective knowledge is constantly evolving, expanding to embrace new knowledge. Study the life of any visionary and you will see he or she did not come into this world with his or her ideas fully formed. Some of the most inspiring visionaries of our time are those whose knowledge has evolved as we have been watching.

Television talk show host Oprah Winfrey is one of those. In her 2005 interview of Jon Stewart, she confessed that when she first set out to be a television talk show host, she just tried to be like all the others. But her personal journey of self-actualization led her to realize she could use her platform for something that aspired to be more than the daily talk show fodder. She made a distinct decision in the early 1990s to accept that higher mission. It's interesting to note that in that same interview, she revealed she was teased as a child, for her unconventional name. Kids on the playground called her *okra*, and now she is so popular she can go solely by her first name.

Study an artist's work over time, and you will see his or her vision becoming clearer. This is true of artists from Picasso to Chagall to Georgia O'Keeffe to Van Gogh to Leonardo da Vinci. It's also true of rock stars. Earlier we mentioned John Lennon, Bruce Springsteen, and Bono because we live in an age in which rock stars have a platform to speak way beyond the typical sex, drugs, and rock 'n' roll. As the nineteenth century transitioned to the twentieth century, actress Sarah Bernhardt became a symbol of the talent, intelligence, and ambitions of women reflected by the blossoming women's movement for suffrage. The wild popularity of The Beatles in the 1960s meant that when The Beatles embraced an Eastern belief system, they opened the American culture to the same. That opened the door for visionaries who have followed, such as Deepak Chopra, to talk about building the bridge between the highest wisdom of Western and Eastern healing.

Tell It Like It Is

In his song "Imagine," former Beatle John Lennon painted a picture of a world that could live as one. He imagined a world with no countries, no possessions, no wars, where everyone lived for today, sharing all that was in the world. He spurred us to really think about it, saying, "I wonder if you can."

When the rock group U2 exploded on the scene in the early 1980s, they were railing against the political violence in Northern Ireland, where the Protestants and

Catholics have fought for hundreds of years. But with their most recent CD, *How to Dismantle an Atomic Bomb*, U2 took on the weighty subject of what life and love mean in the age of high technology. They dismantle the highly destructive technological achievement of the atomic bomb and follow the thread back to the origin of God. "The world was a much more fragile place when they saw what the splitting of the atom could do," Bono said in an interview in *USA Today*. "Suddenly, the world had a sell-by date, perhaps. This album was no time for philosophizing. This is about who do you love, how do you love, why do you love." In their songs, U2 pay homage to Martin Luther King Jr. and Mahatma Gandhi and continue their commitment to activism on behalf of ending AIDS and poverty in Africa, with Bono appearing in Switzerland at the World Economic Forum with British prime minister Tony Blair and Bill Gates of Microsoft in January 2005. In March 2005, Bono won the TED (Technology, Entertainment and Design) award for his work in Africa, an award that honors individuals who have shown they can positively impact life on this planet. He has been nominated for the Nobel Peace Prize multiple times.

Your Evolution

Look at the ways your belief system and operating system have evolved over time. What new wisdom have you allowed in your life? How have your paradigms shifted?

We like movies such as *Forrest Gump* or novels such as the Pulitzer Prize-winning *The Stone Diaries* by Carol Shields because they are excellent examples of the way grander, larger events of our culture influence ordinary people's lives. In both cases, the characters are people who are nearly invisible to the rest of the world, yet the key events of the twentieth century shape their lives; the small choices they make in turn influence the intricate workings of those larger events.

Oracle Advice

Make a timeline of your life, noting key personal events such as graduations, job changes, marriage, children. Also note other transitions such as new friends, joining or leaving a church, or breaking things off with a lover. What events were turning points? What five decisions in life do you most regret? How did these events change you? What major cultural and historical events have marked your life? How did the women's movement influence your life? Vietnam War? Fall of the Berlin Wall and collapse of communism? Stock market boom of the 1980s? Dot.com crash? AIDS? How did these events determine the choices you made and the opportunities that were available (or not) to you?

Translation Required

Modern-day oracles aren't just wise people. They are wise people who have found a way to tap into the collective consciousness and translate it. Each of the examples we have mentioned has found a way to translate it in a way that makes sense for the people who are drawn to their way of conveying it. For some, that wisdom is in a rock song or an afternoon talk show. For others, it's in literature or at a Bioneers conference on ecology.

Think about where you have found insights unexpectedly. Think about where you have found truths that you have applied to your life—truths that you have incorporated into your operating system and that work for you.

Here we want to give a nod to your subconscious. Perhaps all along, your subconscious has steered you to these interests. Perhaps, like Carolyn, you are musical or you love literature, so you respond to that. Perhaps you find your wisdom in going to a conference. We believe that the universe helps us find the oracles we need to come into contact with at just the right time. That is, we believe when you are in alignment with your highest values and your intentions are life-affirming, you bring an abundance of these oracles into your life. It is like the Buddhist saying, "When the student is ready, the teacher will appear."

What's Out There

You are a branch on the tree of knowledge that existed long before you were born and will exist long after you die, as journalist Bill Moyers observed to mythologist Joseph Campbell. You have benefited from that ever-evolving layer of human knowledge, and you have an obligation to nourish and protect it.

Then again, there is a lot of information out there. In truth, there is a whole lot more information than knowledge to be had. There are a lot of oracle spoofs on the Internet. The relatively obscure and somewhat surly Oracle of Starbucks spouts off somewhat insulting insights about your personality based on your favorite Starbucks drink. Then there is the infamous Oracle of Kevin Bacon, which finds a divine pattern in the ubiquitous presence of the movie actor. The oracle is based on a movie-trivia game originated by computer science students at the University of Virginia in which you link any movie actor to Kevin Bacon in the least number of steps. It goes something like this: You type in Humphrey Bogart, for instance. In seconds, the oracle spits back that you can link them in two steps. Bogart was in *The Harder They Fall* (1956) with Abel Fernandez, and Fernandez was in *Quicksilver* (1986) with Kevin Bacon. So even oracles themselves can be parodied. We just hope that most of them have a better sense of humor than the one at Delphi!

The point is, there is a lot of unnecessary knowledge out there, and a lot of it you can get in an instant. If one day you wonder aloud, "Which is the greater number, googol or infinity?" you can get the answer in seconds, more than likely by using Google.com. (The answer, just so you know, is infinity. Googol is 1 with 100 zeros, while infinity is limitless.)

Even as we thrive on the vast collection of human knowledge that is the Internet, we must remember our duty to protect and revere it. Let the lesson of the famed libraries of Babylon be one example of how knowledge can be lost. The grandfather of Carolyn's twins remembers escaping during World War II and finding a copy of *The Communist Manifesto* by Karl Marx and Friedrich Engels in the ruins of a library. Just last year, Carolyn's twins read the children's book *The Librarian of Basra*, a true story about the woman who preserved many of the books in the library at Basra during the Iraq war. These are reminders that we are always on the edge of losing our collective knowledge unless we are cognizant of its value.

> **At Your Peril**
>
> When accessing information through the Internet or from experts, always do so with a dose of skepticism. Check the credentials of the source. Read the information critically. What information does the source leave out to support his point? Has anyone corroborated it?

Knowledge as a Commodity

Just because there's a vast store of information out there doesn't mean we have all the answers. Nor does it mean all the questions have been asked. What it means is that we have an opportunity now, with so much knowledge at our fingertips, to synthesize knowledge and use it in many different ways. One of the latest buzzwords is the *knowledge economy*. That idea says that in the twenty-first century, knowledge is the commodity by which companies will gain the edge. High-tech and multinational companies will have to find ways to use all the knowledge available in an organization in order to compete. It's the idea that each person has knowledge to contribute. From collaboration, ideas take shape and evolve, producing new ideas.

The knowledge economy idea gets the focus on enhancing and magnifying the knowledge within a company as its biggest asset—not the commodity or product but the knowledge that went into making the product. That is what must be nurtured.

A company's ability to synthesize many different forms of knowledge into a new product defines the company's potential to succeed.

Gyhldeptis: Taking the Best

GYHLDEPTIS
SYNTHESIS

The Eskimo goddess Gyhldeptis governed vegetation. Her strength lies in listening to knowledge from all sources. When her people were threatened by a destructive whirlpool, she called all the natural powers of the seacoast together for a major summit. She prepared a big feast and asked all to take part, to break bread with her. She listened to all sides, synthesizing the best ideas and solutions for peace. Eventually, all the powers of the seacoast agreed to work with her. She synthesized their energies and transformed the whirlpool into a river.

What this card reveals is how vital it is for you to play the proactive role in collecting wisdom from oracles and synthesizing it. Take in all the best ideas you receive, but always remain clear on your path. What do you want to create from this? How can you harmonize many competing voices of wisdom? How can you polish off the rough edges of the advice you have received? How can you blend them into one coherent path for yourself?

You want to be open, receiving all potential ideas. Don't dismiss. Don't evaluate. Not right away. Sometimes when you consider an idea, an objection will pop up immediately. Don't listen to it. Just write down the idea. It came to you for a reason. That in and of itself has value.

After you have your list, list the obstacles to doing what you want to do. Ask yourself, "What is the consequence of *not* listening to this need or desire?" Describe what would happen if you continue to let yourself neglect this area of your life.

Using the Collective Wisdom

Now let's get practical. How can you use the collective consciousness for yourself? Let's look at some ways you can put it into action:

◆ Know that someone out there probably has the answer for you.

◆ Build collaboration into all areas of your life. Look at your Nine Wise Ways list from Chapter 1. More than likely you already collaborate in many of these areas. For most of us, collaboration exists to some degree in our working lives. But examine your relationships or your creative self-expression area, and you may not be collaborating.

Suppose, for instance, that your goal is to find a mate. Well, this certainly doesn't seem like something on which to collaborate. After all, it comes down to you and your match, just making sure there is chemistry. But you could call upon your circle of friends in a couple of ways here. One is to ask your friends to give some thought to whether they know anyone who might be right for you and ask them to provide an introduction. Another could be to use your circle as a mastermind group, to help you clarify your values and intentions so you know what you're looking for in the first place. You may find that the group has more wisdom than you do. Your friends know what you like, and they know what you just can't live with. They also keep you honest. They may conclude that as much as you might talk about developing a long-term meaningful relationship, that's not what you really want. You want your freedom more, and you're just not willing to take the steps to grow closer to a potential life partner.

Creative self-expression is another area that can gain through collaboration. Artists and writers may work in solitude most of the time, but they often form strong communities around their interests. Usually, these are for encouragement and for networking contacts, but they can also be for creative synergy. One big break-through for Carolyn in her writing career was when she began to write in community. In 1996, she and another writer formed a group that met once a week to write together, doing free writing. This was different from the critique groups she had been in—some of which had been productive, but some of which had not. The free writing drew lots of energy from its communal nature; and because the goal was merely to "keep the pen moving," in the Natalie Goldberg style, it was a bastion of encouragement.

♦ Encourage community in every area of your life. Over the years, Carolyn has worked very hard to nurture community in her life, but none harder than the years after her divorce, when her twins were still toddlers. She had no extended family in her town, so she had to create a village of love and support around her family. This effort paid off in strong bonds with several communities of friends. There is something quite powerful about building a "family of the heart," with strong bonds, shared memories, and a common vision. It translates most imme-diately to a support system, but in the bigger picture, it translates to a healthy, positive outlook for her life and that of her children. Read: low blood pressure.

♦ Give what you want to receive. Of course, you don't give it to get. Give because you want to give. You know the value of this thing that you are about to give, because you have seen the need for it, and you wish it for yourself. When you give, without attachment to outcome, just for the sake of giving, you have already given the change to the world that you want to see. Remember the words of Mahatma Gandhi, one of our ideal dinner guests: "We must become the change we want to see in the world."

♦ Trust in the higher wisdom of the group. Individually, when left to our own devices, we may make bad choices, at least from time to time. But collectively, we are wise. When you create community around you, where you build a shared vision for your life with others who have similar values, you create a backup sys-tem. You surround yourself with people who treasure your vision for your life as you do. You surround yourself with people who serve as mirrors, reflecting to you the person you want to be.

The Spiritual Principles of Higher Wisdom

Gary has conducted many therapy groups in which people came together to support each other around a shared concern or problem. The substance-abuse recovery community has really made use of support groups, originating with the Alcoholics Anonymous model. When Gary was in graduate school, he co-facilitated a support group for people with substance-abuse problems. He thought he had to be the oracle for the group, and he felt very uncomfortable with the role. He had book knowledge, but he didn't feel all that confident in applying it. Sometimes it didn't feel at all relevant to what the group members were talking about. He pressed himself to say something he thought was brilliant about how to solve their problems and face the week ahead. But he realized that that idea was not about solving their problems but about how Gary could be brilliant.

As time went on, they repeatedly forgave him for his failures, and he realized all he had to do was facilitate. Then he relaxed, and he started discovering all kinds of ways to help them connect with the answers they already had within. He also learned how to facilitate group members in acting as oracles to each other. One woman had experienced an abusive spouse, and she was momentarily an oracle to another group member who needed to hear her message. A man whose wife was physically disabled acted as an oracle to a man who was taking his wife for granted.

Groups can facilitate a connection with the collective consciousness. Each individual has his or her own fears, frustrations, and blockages. In a group, individuals move into a space that is much larger than their limited awareness, and they expand to fill that space.

Marianne Williamson, author of *Everyday Grace*, *A Return to Love*, and numerous other books (see Appendix B), talks about the higher wisdom of a group in many of her books and lectures. Once when she was talking to a group, someone in the audience attacked her verbally in front of the group. Normally, she says, she would have reacted defensively, but she didn't. She remained calm because she felt the higher wisdom of the group. There was a collective, unspoken recognition that some terrible violation had occurred. She felt no need to point it out or defend herself against it. She felt the collective compassion for her, and when she recognized the higher understanding that filled the room, she was able to act in a higher way herself. Of course, the converse of this is the illiterate mob that gives in to fear, such as the fear that Williamson felt when attacked, but this group had come together with the agreement to treat one another kindly and to seek higher wisdom. A group facilitator sets the tone by voicing agreements about why the group has formed and then models higher wisdom.

The Higher Source

Is the aggregate of human knowledge enough? Well, we don't think so. First, you must apply your own critical, clear-minded, life-affirming thinking to any knowledge you receive. Make sure the thought process is supporting your goals in the best way possible—not the easiest, but the wisest. Ask yourself, "Is the way I put this into action making me happy?"

And second, tapping into the highest human wisdom is only the first step. The collective consciousness is a map to lead you the rest of the way—to your highest source of wisdom. Meditation or prayer are excellent ways to access it. So is your subconscious, a place that often directs you to your highest wisdom. This highest source of wisdom, however you choose to define it, is embedded in you, and it helps you to find the oracles with which you need to come into contact. It guides you to the right place and the right time. The universe wants you to have the answer.

Minerva: Sharp Vision

Take a few moments to contemplate the Minerva card in the Goddess Oracle Deck. Minerva was the Roman goddess of wisdom and knowledge. She ruled all intellectual activity, including schools, and she was considered the keeper of Rome, perhaps not unlike a librarian, a protector of the highest knowledge of the Roman society. She was the patroness of physicians, considered in ancient Rome, as in our times, to be one of the most knowledgeable professions.

MINERVA
BELIEFS

Minerva's sacred animal is the antelope, which was thought to have powers of prophecy. The antelope's eyes are associated with sharp vision.

Minerva represents belief and sharp vision, which go hand in hand. Belief allows us to imagine and create a vision for our lives—when we belief it can be so. Sharp vision affirms the belief, gives us a clear picture of what we want to create. Sharp vision gives us the acumen to put the vision into action.

Write a vision for one of your Nine Wise Ways goals. Make it as specific as it can be. Put yourself in a picture where your goal comes to fruition, and describe it.

Cement your vision by bolstering your belief that this vision is right for you and that it will come. *Act as if it has already happened.* You may want to use some affirmations: *I am embracing all the wisdom and clarity that is coming to me now.*

Go Forth and Multiply

Ultimately, oracle wisdom is a divine message, but you exponentially magnify your experience of oracle wisdom when you tap into the collective wisdom. It's like taking wisdom to the power of infinity.

The Least You Need to Know

- ◆ Visionaries serve as tools for the Divine to advance our knowledge of the Divine.

- ◆ Our collective knowledge base is constantly evolving.

- ◆ By taking note of the ways in which you access your knowledge and insights, you can better understand what speaks to you.

- ◆ Synthesizing means being open to all ideas, taking the best and leaving the rest.

- ◆ The highest human layer of wisdom is only the first step in accessing messages from the Divine.

Chapter 6

The Oracle Is the Answer

In This Chapter

- Layers of meaning
- Meeting your oracle halfway
- Interpreting the messages
- Creating a clear channel

No matter whether an oracle takes the form of a person, place, or thing, it can be a great mystery. Whatever the source, it's still up to you to ponder and decide what oracle wisdom means for your life. Only you can truly know when you have received a message, and only you can decide how best to put it into action.

Many of the oracle messages in various traditions are downright puzzles. And that is true today with modern-day oracles. It seems some things never change. Why can't the answer to your question just appear in sky-writing? In this chapter, we show you how to make sense of it all.

Message in a Bottle

Recently, Carolyn took her son and daughter to a Chinese restaurant. At five, the twins were just learning to read and really starting to learn about the world, so they were into exploring the chopsticks and fortune cookies, if not the moo goo gai pan. Carolyn's son, who had decided his ambition in life is to become governor of New Mexico, was thrilled to receive a fortune that said, "You have the skills and talents to succeed." "Wow, Mom," he said, "I got just the right one!"

How did that happen? Well, of course, you know … Carolyn's son provided his own interpretation.

When it comes to oracles, whether they come as a fortune cookie, a message in a bottle, or nighttime dreams, it's all in what you bring to it. No matter what the tradition, whether it's from the West, as with the Greeks, or from the East—no matter whether your oracle derives from ancient or contemporary sources—when you take counsel from an oracle, you must be in harmony with the governing principles of the physical and spiritual worlds. This is the natural law of the universe that says like attracts like. The five-year-old with altruistic intentions of being governor someday hears the message he wants to hear. He wants to believe he one day will have the skills to do that. He put the energy of his good intentions out into the world, and it came back in the form of a message of encouragement.

But many oracles can be downright mysterious. They may require many months or even years of pondering their meaning. And that's especially true when it comes to the big stuff in life. We've noticed that oracles that come to you out of the blue often tend to be clearer. These are the ones that are so definitive, you change your life. This is the epiphany—the quantum leap of conscious, the miraculous shift in perception.

Other oracles, the ones you have sought out, contain layers of meaning that you must ponder over time. They are like onions that you peel back one layer at a time.

Why would some oracles be absolutely crystal clear, but others impossibly inscrutable? Why would some oracles have such deep layers of meaning that their message transmutes over time? (Some dream oracles are like this! We talk about them more in Chapter 18.)

The answer to that lies in the definition of oracles as a message containing divine wisdom. Oracle messages themselves have their unique divine curriculum. Understanding them is a path that you may choose or not choose to undertake.

Mysterious Messages

When mid the rocks an eagle shall bear a carnivorous lion,
Mighty and fierce, he shall loosen the limbs of many beneath him
Brood ye well upon this, all ye Corinthian people
—Oracle of Delphi

This is a joke, right? That's what you might be saying if you have received an oracle message like this one. Maybe you have sought long and hard for an answer to this question, but nothing about the message makes it clearer. Yet you know you have some kind of answer.

Is it really so necessary for oracles to be so beguiling? Agamemnon, the king of Mycenae, probably wondered the same thing. He asked the Oracle of Delphi for advice when he was strategizing the Trojan War, and the oracle told him that he would know he was about to defeat the Trojans when his own captains began to quarrel. "Okay …" he might have said.

The timing of the Oracle of Delphi's dispensing of wisdom was equally bewitching. The oracle opened for business early in the morning on the seventh day of each month. It was closed down during the winter months, which meant you had to get your questions in way ahead of time, before the cold set in. The messages were spoken in dactylic hexameters—which, for the poetically challenged, means a line of verse with six metric feet, each one with the first syllable accented. For this reason, the Oracle of Delphi had a cadre of poet-philosophers, who would interpret the oracle and give direction about how to apply the message.

Still, Greek history is full of examples in which misinterpretation of an oracle led to calamity. Or in the case of Oedipus and the Sphinx, certainly where the seeker was tested. In that legend, which you'll remember from Chapter 2, there was a creature with the body of a winged lion and the head of a woman who inhabited a cliff towering above the road leading to Thebes. To pass, you had to answer the riddle of the Sphinx, which was, "What animal is it that in the morning goes on four feet, at noon on two feet, and in the evening on three feet?" If you couldn't answer the question, she destroyed you. Oedipus, though, gave the answer: man himself, who in infancy crawled on his hands and knees, in manhood walked on two feet, and in old age used a cane. When Oedipus gave the correct answer, the Sphinx cast herself from the cliff and died.

Tell It Like It Is

There is a second, more spiritually transcendent definition of the answer to the mythical Sphinx's riddle, using Pythagoras's values (remember him from Chapter 2?) to the numbers in the riddle. The numbers four, two, and three add up to nine, the natural number of man. The four represents the ignorant man, the two the intellectual man, and the three the spiritual man. Infant humanity evolves into the power of the mind, the adult man. To that, the spiritual man adds the staff of wisdom, which redeems and illuminates. In this interpretation, to solve the riddle of the Sphinx is to attain the highest personal wisdom, or enlightenment.

An Oracle Is a Two-Way Street

Oracle messages are not mysterious for the sake of being confounding or for the pure delight of watching us search—and falter. Oracles are mysterious because they make us work. In other words, an oracle is not a one-way message.

Because oracles require interpretation, they require us to meet them halfway. They require you to engage with your Source of divine wisdom. They are interactive, which makes them decidedly twenty-first century.

So get out of your head any sort of notion that using oracles is passive. This is most definitely a proactive application of wisdom. Oracles make you think. For Gary, the sign of an oracle is not someone who gives him specific advice or tells him what to do. Instead, an oracle is someone who makes him look at the situation in a different way—or even turns his expectations upside down. In fact, this is a litmus test for Gary when he's receiving a message from an oracle.

Oracles call on you to ponder their meaning precisely because they ask you to examine what you might be willing to change. The Buddhist tale of the search for a mustard seed (see Chapter 1) is a prime example of the process of changing a perception about a situation.

When Gary hears a different perspective, when he is challenged, he is more likely to examine what he thought, what he wanted, and what he expected. It doesn't necessarily mean it changes his course—just that he does go forward more thoughtfully. It means he has deepened his understanding of himself and of the situation. (Perhaps this was the case for Agamemnon as he waged the Trojan War knowing he would recognize the sign of the beginning of the end when it came.)

Oracle Advice

Another reason oracles are embedded with mysterious messages, quite frankly, is because you might not like what you hear. In the case of Apollonius of Tyana, he consulted the Oracle of Delphi, asking whether his name would be famous. The Pythia said yes, but his name would always be calumniated. Apollonius stormed out of Delphi in a rage, but it turned out to be so. Many of the early Christian church founders believed him to be the Antichrist. Now, although we doubt you'll hear you're the Antichrist, you may hear some oracle advice that shakes you up—and demands that you change your ways in an area of your life. Are you willing to look at the full package, good and bad?

Random Acts of Wisdom

Many oracles seem to come to us at random. A big dramatic example is Paul on the road to Damascus, when he was hit with the blinding light of wisdom. It's safe to say that the oracle appeared just when he least expected it. If God had warned him ahead of time, it would have given him time to build up his defenses. It would have given him time to embellish or weave in his own interpretation of the message, depending on his comfort level. Were that so, Paul could have easily minimized the encounter, interpreting it as "Could you just lighten up a little on persecuting the Christians?" Instead, he got a message from out of the blue, and it really got his attention. Paul's interpretation led to much bolder action.

But even less-dramatic oracles can get our attention when they come in unexpected ways. Wise people come into our lives every day. Each one has something to say, but not necessarily all the answers we want or need. Sometimes if we are waiting for "the one," we overlook the little oracles in our lives that give us a piece of the puzzle at a time.

Oracles cannot speak to us if we are too comfortable. If we are too comfortable, we might not even hear them, and we are certainly not open to change. And oracles are not about making us more comfortable. They ask us to change.

Then again, oracles can be quite gentle. This is another reason oracles leave a little to mystery: if we knew the whole path before we set out, we might not take it. When we receive a little bit of wisdom as we go, and just enough encouragement, the journey to usher in changes to your life seems less daunting.

Our daily lives are full of these small, gentle encounters with oracles. Gary can find wisdom in professional contacts or someone who happens to be on the same elevator at the same time. Oracles can even be strangers.

Once our book producer, Lee Ann Chearney, was on the eve of moving out of New York City to Maryland's eastern shore. She was looking forward to the move, but with New York in her blood, she felt the tug of regret. Doubt and exhaustion descended on her in the last days of bustling about preparing for the move. One morning she was sitting on the front steps of her Park Slope brownstone apartment sipping tea when a man about eight years younger than she rode by on a bike. He called out "Hey beautiful" in a way that was not obnoxious or threatening, and it made Lee Ann laugh out loud. They ended up chatting about what a lovely spring day it was. Twice while they were talking, he greeted passersby as though he knew them, and they responded as though they knew him, though they were very different types of people. They talked about five minutes more, and then the man said, "You look like you need a hug. May I hug you?" Sensing her New York defenses kicking in, he said, "You just look like you need some loving energy." Amazingly, Lee Ann let him hug her. As he hugged Lee Ann, their hearts pressed together. He held her for up to a minute. "That's better," he said. "For your heart." And he rode off with a wave and a smile.

Lee Ann's story is an example of how *right* it feels when you receive a message. You know it is exactly for you. Oracles can come in encounters that are unique in their probability and distinct in their message. Lee Ann had a big question on her heart that day, and the universe was going to give her the answer.

We call it random wisdom, but we believe it's not random at all. It's meant for you. You just were not recognizing all the sources available.

A Guide to Interpretation

Oracles may not always be crystal clear, but that doesn't mean you cannot develop your own personal code for interpreting them. Like anything mysterious, it helps to develop criteria for cracking the code. And with anything involving your personal growth, it must be uniquely for you.

Coming up with a personal code for interpreting your oracles is not about developing a formula. It's about developing a personal set of operating techniques that give you confidence in your interpretations.

Take a few moments to identify your personal interpretations to these symbols:

The color red _____

A cathedral _____

A lotus petal _____

A rose _____

A candle _____

The sun _____

An apple _____

A caterpillar _____

A gateway _____

A spiral _____

An eagle _____

The forest _____

Keep this list handy. We come back to it in subsequent chapters.

Putting the Messages Together

Sometimes it takes putting the oracle messages together for them to make sense in how to act. The story of Aetion is an example in which he was able to save the life of his son. Aetion wished for a child, so he went to Delphi to consult the oracle. The moment he entered the temple, the Pythoness uttered these words:

> No one honours thee now, Aetion, worthy of honour—
> Labda shall soon be a mother—her offspring a rock, that will one day
> Fall on the kingly race, and right the city of Corinth.

Great news, right? But the words of this oracle came to the ears of Bacchiadae, who had received an earlier prophecy that pointed to the same event about the fate of Corinth:

> When mid the rocks an eagle shall bear a carnivorous lion,
> Mighty and fierce, he shall loosen the limbs of many beneath them—
> Brood ye well upon this, all ye Corinthian people,
> Ye who dwell by fair Peirene, and beetling Corinth.

At this, the Bacchiadae began to plot to kill the son that was coming to Aetion. As soon as the baby was born, they sent 10 soldiers to his house. His mother, unaware of their purpose, brought out the child and placed him in the arms of one of the soldiers. The plan had been that whoever received the child would dash it against the ground, killing it, but the happy mother gave him a glowing smile that tugged at his heart, so he could not kill the child. He passed the baby to the next soldier. And so on, with the baby being handed through the arms of the 10 men, with none choosing to be his murderer. After they left, they stood near the door, reproaching one another, and the child's mother heard as they plotted to storm the house and take the child. The mother hid the baby in the corn bin. When the soldiers returned, they searched the house up and down but did not find him. They decided to return and report that they had done the deed anyway.

The boy was named Cypselus, which means corn bin. As a man, he went to Delphi to consult on a matter of a man's estate. This was the oracle:

> See there comes to my dwelling a man much favour'd of fortune,
> Cypselus, son of Aetion, and king of the glorious Corinth—
> He and his children too, but not his children's children.

Cypselus became master of Corinth, though history shows he was a harsh ruler.

When you put together the little pieces of oracle messages, you may find they make more sense for your life. The connection may not be direct. There just may be something in one oracle message that resonates with another, and you may not know why it sticks in your mind. But listen to it. The missing piece of the puzzle will come to you.

Don't Talk Over Them

Oracle messages become easy to interpret if we sit still and stop trying to talk over them. This reminds us of the line from the song by folk singer Nanci Griffith, "I Don't Want to Talk About Love," in which she says, "I don't want to talk about love, because I've heard it before, and it talks too loud." She sings some more, "You can hear it in a disco at midnight, shouting." In that song, Nanci Griffith does indeed want to hear about love, just not the message she's heard before. We tend to want to drown out messages that don't fit our picture by talking louder, talking them down, so that what we truly want is just a small, still voice. If you have an agenda, you may be so locked into it that you crowd out the genuine messages leading you to what you really desire. We have to let go of what we want oracle messages to tell us and just listen to what they have to say. They are probably a lot clearer and more direct than we think.

Get out of your routine. Have an open mind. Be open to growth. When you are locked into a path, you strangle your dream.

Inanna: Survivor

INANNA
EMBRACING THE SHADOW

Inanna was a Sumerian goddess who was described as the queen of heaven. In her myth, she descends into the underworld, the dark domain of her sister Ereshkigal. At each of the seven gates during her descent, she is required to surrender her robes and jewels and regalia. Finally, naked, vulnerable, and stripped of the trappings of power, she enters the presence of the queen of the underworld. Ereshkigal kills her with a glance and leaves her hanging like a piece of meat on a hook, where she hangs for three days until she is rescued and revived by her father, Enki, the god of wisdom. She ascends from the underworld into heaven, and at each gate, she regains her jewels, her robes, and her royal powers.

Inanna represents the survivor in us all. She has quite literally "been to hell and back." She personifies the process of transformation—first of being stripped of her identity, then of being restored with a new identity. The process of personal transformation is one of getting to your core. When you go through the tough stuff, you develop a steel-hard center. You find your resolve. You find out what you are made of.

To bring the power of Inanna to your Nine Wise Ways, make a list of the trappings of power in your life. These can be things like your nameplate on your desk or your job title, which may mean to you that you have achieved stability and status in your professional life. You have arrived. You are to be taken seriously. This can be the part of town you live in, which may indicate a certain kind of socioeconomic status. Or it may be the way you identify yourself when people ask you what you do for a living. Ask yourself, if you had to relinquish these things, how would that change you? Would it change who you really are?

Clearing the Channel

What can you do to create a clear channel? Certainly there has to be a way to optimize the kinds of oracle messages you receive.

Oracles can be like *Zen koans*, which are questions that the Zen student must ponder. The most famous Zen koan is "What's the sound of one hand clapping?"

The act of pondering, in and of itself, is a way of clearing your mind. By meditating, you clear your mind of all the mental debris that clouds your everyday thoughts. Have you ever noticed how quickly your mind calms when you are led in meditation?

> **Wise Words**
>
> Zen koans are puzzles or seemingly paradoxical stories that prompt you to ponder until you internalize the lesson. Because they are puzzling, they require you to understand them on a level beyond logic and reasoning, way beyond the ability to verbalize the lesson. They also can serve to keep a wandering mind on track.

The Zen of Oracles

In Zen thought, you are always seeking to bring yourself back to zero. This means relinquishing your attachment to who you are and what you think your world should be. Zero means you have neither an inflated view of yourself nor low self-esteem. In Zen, it's about staying on an even keel, in this state of calm mindfulness. Calm and mindfulness go together, because Zen meditation isn't just about being calm and serene, retreating from the world outside. Mindfulness is about still being engaged—but you are engaged with life in the present moment. You are not trying to change it or control it; you accept it as it is.

For many years, Carolyn has practiced Natalie Goldberg–style writing practice, sometimes blending it into the writing workshops she teaches. Goldberg, a Zen Buddhist, emphasizes the importance of reading your writing practice aloud in a group. A group free writes together, using a prompt, for 10, 15, 20, or even 30 minutes. The only rule is to not judge. You must always keep the pen moving, even if the only thing you can think to write is "This is crap. I don't know why I'm writing this." Inevitably, you will only stay in this for two, maybe three, sentences before your imagination sparks, and something intrigues you, and your horses are off and running. Goldberg teaches her disciples that this is the way through "monkey mind," that negative self-chatter that blocks us from our truest expressions.

Reading your piece immediately afterward to the group is a way of cleansing the palate of the mind. It brings you back to zero if you thought every word was grand, and it was the best piece you have ever written. It brings you back to zero if you thought no one could possibly want to hear this and you could never be a writer so why bother. Getting back to zero has proved time and time again to help Carolyn as a writer, breaking through writer's block (she never has it), and giving her encouragement and insight into her muse.

At Your Peril

Don't let your expectations of the future you want color your interpretation of an oracle. Oracles tell you the truth, whether you are ready to hear it or not. When you have a preconceived notion of how it's supposed to happen for you, you impede the wisdom of oracles. Even if you think you don't have expectations, you generally do. Sometimes what you want shows up—just in disguise. Keep an open mind and be aware of your expectations, and you'll find the bliss you are seeking.

Our preconceived notions of what the moment is supposed to be—whether it's a perfect piece of writing or a first date or a dream job—get in the way of oracle messages. Being in New York City, Gary has many clients who have clear images of their dreams in performing or writing. They have this image, and all evidence to the contrary is ignored. They seek signs everywhere that they are headed the right direction. They hear constructive criticism and either ignore the speaker or reinterpret the message to suit them. People who say what they want to hear are revered as oracles. Self-help gurus, tarot card readers, astrologers—you name it.

Gary will encourage these clients to detach from what they think they must be. He doesn't tell them to give it up, but from a Zen perspective, he tells them they are strangling their dream to death. He encourages them to let their dream breathe.

The Zen ideal is high participation, low attachment. Attachment is different from desire. Desire is good, but let it fuel the participation aspect of your dream—not the attachment. Often we become attached to a certain outcome, and we decide the form it will take—only to completely block off the wisest way to our dream.

A Zen koan forces us to ponder, to admit we don't know. It brings us to humility. Humility is another way of saying bring your mind to zero. A koan prompts our logical, all-knowing left-brain to focus on pondering something unknowable. It creates open space in the right side of the brain to listen, grow, and imagine without being shut down by logic.

What You're Willing to Do

To clear the channel, get clear about what you are willing to do. How far would you go to reach your goal? Would you try, and try again?

- Be willing to change your frame of reference. Listen to ideas that challenge you. Listen to sources of unconventional information.

- Be willing to say you don't have all the answers. Be willing to say you don't know the path ahead.

- Be willing to notice, just notice, the message. Notice your feelings about the message. What enlivens you? What scares you?

- Be willing to wait. If you don't get a clear interpretation right way, be patient. It will come. Be receptive. Open your mind. That is all you need to do.

- Be willing to ask for more understanding. Trust that the source of your oracle is divine wisdom. If so, your source has your best interest at heart. So ask.

Recently, Carolyn had a conversation with a man who was discouraged about his search for the right romantic partner. He was questioning his strategy. Should he be more patient? Should he be more open? Carolyn didn't know him well enough to give him good advice—or so she thought. But it came to her to say in reassurance, "A question like that doesn't remain unanswered for very long." She didn't know where that thought came from—maybe it was an oracle!—but it is true that our deepest desires do not remain mysteries for long.

It's difficult to be patient, especially when you know you have received a message that you do not fully understand. Gary admits he's an impatient person. But Gary has often found that he doesn't know the exact time frame a goal will be reached. Humans are time-bound, and that limits our perceptions. The universe is not.

Gary admits he has been frustrated to have to wait months, even years, for something to come to fruition. Going out on his own to be self-employed is one. But he realizes now that though he thought he was ready, the universe was sure he was not. When people suggested that Gary might want to wait before making his move, he viewed them as limiting him. It's a fine balance. He doesn't accept the limitations others attempt to impose on him, and he advises his clients the same. He tries to remain open to a greater vision that extends beyond what he can see at the time. By and large, Gary has been pleased—and even relieved—that events unfolded in his life on the universe's schedule, not his own. The results were that much greater.

Again, we don't know what we don't know. Our vision is limited by the past and colored by our wants and needs. We perceive limitations where the universe does not. An oracle—especially if it is a real person—bursts through those limitations.

Lakshmi: Taking Steps

Lakshmi is the Hindu earth goddess who represents good fortune and prosperity. Lakshmi was one of the treasures born of the churning of the sea of milk. She emerged holding a lotus and proceeded to bestow blessings on the universe. Deities were dazzled by her brilliance. Invite her abundance into your life. Invite her to break down the limitations of your perceptions. As you contemplate her card from the Goddess Oracle Deck, invite abundance into your life.

LAKSHMI
ABUNDANCE

Lakshmi is often referred to as the red goddess. She is believed to be the culmination of the three goddesses of the Indian rivers, Ganga, Yamuna, and Sarasvati—another triple goddess. The Hindus celebrate Divali, a festival of light, on the new moon that ends the month of Ashvina (late October to early

November). They light lamps to invite Lakshmi into their homes to bring the family good fortune in the coming year.

Blank Pages

The first step to interpreting an oracle message is opening your mind. Clear the channel by accepting you don't know everything—not even who might have the answers you need. Focus on the present. Focus on what you're willing to allow in your life. Get out of your routine. Get out and participate in life.

The Least You Need to Know

- No matter the source of an oracle, you must be in harmony with the governing principles of the physical and spiritual worlds.

- Oracles are not one-way messages. They require us to do the work of interpretation, and in doing so, we learn and grow.

- Oracles can come to us dramatically. Often these oracles are clear and prompt us to bolder action.

- Oracles can come to us as pieces of a larger puzzle. It may take several small messages that resonate with each other for you to fill in the big picture vision and act on it.

- Borrowing a little from Zen philosophies in interpreting your oracles can help them become clearer faster. Practice mindfulness, patience, and acceptance and see what it yields in your understanding.

- Be willing to be humble. Be willing to change. Be willing to hear a message that comes from outside your frame of reference.

Chapter 7

Put Oracles in Their Places

In This Chapter

- ◆ A place with presence
- ◆ Planning a pilgrimage
- ◆ Sacred space at home
- ◆ Sacredness on the road

The sacred is everywhere. Thoreau called the sacred "the divine energy everywhere," while Tao-te Ching said the sacred is "hidden but always present." But it is not always apparent to us in every place.

There are certain places where we can experience the sacred, where we recognize the presence of a special energy connecting us with the deeper meaning of life. In these places, we recognize a higher presence and surrender to it. These sacred places have messages of enlightenment and wisdom for us. They can serve as oracles, revealing the mysteries of the future and the now.

Finding the Sacred

A sacred space confers its wisdom on you wordlessly. Whatever the personal message you receive, it's beyond words. You absorb it. You experience it. You enter with a questing heart. You leave with the answers embedded deep within. It may not immediately be apparent, but the sense of calmness generally is. It's like Gary says: he knows he has received an oracle message because he no longer has the question.

In a sacred place, you immediately sense a divine presence. A sacred place has a clear spiritual focus, and often, upon entering, you sense a spiritual charge. It's almost palpable. Whatever your concept of the Divine, suddenly you experience that it's touchable.

A sacred space very often is set apart, physically, from the rest of the world. The location itself may be remote, as in Chaco Canyon in New Mexico, Stonehenge in England, or Angor Wat in Cambodia. The building itself may be set apart from others, or its stately and serene architecture may set off the building even though it sits amid a bustling metropolis, as in St. Patrick's Cathedral in New York, a sacred space Gary often visits.

The architecture of a sacred space must reinforce the natural spiritual charge. Often a sacred space has the element of lifting the eye upward to heaven, as in the dome of a great cathedral such as St. Peter's Basilica in Rome, Chartres Cathedral in France, the Hagia Sophia in Istanbul, or the Blue Mosque, also in Istanbul. The space must capture the reverence of the person who is entering.

A sacred space, whether it's a building or a mountain, a monument or a river, inspires a feeling of calmness. When you are in a sacred space, you find your center.

The Road to Sacred

Understanding how places of the world became sacred can give us insight into how to find and create sacred spaces in our lives. First, understand that the Divine is always trying to reach us. And truth be told, even if you do not consider yourself a spiritual person, you more than likely share the desire to experience something beyond your own mortality. That desire to reach out to a higher presence and find deeper meaning for your life exists in all of us, we believe.

It is in these two eternal desires—Creator pursuing us, us reaching out to Creator—that a sacred space is born.

When we look at some of the famous sacred places in the world and examine how they came to be so, we find there are several paths:

◆ **Natural phenomenon.** Throughout time, geological formations have provided a window to the sacred. The fissure at Delphi is one example, of course. Know that one translation of the word *Delphi* is "womb," which suggests it is the birthing place for ideas and dreams. Another sacred place is Iona, one of the smaller islands of the Inner Hebrides off the western coast of Scotland. The island is strikingly different from the neighboring islands and it is known for Iona marble, a near-pristine white rock with streaks of celadon. Geological formations such as this inspire awe in us. Many describe Iona as a place on Earth where the veil between the material world and divine world is thinner. Other such spots: Sedona, Arizona; and Glastonbury, England.

◆ **Alignment, with intention.** The ancient circles of massive stones that stand on the plain in Stonehenge, England, are lined up with the solstices and equinoxes, the movements of the sun. It is still a mystery about who shaped, carried, and set the stones in place—and how. But what inspires reverence to those who visit the site is evidence of a steadfast intention to align oneself with the Divine to gain a deeper understanding. There are many such sites in the ancient world, from the Egyptian pyramids to Aztec pyramids to the Anasazi ruins of Chaco Canyon in New Mexico.

◆ **Sacred experience.** Many sacred sites that inspire pilgrimages are based on the experience of one believer, or many. Lourdes, France, is one such site, where pilgrims come from near and far because of the experience of one peasant girl named Bernadette. In the mid-nineteenth century, Bernadette said she experienced visions of the Virgin Mary at a grotto near Lourdes, a village in the foothills of the Pyrenees in southern France. When she told others of her experience, leading them back to the grotto, a spring spontaneously appeared. Since then, many have believed the water has healing properties, and the site draws millions of visitors each year.

In Oaxaca, Mexico, pilgrims flock to the shrine of the Juquila Virgin, paying tribute to her with *milagritos*, small charms that represent little miracles in their lives. (*Milagritos* means "little miracles.") The legend of the Juquila Virgin is that an image of the Virgin was in a cave, but a fire burned down everything in the cave, even the Virgin's face—but not her dress and veil, which stood, white and immaculate amid the ashes. Pilgrims come to touch her dress and veil and promise to perform some act of kindness in her name. The hand-embroidered dress is magnificent, and the veil is so long that the people built a little room on the back of the shrine so that her veil is extended, like the roof of a tent, over the room.

♦ **Making a shrine.** The building of a shrine or temple, no matter the culture or belief system, was an undertaking to create a meeting place between the human and the Divine. In ancient times, the *way* these temples were built, such as King Solomon's temple, was just as important to the result. For instance, all brass, wood, and stone for the temple was prepared before being brought to the site, so that the assembling of the temple itself was done "without the hammer of contention, the axe of division, or any tool of mischief," according to George Oliver, author of many texts on freemasonry.

In the midst of Solomon's temple stood the holy of holies, sometimes called an oracle. The shrine or altar is a threshold, a common ground where the human and the Divine can convene. It's the place where you can invite the presence of the Divine into your heart.

Architectural and the Divine

Sacred spaces often contain similar architectural elements. An upward focus—such as the dome of a cathedral, a cross on an altar, a sculpture such as Michelangelo's *Pietà*, the inscriptions of Allah on the dome of a mosque, or the height of a great monument such as the pyramids of Egypt or Stonehenge—brings our eyes off of our navel to acknowledge a higher presence.

The circle is a universal theme because of its calming effect. Psychologist Carl Jung said circles, or mandalas, have this effect because they work as magnets, drawing us forward to the Divine, allowing us to discard any contradictory mental chatter as we near the center. In the mandala, he saw the expression of the structure of the soul. In moving through that structure, either visually, as you contemplate a mandala or the dome of a cathedral, or physically, as you walk through a labyrinth, you reach the point where you surpass your individuality and enter the realm where you can experience the rhythm of the universe. (We talk more about how you can use mandalas and labyrinths in Chapter 14.)

We don't think of architects and builders this way in our culture, but in ancient times, sculptors and architects were revered for the profound knowledge they possessed of the Divine. To be a builder in those times, one had to be an expert in mathematics and astronomy. All measurements of buildings and all ornamentation were based on knowledge of the laws controlling the universe. Scholars have detected many of these symbols of their knowledge of divine doctrine in structures such as Cleopatra's Needle in Central Park, New York City, or the rose line in the Rosslyn Cathedral, often called the Cathedral of Codes, in Edinburgh, Scotland, which figures in the best-selling novel *The Da Vinci Code* by Dan Brown (see Appendix B).

> **Tell It Like It Is**
>
> Many sacred places represent layers of different doctrines. Jerusalem is the most notable example of the way many belief systems converge on one place. Other examples are the Chartres Cathedral in France, dedicated to the Virgin Mary but believed to be a goddess site in pre-Christian times. Another is El Sanctuario de Chimayó in New Mexico, which is believed by some to have been a sacred Native American site before the church was built there. Sacredness transcends culture and time.

Going on a Journey

What if you'd like to go on a pilgrimage? Millions of people choose to do just that every year, in search of healing, understanding, or just a midlife gut check. If the previous discussion of sacred spaces has you wanting to book a flight, then let's take a look at what you need to do.

How to Do a Pilgrimage

As you might imagine, the first step is to prepare your heart. Take some time to set your intention for the pilgrimage. Is it for healing a past relationship? For healing a physical illness that has depleted your body and your spirit? Is it for insight into a change you want to make in your life?

Setting an intention is not the same thing as creating expectations for your pilgrimage. It's important that whatever journey you take, you take with mindfulness. Mindfulness means staying in the present moment and taking the experience as it is. Often the sweetest moments of life are those we do not create through our own effort and expectations, when we just let the presence of the Divine take hold. We are reminded of the pilgrimage Jean Shinoda Bolen takes in *Crossing to Avalon* (see Appendix B) to

Chartres Cathedral. She expected to see the famed labyrinth immediately. Instead, she stumbled on it, somewhat by serendipity, as she broke free from a tour group, finding it underneath folding wooden chairs that she had to move, one by one, to walk through the labyrinth.

Before you set out on your pilgrimage, examine your motives. Your aim must be life affirming, not just for you, but to everyone you are connected to. This is important if you are seeking healing, whether emotional or physical, because there may be parts of you that hurt and feel angry. Just know that they are there.

Sulis: Sunlight and Healing

SULIS
ILLNESS/WELLNESS

Sulis is a British goddess depicted in the Goddess Oracle Deck, and she was known for her healing powers. She had a shrine in Bath, England, that was a spa with healing waters. Legend has it that her healing waters were miraculous in their powers. Her name derives from *sul*, Celtic for "sun" and "eye." In that, she represents the healing power of sunlight. On this card, she is depicted swimming through her healing waters, up through the light, reaching to the sun. To us, she represents optimism.

To bring more of this kind of energy into your life, schedule yourself some time at a spa or natural hot springs with thermal mineral waters. Or schedule yourself for a hot-stone massage.

Sulis reminds us of the importance of self-care, of creating a *sanctuary* in which we can tend to our body, mind, and spirit. She also reminds us of the power of optimism to encourage us to reach for the healing that we need. Miracles are all around us, in everyday life. If you seek the miracle of healing, consider the words of Buddhist teacher Thich Nhat Hanh to restore your innocence and optimism: "People usually consider walking on water or in thin air a miracle. But I think the real miracle is not to walk either on water or in thin air, but to walk on Earth. Every day we are engaged in a miracle which we don't even recognize: a blue sky, white clouds, green leaves, the black, curious eyes of a child—our own two eyes. All is a miracle."

Wise Words

In a religious context, a **sanctuary** is generally a holy place set aside for worship, but in the larger sense, it's a sacred place that focuses your heart and mind on the Divine. In some definitions, it's a refuge, a place in which you can shut out the dangers and worries of the world and feel safe. It's a place where you allow yourself to be humble. You can be vulnerable and reveal your inner self. In this place, you can commune with a higher presence.

Creating Your Own Sacred Space

You don't have to go on a trek to find sacred space. You can work to create that in your own life, right where you are. Mythologist Joseph Campbell urged people to create their own bliss station, a place of creative incubation, where you are free of knowing what was in the newspaper that day, where your friends and family can't intrude, and you don't think about anything you owe anyone. You are in a sanctuary where nothing is required of you. It is a place where you can simply just be. It's a retreat for the soul.

If You Build It ...

The phrase "nature abhors a vacuum" applies here. If you create a space in your life, in your home, with a specific intention behind it, then the universe works with you to fill that space. In other words, if you build it, the Divine will come.

But it does take some effort. You must put real action behind your intention. It means making time to contemplate, meditate, and read. It might mean saying no to social events, working smarter, or cutting back on projects.

Intentionality means not only having good intentions but taking actions that demonstrate to the universe that you are serious. We think you get back in equal measure what you put in.

A Sacred Space in New York

Gary lives in a studio apartment in Manhattan, which presents a challenge for him to have a separate sacred space. In his apartment, he has one expanse of wall (expanse in a studio apartment means about 10 feet) that he painted orange. He bought a small table that fits proportionally to the wall, and on that table, he has a single lamp, a beautiful bowl, a candle, and nothing else. On the lower shelf of that table, he has a small statue he bought in Japan. It has no religious significance, but nevertheless, he looks upon that small area of his apartment as a kind of sacred space.

Gary draws upon feng shui, the Chinese art of arranging space, as well as the principles of Zen living he discussed in his previous book, *The Complete Idiot's Guide to Zen Living, Second Edition* (see Appendix B). He keeps his office space sacred by keeping it simple, balanced, and uncluttered, and he's quite diligent about it.

Another way Gary creates that sacred space in his life is to light candles or play chant music. Carolyn does this, too, at her sacred space, the jetted tub in her home, where she has candles and a window that looks east to the Sandia Mountains, where she can watch the moon rise. Candles are an excellent way to bring your contemplation to the source of light. As Taoist founder Lao-Tzu said, "Use your own light and return to the source of light. This is called practicing eternity."

Artemis: Finding Sanctuary in Nature

ARTEMIS
SELFHOOD

In Ephesus, Turkey, there is a Temple of Artemis, the Greek goddess of the hunt, the forest, and the moon. Artemis was one of the super-goddesses of Greek culture, a daughter of Zeus, who loved nature so much that she is described as the virgin goddess who made love in the woods. By virgin, though, we mean whole and complete to herself—not in the sense of a maiden who has not yet experienced the full expression of femininity. For in Artemis, we find the divine feminine principle. For this reason, she was the goddess of childbirth.

Carolyn has been to the Temple of Artemis and seen the totem to Artemis, who was known as the "Lady of All Wild Things" and was worshipped by the totem clans. The Greeks offered her sacrifices of animals, birds, and plants. She represents the home we can make in the natural world, the communion with the forest and the wild animals. She represents the bliss that we can feel when we bring ourselves in harmony with nature.

Everyday Sacredness

Why do we need a sacred space if the whole world is sacred? Isn't a sacred space something we create in our own minds?

What you call a sacred space may not feel sacred to another. What is special about sacred places is that they are personally meaningful to us. They may evoke a memory or a feeling, or they may be awe-inspiring in a way that helps us get into a place spiritually and emotionally where we are more open. Why we do or don't make a connection with a sacred space is as complex as why we have more chemistry with some people than others, or why a novel or a poem might affect two people completely differently. It is a question without an answer, but then it probably doesn't need to be answered. You may need to slip into a spot in nature, but Gary might find a small bench positioned between two buildings to be sacred for him. Focus on how you are affected, and not on whether a space is "supposed to be" sacred.

You can find sacredness in everyday life, even in New York City. Sometimes Gary slips in to St. Patrick's Cathedral, though he is not Catholic. Or he will go to Central Park, to the Japanese garden at the Brooklyn Botanical Gardens, or to the Egyptian wing of the Metropolitan Museum of Art, and many, many other special places the city harbors.

When you travel a lot, as Gary and Carolyn do, you find these little sanctuaries. When Carolyn was in Portland, Oregon, she found a Zen garden in the Japanese gardens there. When she was on the south Gulf Coast of Florida, she found a little strip of beach where there were very few people at the end of the day. Sometimes she goes to the garden behind the Fenn Gallery in Santa Fe; the sculpture garden at the Santa Fe location of Ghost Ranch; the little canal in the courtyard in Arroyo Seco near Taos, New Mexico; or a *sanctuario* in Arroyo Hondo. All of these are little places she's discovered, but these little places are everywhere. The reflexology path, a path of stones at Bastyr University near Seattle, or the Sound Garden, also in Seattle, are other examples. It's just a matter of exploring. It can be as simple as the little corner of your favorite independent bookstore.

Once when Gary was on a business trip to Los Angeles, his driver asked him whether he wanted to stop and visit a sacred garden. Gary said yes, and the driver took him to the headquarters of the Self-Realization Fellowship—Paramahansa Yogananda—where there were beautiful buildings and a garden that is open to the public. The path through the garden is tended by followers, all of whom greet you as you pass through. The experience meant a lot to Gary. It was a pilgrimage that presented itself to Gary when he hadn't even asked for it.

Going back home can sometimes be a pilgrimage, if you are in the right frame of mind. For Gary, that means going back home to Michigan. For Carolyn, that means Bluegrass horse country in Kentucky. Going home can be tricky if you are focused on resisting the differences between you and your family and your past. So you must prepare yourself ahead of time, or often those issues will present themselves to you in dramatic ways that you will choose to avoid.

Carolyn used some of the techniques from the book she co-authored with Shari Just, Ph.D., *The Complete Idiot's Guide to Creative Visualization* (see Appendix B), when she returned home for the holidays with her twins. Instead of focusing on the differences that existed in her family as it was in the present, she chose to collect in her mind instances of positive family experiences from her childhood and through times of crisis. In visualizing moments from her happy childhood, she remembered the feeling of growing up in a secure, loving family. In visualizing ways her family had really been there for her when it counted—and she for them—she got in touch with the glue that keeps her family together, despite distance and different viewpoints.

Reconnecting with the small moments from your childhood—seeing friends and relatives from your past, even sleeping in your childhood room, driving past your old school—can restore depth to your life experience. You can feel whole again. And you can see how far you have come.

We return to the idea of creating sacredness in everyday life in Chapter 20, but use some of these ideas for now to begin connecting to the wisdom that comes from sacred spaces:

- **Simplicity and harmony.** Read up on feng shui, the art of arranging your space to create harmony in your environment.

- **Tranquility.** Find a Zen garden in your city or create one in your own backyard. You can even create a desktop Zen garden, usually just a small tray with white sand and smooth stones. (Kits are available at home furnishing stores, at gift shops, or on the Internet.) Or you can find virtual versions of Zen gardens on the Internet and "rake" your Zen garden with your computer mouse.

- **Light.** Lighting candles, bringing the sunlight into your home, or just noticing the plank of afternoon sunlight falling on your living room floor—all of these keep you in touch with the undercurrent of sacredness in everyday life.

- **Intention.** Set up your own personal altar in your home where you bring items that signify your devotion. Make this your meeting place with the Divine.

◆ **Reverence.** Seek out cathedrals, gardens, and other sacred spaces that inspire reverence.

◆ **Emblems.** Like the milagritos that pilgrims bring the Juquila Virgin in Oaxaca, emblems pull your thoughts into a spiritual focus. Mala beads, in the Tibetan tradition, work the same way. Emblems keep your wishes and desires close to mind; and they keep you close to the Divine. We talk about these more in Chapter 20, so stay tuned!

This Way to Wisdom

Sacred places can increase the quality of your thinking and your contemplation. If you are stuck on finding the way in your Nine Wise Ways, you may not need to seek an oracle that comes in the form of a message or a person. You may just need the change of scenery that sharpens your thinking and brings you clarity. Let your test for a sacred space be the place that enlivens you and inspires renewed reverence for the Divine and for yourself, as part of creation. In the words of mythologist Joseph Campbell, "Your sacred space is where you can find yourself again and again."

The Least You Need to Know

◆ Certain places in the world are sacred because we more readily sense the heartbeat of the Divine, but in truth, sacredness is everywhere.

◆ A sacred place brings you into a clear spiritual focus and a heightened awareness of a higher presence.

◆ Going on a pilgrimage to a sacred space can provide you with a quantum leap of consciousness.

◆ You don't need to go on a trek to find the sacred; you can create sacred space in your own home.

◆ Tune in to find the sacredness in everyday life, wherever you are.

Chapter 8

The Oracle Is the Messenger

In This Chapter

- ◆ Selecting oracle messengers
- ◆ Reaching out to messengers
- ◆ Facing the tough stuff
- ◆ Is it working for you?

Some people just embody wisdom. We instinctively know that, and in this age of global media, we often make them instant celebrities.

King Solomon, the Hebrew king of the Old Testament who chose wisdom over health and wealth, is one ancient example of the embodiment of wisdom. The syllables of his name, Sol-om-on, are believed to symbolize light, glory, and truth.

Many people act as messengers who blend light, glory, and truth into simple messages. They act as translators of oracle messages, taking what might be esoteric to us and making it make sense. In this chapter, we show you how to select them and how to use them.

Choose Well: How to Find an Oracle Messenger

You already have a wealth of oracle messengers in your life. But taking the step of identifying them and understanding what they might represent to you will allow you to use them more thoughtfully. Here are some steps to take:

1. Make a list of people who seem to fit the bill, identifying people from your personal life as well as public figures. Don't limit yourself to only people you know, or who are living. Some of the goddesses we have introduced, or other wise figures from the ancient world or from history, might be just right for you. We encourage you to make at least some of your oracle list from the ancient world.

2. Examine your goals under Nine Wise Ways (see Chapter 1). Try to identify several knowledgeable people for each one. Look to your personal life for wise advisers. Look on your bookshelf for books that have inspired you. Ask among your friends and acquaintances for the person who can tell you about what you need to know. Get recommendations.

3. Identify some specific things that they have said that you agree with, that have helped you.

4. Looking at that list, ask yourself what values you share with this person. What might be similar about your backgrounds? In what way do you feel familiar with this person? It could be his face, her voice, the fact that she also is from the Midwest, the fact that he also has two daughters. Whatever it is, these commonalities form the basis for an interchange of wisdom.

An Expanding Circle of Wisdom

This first circle of oracles is those people who espouse views similar to yours and with whom you have a sense of familiarity. They are your inner circle of oracles. They provide security for you. They are the ones you can trust with your most vital needs, wants, and desires.

Next we want you to make a list of people who have surprised you or provoked you to change. They can be people you interact with regularly, or it could be someone with whom you had one encounter. These are the people who keep you honest. They remind you of your true worth and your most heartfelt desires when you lose sight of them. They spur you to think again when you are contemplating an act that might compromise your integrity.

Write what you like about these people. Some examples might be:

Always tells it to me straight.

Always has my best interest at heart.

Doesn't always say it tenderly, but his heart is in the right place.

Next compile a list of people who are outside of your normal realm of activity, both in your personal life and in the public eye. When it comes to experts who might serve as oracles to you, you might tend to gravitate to people in your field, or in the field of knowledge that relates to one of your Nine Wise Ways. For instance, if you are looking for your calling in life, you might turn to an author who takes a business-oriented, practical approach to changing jobs, such as Barbara Sher in *Wishcraft* (see Appendix B). It's possible a spiritual self-help book doesn't quite cut it for you when you're looking for a better-paying job. Or it may be that you need to go more spiritual to get out of the box: a book such as *Sacred Contracts* by Caroline Myss (see Appendix B) may help you look inward to see what agreements you have made with yourself that hold you back from even *imagining* a better job.

Tell It Like It Is

Author Caroline Myss defines a sacred contract as your overall relationship to your personal power and your spiritual power. You have made agreements with a set of beliefs, and those agreements determine how you will use your energy and to what and whom you will give it. These beliefs also determine how much you are willing to submit to divine guidance. By examining this information about yourself, you can make different choices for the path of your life. Oracles can be windows into these beliefs that shape us.

In your personal life, make a list of people that you have limited friendships with, or people you know only casually. Is there anyone who intrigues you, anyone you'd like to know better? Is there anyone you shy away from in a social setting? It's worth it to take a moment to examine why. It may be merited on the surface—the person may convey a value you disagree with, such as rampant materialism, in the way she dresses or what he talks about. Or he may seem judgmental, and you instinctively steer clear of negative people. But know that sometimes first impressions can be wrong. What may frighten you about this person is that he or she may tell you something you don't want to know yet, but that something may help you very much. We're not suggesting you make bad friendships or seek bad advice—just be a little more open and know that people with very different values from you can sometimes be quite helpful.

Cultivating Your Messengers

Okay, now you have a list. How can you bring more of this wisdom into your life? Of course, if the person has written a book, produced a tape, or hosts a television show, you can write that person. Or you can collect his or her work.

Writing a letter to your oracle can work, whether your oracle is living or dead. Go ahead, write a letter to Isis or Sulis, Gandhi or the Dalai Lama. Pour your heart out.

For oracles who are in your personal life, two vital steps predicate your first approach to your newfound oracle. One is to develop an emotional bond with your oracle. Two is to have the proper attitude—meaning one of nonjudgment. Take a moment to note what judgments you have about this person, even if you think you only have the utmost admiration for this person. Notice what your differences are—and neutralize them. They are neither good nor bad. You are just aware of them as possible places where there are limits on the wisdom you may receive from this person—unless you choose consciously to bridge those differences.

Now focus on what you admire about your oracle's work. Ask him how he does it. Ask how she gets engrossed in her work and shuts out distractions. Ask him how he gets a team of people to cooperate with him. Ask her how she keeps all the details in her mind at one time. Ask for suggestions on how you might develop some of the same qualities. Open yourself up to a constructively critical analysis of your approach.

Also make a point of seeking out oracles whose wisdom sometimes rubs us the wrong way. We tend to shy away from people with whom we are not comfortable. Sometimes we criticize them, faulting them somehow for our discomfort. Maybe we judge them as too aggressive or from a different social class.

Know that every person has something to teach you. Sometimes it's a negative—the way *not* to be in your own life. These people can teach us another dimension of what it means to be compassionate. Or they can teach us about a challenge to add to our lives.

Gary finds himself turning away from really aggressive, take-charge people. But this is also a characteristic he has had to cultivate in himself, certainly, as a self-employed person. So that take-charge attitude may frighten Gary, but it is something he has envied at the same time. By looking at his reaction to aggressive people, he has learned to ask people who have take-charge attitudes how they do it. Sometimes they admit that they are as frightened of that quality as Gary is, but have had to harness this ability for survival.

At Your Peril

Why go through a messenger? You may feel that way if you got a cryptic message like Oedipus got at Delphi—that he would kill his father and marry his mother. (This may be the origin of "kill the messenger.") But the answer is, yes, you could receive the message directly, and you are perfectly capable of doing so. (We even show you how in Chapter 12.) But the people we call oracle messengers have prepared intellectually and spiritually for their role for many years. The short answer is that oracles can get you there faster. They provide the quantum leap of consciousness. They can collapse lifetimes of learning into a cosmic instant.

Oracles by Example

Some people of wisdom are not the kind to take the spotlight, and we caution you not to overlook them in your quest to collect personal oracles. Some people are oracles in how they lead their lives. They provide messages by example. There are many reasons they can't or won't speak to us directly. In some cases, they have been silenced or suppressed. Nelson Mandela is one example, until he was freed after spending 26 years in prison, before he became president of South Africa from 1994 to 1999. But it was while he was imprisoned that he gained the esteem and admiration for continuing to fight apartheid. He won the Nobel Peace Prize in 1993. Others have chosen to remain silent, choosing instead the path of humility. St. Teresa de Avila is one example. Her writings speak to us across the centuries, transcending the limitations that she faced, as a woman in the Catholic Church. For others, humility was absolutely a vital part of who they were and formed their message, such as St. Thérèse of Lisieux, often called "the Little Flower."

We use the goddess cards in the oracle deck as examples—archetype oracles, if you will. Archetypes transcend time and culture and recognize that we all hurt, learn, and grow. Our initial understanding of Isis, for instance, is situational, another goddess of the earth, daughter of Ra. But we find out what she is really made of when her husband is hacked to pieces, and she must revive him. That's when we learn of her undying dedication. That's when we connect, with compassion, to universal emotions: love and sorrow.

The following three goddesses show you how to use the goddess cards as archetype oracles. Notice once again, we have a triple. This triple reading represents the cycle of growing into your emotional power, moving from victim to protector to healer.

Sekhmet: Facing Your Anger

SEKHMET
ANGER AND RAGE

Sekhmet is the Egyptian goddess of anger and rage, known as the one who punishes for mortal sins. In later, kinder incarnations, she was the protector of righteousness. Her name means "Mighty One," and she is often depicted as a fearless warrior who uses arrows. Egyptians described the hot desert winds as her breath, and they depict her with a fiery glow emanating from her body.

You can call upon the strength of Sekhmet to help you face your anger about the injustices and disappointments in your life. It's okay. Go ahead and acknowledge the messages you have not wanted to hear. She reminds us we can feel safe in bringing up the things we don't want in our lives.

Acknowledging your anger is the first step in transforming it. Righteous rage is the signal that something is out of balance. What did you let get out of balance in the situation that provokes your anger? Knowing what it is will give you insight into changing it.

Durga: Facing the Threat

DURGA
BOUNDARIES

A major part of using oracle messengers in your lives is employing the strength of the messenger to do for you what you cannot yet do. The messenger acts as an intercessor. In the case of the Hindu goddess Durga, she goes as the warrior goddess to the places you can't or won't go.

Durga is described as the invincible destroyer—someone definitely to have on your side. She is said to be formed by the flames in the mouths of Vishnu and Shiva, two of the central Hindu gods. Time after time in Hindu mythology, she went into battle to fight demons that no one else would face. She is usually depicted riding a tiger or lion and shown with 2 to 10 arms. Sometimes she is depicted as a beautiful woman holding the disk of the moon and a skull. But most often, she has eight arms, and she holds a sword, arrow, chakra, shield, noose, javelin, bow, and conch shell. So she was armed!

Durga is said to be the goddess of boundaries because she is the energy that goes out and fights for your rights.

As you contemplate Durga, identify the threats you are facing. Use the depiction of her energy—going into battle fully armed—to direct your thoughts to your higher source of power, the power that transcends threats and holds true to who you are.

Coatlicue: Facing Your Grief

COATLICUE

GRIEF

This Aztec goddess is the story of mother-daughter love. Coatlicue had 400 sons and 1 daughter, all of whom were gods in Aztec mythology. One day she placed some white-plumed feathers on her bosom, and she became pregnant. The jealous sons plotted to kill her so there would be no other son to threaten their place as gods. But her daughter, Coyolxauhqul, the moon goddess, warned her. The sun god decapitated her daughter. In the depiction of this card from the Goddess Oracle Deck, Coatlicue is placing her daughter's luminous head in the sky.

Let her story be an encouragement for you to face your grief. Grief need not be about a death. It could be a divorce or a missed opportunity. Perhaps you always wanted to have a child, but the time and circumstances never seemed right. Perhaps you nurture the dream of a career or calling that has not yet materialized. Letting yourself grieve is vital to clearing the channel. Face what will not be in your life. Know that acceptance leads to forgiveness, and forgiveness heals.

Oracle Advice

Take a few moments to write in your Oracle Journal about people who have earned your admiration for their fortitude and grace in facing a life crisis. Again, these can be people in your personal life, can be people in the public eye, or can be important figures from history or ancient mythology. Maybe they faced their situation with courage and optimism. Maybe you knew their despair but saw that they did not give in to it. What do you think was in that person's character that made him bounce back so quickly? What attributes do you share with this person? What would you like to be able to do?

Unique Qualifications

We have touched on the idea that people who serve as oracle messengers have unique qualifications. Some of that comes from life experience that shapes their view of the world, as in Nelson Mandela or Viktor Frankl, who wrote *Man's Search for Meaning* from a German concentration camp. It was that experience that prompted him to write, "The one thing you can't take away from me is the way I choose to respond to what you do to me. The last of one's freedoms is to choose one's attitude in any given circumstance." These are the experiences that separate oracles from the rest of us. Let's take a closer look at what shapes them.

Courage, Mate

Courage sets apart those who think and those who act. Courage comes in many musical strains, loud as a symphony or quiet as the plucked strings of a harp. Martin Luther King Jr. lived a life of courage. Rosa Parks made one courageous choice—not to move to the back of the bus—that arose out of her everyday life.

There are people who are willing to be vulnerable with us, as Princess Diana was about her bulimia, depression, and unhappy marriage; as Oprah Winfrey has been about her difficult childhood. Their courage to reveal personal pain inspires us.

Then there are people who have the courage not to mince words, to just tell it like it is. Dr. Phil of television talk show and book fame is one example. Like him or not, Dr. Phil tells people plain to their face how they must change to make their relationships work, and this truth resonates with many people. His famous line, which often spurs people to change, compromise, get real, and get honest, is "Is that working for you?"

Some people inspire us because they talk about difficult subjects that we can't talk about, and they make them universal. The way writer Susan Sontag spoke about AIDS in her book *AIDS and Its Metaphors* (see Appendix B) gave us an understanding of this terrible disease. Basically, Sontag said that we speak in metaphors about illnesses such as cancer and AIDS to create an artificial boundary between us and the illness. As a result, we use warlike imagery—"fighting AIDS"—and we make people who have these illnesses feel isolated and even blameworthy. By trying to keep the illnesses away from us, by not talking about them, we isolate the sufferers. In her lifetime, Sontag was certainly an oracle. She basically admonished us to be honest, courageous, and forthright and see illness as affecting all of humanity rather than only those stricken with it.

Some people have a way of striking that chord of compassion that brings about unity, such as Nelson Mandela did or Mother Teresa, who was, in her life, the human embodiment of compassion.

Gary works a lot with cancer patients, and they serve this purpose for those around them, even though they are not recognized as oracles. By dealing with their illness in a direct and positive manner, they influence others in a manner similar to Mandela. Gary had breakfast recently with a man in his 30s with a jaw cancer that required some bone replacement as well as skin grafts. His positive attitude and his joy at being able to return to his children and his wife and his job were awe-inspiring.

Tuning In

The people we can turn to as interpreters of divine wisdom are those who have found a way to tune in to oracles. Up to now, we have skirted the subject of whether oracles are psychic. Psychic, in our minds, is not limited to someone who knows about astrology or tarot, but someone who is tuned in to deeper wisdom. So instead, we would rather look at the role intuition plays in the qualities of an oracle messenger.

People who we might call psychic seem to have their finger on the pulse of knowledge that vibrates differently—knowledge we cannot all immediately access. Much of what we talked about in Chapter 4 on skepticism is about freeing yourself from the limits of the rational mind so that you, too, can cultivate a wider range of knowledge. *Intuition* is defined as knowing without conscious thinking. But when you cultivate it, you can start to discern the information you have taken in that forms your knowing. It can become conscious, though that is not necessary. To become more intuitive, you must simply practice noticing your intuitions and exploring them. With practice, you'll come to trust your intuition more and more. And with that, you'll come to trust the knowledge of other intuitive people.

> **Wise Words**
>
> **Intuition** is direct knowing that comes without conscious reasoning. Intuition comes in the form of impressions, inklings, and little glimmers of insight. Some people describe it as instinct, a gut reaction, or a hunch. On the surface, it seems independent of previous experiences or empirical knowledge. But it comes from a deep knowledge from within.

Gary asks clients to recount events from the past when they have used their intuition and been correct. Gary helps them compare the decision they have to make now and decisions they have made in the past. How does this feel the same? How is it different? At what stage, in past situations, did you feel ready to move forward based on your intuition? What had to happen first? What doubts remained?

Looking at the consequences of making the wrong decision can also be helpful. What is the worse thing that could happen? What would you do then?

It is all about understanding the implications and the ramifications, and building confidence in trusting your gut. What does it feel like when you decide to go in *this* direction? What does it feel like when you decide to go in *that* direction? What is that telling you? Use your Oracle Journal to play out the two scenarios.

Part of learning to use your intuition is learning to sort out information from your head versus your gut. One question Carolyn applies to situations of uncertainty, such as meeting a new person or visualizing a future event, is "What does the energy feel like?" She will examine whether the energy around this subject feels unmovable, or if it feels like it is flowing, or possibly light. Carolyn uses this to get clear on her sense of trust with people.

If you are a highly verbal person, as Carolyn is, this technique might be useful to you. Many of us, in the information age, even if we aren't writers or psychologists, spend a lot of time in our heads. The talk in our heads can sometimes drown out our gut sense of a situation. Asking these kinds of questions can get you back to a centered, calm place where you attain some certainty.

Carolyn used this technique with a boyfriend when he was facing the issue of a career transition and she was still getting to know him. The technique proved useful in helping her create her own sense of centeredness and not get caught up in the daily fluctuations as he faced the issues of a midlife transition and a changing identity. When she would listen to him talk, she would pay attention to whether the energy seemed solid and true or light and changing. She learned that one day he might talk about a career prospect with great excitement, but then completely drop it and never mention it again. Some prospects seemed like fantasies, whereas others seemed more in line with the man she was getting to know. In a short amount of time, Carolyn was able to arrive at some certainty about his future and find her own equilibrium within the relationship, despite the changing day-to-day prospects.

Personalizing Your Messages

Our discussion on intuition leads us to the next dilemma. There are many visionaries and messengers out there. We may call Warren Buffett the Oracle of Omaha, but how many of us would have trusted to stay away from dot.com stocks when he did? For some of us, the answer would be yes; for others, it would be no. The point here is that not every person that would be considered an oracle has the message that's right for *you*.

Consulting an oracle is a very personal experience, and that's where intuition comes in. You must know in your heart of hearts that this oracle messenger is right for you.

With clients, Gary uses an approach similar to the one Carolyn took with her boyfriend. If the client is listening to various people, Gary discusses the advice they are getting and raises their awareness to how it sits with them. Does it get them excited? How? What about after the emotional rush wears off? And what does the advice stimulate in terms of action they need to take? Gary is always wary of "believe in yourself" kinds of messages. And the same for advice that is discouraging. Instead, he asks, "does this person want to give up and go in another direction?" Why? Or did it introduce a jolt of reality that this person didn't really want to look at? Again, there is often at least a kernel of knowledge to be gained in every situation.

It's paramount to be selective about the people you seek out as oracles. Use the exercise earlier in this chapter to clarify your values and see where you match—and don't match—with this oracle.

Another obstacle might be if the oracle is of a different belief system from you. You may be unwilling to accept the wisdom, no matter how true it is, if it comes with the trappings of a different religion or culture. Then again, you may be the kind who can sense the current of wisdom no matter the trappings. It's neither good nor bad if you are one way or another, just something you should know about yourself.

Use your intuition to take the best of an oracle message and make it work for you. And leave the rest behind.

Customized Oracles

Oracle messengers work in our lives to be guides to the wisdom we all seek. They also help unlock the wisdom you have within. By getting clearer about which oracle messengers provide the most insight for you, you can gain better facility with using oracles as tools to manifest what you want in your life.

The Least You Need to Know

- Make wise choices in choosing oracle messengers. Know what values you share and know how they will challenge you.

- Cultivate oracle messengers in your life by striking up a conversation with them, either directly or through correspondence.

- Many oracles lead by example, providing their lives as a blueprint for how we might build ours around the same values.

- Oracle messengers have unique qualifications. They possess the courage to hold fast to their convictions, the willingness to examine painful experiences, and the openness to tune in all dimensions of life.

- Tune in to your intuition to know whether the message an oracle has is right for you.

Part 3

Wise Oracle Knows All

Know thyself, and you will know your oracles. In this part, we show you how to get the most out of your oracles. Know your questions, examine your intentions, and find the most life-affirming desires within. And be good to your oracles, being generous of heart and mind. They will take you there, whatever happy place there might be, and they will give you the wisdom to solve the puzzle of their truth. You might even learn to become an oracle yourself!

9

What Do *You* Want to Know?

In This Chapter

- ◆ Get your story straight
- ◆ Asking the tough questions
- ◆ Taking the inner path
- ◆ Going on a quest

People consult oracles for many reasons, some of them highly personal, some of them with an outward focus on societal issues. Sometimes people consult oracles to resolve conflicts, either interpersonal, as in the case of a marriage counselor, or between nations, as in the case of a shuttle diplomat. Throughout the ages, people have consulted oracles about the timing of things—about when to set sail on a journey, when to plant the corn.

All in all, the key is to know the right question. Sometimes the answer you need depends on the intention and clarity of your question. In this chapter, we teach you how to get in the right frame of mind so the questions you ask yield the answers you seek.

What Are You Asking?

If you are the self-reliant type, you may not recognize the ways you consult oracles, but more than likely you do. Some of the most resourceful people in this world are not those who hold all the answers within themselves but know *who* to turn to for the answers they need.

If you look over your list of goals in your Nine Wise Ways, you'll probably find you are more self-reliant in some areas and more interdependent in others. You might also find that the types of oracles you consult in certain areas are very different. For instance, you may turn to rational, cognitive thinkers in one area, but rely on intuitive thinkers in another.

When we hear stories about how oracles were consulted in ancient times, we imagine that one wise person who knows all. Somehow the idea gets imprinted on us that there is one powerful, visionary person who knows us so well that he or she has all the answers for us, can see the future, and knows this world better than we do. But more than likely, the oracles we read about in ancient history were composites that became archetypes of wisdom as the stories were handed down over time. And more than likely, in real, contemporary life, the oracle that helps us most is a composite of many and is individualized for our unique questions.

Your Questions

There are some fundamental reasons we all consult oracles, and we have categorized them into these two essential reasons:

◆ To resolve inner conflicts

◆ To help you make decisions and act

Let's take a few moments, then, to get clear about the reasons you might consult oracles. To personalize it for you, look at each of the following questions through the lens of your Nine Wise Ways. For instance, take the first one, love, and break down what you need, want, and desire. Need is your security needs. It could be something concrete such as a low mortgage on the home that you share with your life partner. Want can be your emotional needs, such as good, open, honest communication or sweet affection. But desire might be what fuels the commitment you have, or want to have, with your honey. Desire is your soul need—a deep desire to be heard, to be loved for who you are, or to be allowed to make mistakes and be forgiven. Go through each area, answering each of these questions.

What do I need?

What do I want?

What do I desire?

Then ask yourself what feels unknown about this area. What seems remote about this idea? What hardly seems possible? Write these out as questions. It may be hard to answer this, especially in the desire department—because you may not realize how deeply you desire it or how much you need it, and it can be painful at first to get in touch with that. Start with the easy, direct questions, such as "Should I move to a new city this year?" Then work deeper into the harder questions, such as "If I move to a new city, will I thrive financially?" or "If I move to a new city, will I find love?"

Looking at your list of questions, can you make them more specific? In the example of moving to a new city, notice that we asked "should I move to a new city *this year?*" Getting specific puts a finer, more practical point on your question. You may already know in your gut that the right thing to do is to relocate. But what you might not know is *when* you will be ready—or, even more beyond your control, when your family will be ready.

> ### At Your Peril
>
> Many counselors such as Gary can serve as oracles to help people resolve inner conflicts. But you must find someone who has your best interest at heart. The oracle who just gives you the answer is not as helpful as the oracle who helps you connect with the answer that's already within your truest self.

The Question You Won't Ask

Just as it's important to know exactly what you want to know, it's also important to know what you don't want to know. Once Gary was doing a time-management presentation to a group of people who worked the customer-support telephones for a large company. It was their job to field customer complaints, and these employees were angry themselves, burned out, and working dead-end jobs. So he walked in to teach time management to people who had no control over their time. He sensed they were unhappy and took the approach of encouraging them to think about their priorities in life, imagine what would add more pleasure to their lives, and focus on managing their time so they became more *centered.*

But the group wanted a more practical, step-by-step plan for just getting through the day. They weren't ready to think about the big picture. They couldn't see it. Instead, Gary was there to spur them to start with the big picture and inform them there was no magic formula for managing every second of the day. He asked them to take responsibility for their personal priorities and examine changes they could make. He didn't just wave a magic wand and take their dead-end jobs away. So, needless to say, they didn't like him very much. He was the wrong oracle at the wrong time.

Wise Words

To be **centered** means to see your place in the calm center of your life, like the hub of a wheel. It does not mean to be self-centered, as though the whole world revolves around your needs, wants, and desires. Rather, it means that you can find calmness amid the interchange of needs, wants, and desires or those around you because you are clear on how you interact with others. You choose how much you let the external world influence your thoughts and actions. Many people find the key to being centered is to connect with a higher presence, the Divine as you define it.

If you can allow yourself to see what you *don't* want to know, you can reap the benefit much faster. Or because it's hard to see what we don't want to see—thus the term "blind spot"—allow your oracles to show them to you. Notice what you react to most strongly. Listen to the "but" as in, "That's a great idea, but ...."

The Central Question

If you'll remember from Chapter 7, when we discussed sacred spaces, we defined the circle as a universal theme of sacred wisdom because of its calming effect. The circle is a great tool for the questions and answers of oracles, because the closer you get to the center of a question, the closer you get to the answer.

For this reason, many people use circles to get centered, either by contemplating or creating a mandala or walking a labyrinth. In Jung's description of a mandala, or circle, the closer you get to the center, to the Divine, the more you discard the chatter—the information you don't need, the questions, doubts, and concerns that don't serve you. As you near the center, the questions become more pointed.

The journey toward the center, toward the inner you and your deepest desires, is one of many steps. Many people shy away from solitude or contemplation out of fear of loneliness, but using mandalas can make this journey on the inner path be done with ease. Try spending some time just coloring a mandala. (We explain how to get set up for this in Chapter 14.) It will help you disclose to yourself the spaces inside yourself that you protect so well and discover a whole new wealth of personal energy and insight. Walking the inner path will serve you well in getting your questions just right. Part of the process on the inner path is letting go. It may mean letting go of limiting or negative thinking. It may mean examining what's working and what's not and letting go of what no longer serves you. The introspection of the inner path may surprise you. You may find that something that once served you very well, enriching your life and creating a positive identity, no longer does enrich you but actually limits you.

That was the case for a friend of Gary's who had taught writing for many years. She knew it no longer suited her, but she was spending a great deal of her time teaching, along with grappling with the planning and paperwork that goes with that. She knew in her heart of hearts that she wanted to return to her own writing. So she cut back on teaching, and that helped—a little. The more she focused on writing articles, the more excited she felt. So she decided to devote more energy to it, giving up teaching. This has allowed her to pursue writing with energy and enthusiasm. But first she had to create the space. It's another example of "nature abhors a vacuum." When she created the space by letting go, just a little, of teaching, she found the energy to move ahead with writing; her motivation was reinforced by the enthusiasm she felt, and she was able to take the next step and relinquish teaching completely.

Finding this center is not just a process of self-discovery. It's also a process of rebirth. As poet Adalbert Stifter wrote, "The great deeds of humankind are not those that make a lot of noise. Great things happen simply—like the trickling of water, the flowing of air, and the growing of grain." When you find the center, that is the place from which you can grow.

Unless we can let go of what isn't working—whether that's specific actions or ways of thinking and feeling—we can't be open to what we can learn from oracles. The risk, if we are not willing to let go, is that we will twist and turn the interpretation—or simply ignore it—if we don't want to hear it.

Solitude: The Softening

We're not saying this is easy. Letting go can be the hardest thing in the world. Sometimes the things we must let go of to get the questions right are the very things that made us successful in the past. These ways of being feel right, easy, and good. Or at least they did at the time. And we just haven't received the new information, because they became part of our identity or they became habit.

Spending time in solitude is a good first step to softening your resistance to changing. Solitude gets you in touch with your compassion for yourself. It softens your self-talk, if you tend to live with a lot of "shoulds"—ideas about how you are supposed to live your life and be in control. Solitude gets you accustomed to the amplitude of your own thoughts. It leads you on a journey to the deepest truths about your needs, wants, and desires. Solitude gets it down to its essence.

Releasing: No More Resentments

Let's be honest here. We have to get to the tough stuff. It's human nature to have resentments. But nursing an old grudge can keep our eyes looking down at the ground and not toward the sky. How can you benefit from new wisdom when you are grinding and regrinding the same old axe? Releasing resentments is a way to create that vacuum in your life that empties out the old and creates space for the new.

Many people Gary has worked with are unhappy in their jobs but are focused on nursing a resentment. It could be against their father for steering them toward business and away from the arts, or their boss for mistreating them in some way. They are so enmeshed in maintaining this resentment, giving it energy even when it's not conscious, that they are immobilized. Cognitively, they know they need to create change in their life, but their need to prove themselves right and someone else wrong means they have created the ultimate boomerang. All efforts they put into changing the situation come back to them and hold them in place. The resentment at that point starts to become a form of protection—protecting them from taking a risk.

At Your Peril

Resentments weigh down your spirit. Whether you cloak them or restrain them, they are negative energy that you carry around with you. They are embedded in the thoughts that rattle around in your head. It's infecting no one but you.

There is no room for new wisdom when the vessel is filled with so much poison. If you have resentments in your life, try this exercise of compassion Gary uses with his clients. Write a letter addressed to yourself from the person to whom you have directed this resentment. When you sit in the other person's head for a moment, it makes you think about the pressures and disappointments he or she might have faced. How might those factors have caused them to act in hurtful ways? Sometimes the letter may outline what this person perceives *you* did to contribute to the hurtful behavior. This exercise can help you open up to seeing that everyone has limitations that keep them from living up their higher self.

Carolyn lives by the belief that we are all doing the best we can. We are all in this together—the pressures, the pain, the victories. And we are all responsible for creating our own path.

Baba Yaga: The Wild Woman

BABA YAGA
WILD WOMAN

Baba Yaga, from the Goddess Oracle Deck, is a Russian/Slavic deity who represents the wild woman in us all. She is described as the thunder witch and the grandmother of the devil. In some depictions, she lives in a house with a picket fence tipped with skulls. She is said to eat or petrify her victims and to sweep away any trace of her path with her broom.

Baba Yaga reminds us we may be so self-protective, so tightly wound, that we are smothering our own spirits. This protectiveness can be the result of fear of misbehaving and being punished, or fear of getting in touch with feelings that we are afraid of, such as anger and sadness, or fear of admitting that we want more than what we are or what we have. We all have an inner wild woman (or man) who wants to be released if we can only allow her (or him) to break loose. Most likely, we fear that if she peeks out, she will become out of control and take us down with her. In some ways, she represents an inner child who wants to have fun and be self-expressive but also wants to connect with others and be loved. To hold her under your thumb is self-destructive.

Exercise! Dance, run, or talk with someone who can hear your innermost feelings. All of this can help release your inner Baba Yaga. Are you grinding away at something that no longer nourishes you? Gary tells his clients, "Go ahead, have your feelings." After all, they're only feelings. They aren't necessarily reality, and they won't destroy you. Let them out. And clear your mind.

THE ERINYES
CRISIS

The Erinyes: A Sense of Justice

The Erinyes are parallel to the Roman furies, a trinity of goddesses who rule retributive justice. They are a combination of harsh and benevolent. They represent hate, jealousy, and revenge.

Our own personal resentments can be nurtured to the point that our own internal furies are constantly howling. Although it's okay to have a sense of righteousness, when our furies howl this is a sign of an imbalance that we need to correct.

This card is a checkpoint. Have you allowed your thoughts to decline so that you are in a constant state of rage and frustration? Do you relive memories? Do you rehearse what you'd like to say or do? This card reminds you not to be stuck. Practice going to your sacred place, getting calm again, working on forgiving those you have resentments against, and rewriting your self-talk. A counselor or therapist can help, but so can keeping a journal, meditating, joining a discussion group, or joining a spiritual group.

Oracle Advice

Are you bound to an oracle just because it predicts a certain path for you? That might be what Oedipus wondered when the Oracle of Delphi told him he would kill his father and marry his mother. You always have free will, whether you choose to act or you choose denial. In *A Course of Miracles*, a psychological-spiritual belief system, it is said that you do not choose the curriculum, but you do choose how much of it you do at any given time. This means that *true* wisdom waits until you are ready to receive it wholly.

Your Quest

Your quest will be individual, assigned only to you and done at the pace you choose. Though you may listen to oracles who suggest this or that, and though they may speak with certainty, the way in which you take it in is entirely up to you.

We always have free will regardless of what others tell us or suggest. Using the "gut" test can help us to know whether we are headed in the right direction by trusting someone. It is human nature to assume that if someone is somehow smarter or more experienced or more spiritually aware, then they know more than us and we should do what they suggest. Gary has certainly felt that way in his life. In a way this is a primitive need to have "Mommy and Daddy" tell us what to do so that we don't have to take personal responsibility. But we have both free will and responsibility, and we also have inner resources that we can learn to listen to that will help us navigate the world.

Even when Gary's clients who have an illness see a specialist with highly reputed skills, he encourages them to remember that they still have the power to make the ultimate decision. They can work with that specialist, or they can decide to consult others.

Vision Quest

A vision quest is a method by which many Native American cultures sought knowledge or received answers to questions. A vision quest is a journey that is set up to create the conditions in which the seeker experiences dreams or visions that answer big questions. They can be about which path to take in life and who you are. Or they can be about specific problems, about making a this-or-that choice.

The conditions of a vision quest are set up to test the seeker physically and spiritually. In traditional Lakota culture, it is called the Hanblecheyapi, which literally means "crying for a vision." The aim of a vision quest is to lead the seeker across the threshold between the physical and spiritual worlds. Often, they involve physically demanding practices such as a sweat lodge, hunting, or being branded. Or they involve life-endangering practices such as fasting, walking on hot coals, or walking through fire. Sometimes they involve a deliberately induced altered state, with hallucinogenic drugs.

By creating a test in the physical world, you alter your awareness. It has something to do with the fact that life is sweeter when it sits near death. And it has something to do with the transformation of our perceptions when we get out of the physical body.

It's not just a Native American tradition. When you look back on many spiritual traditions, the vision quest is an integral part of the story, as when Christ faced the three temptations in the desert, Mohammad retreated to the cave, or Buddha sat under the bodhi tree.

The purpose of a vision quest is to get in touch with the sacred. In a vision quest, you set out with no vestige of your civilized life, and you are tested to summon your inner source of strength. In finding it, you experience empowerment and find inspiration. A vision quest can produce powerful changes. Like an oracle that is a message or a person, a vision quest helps you get in touch with the essence. It strips you to your core, relinquishing what you no longer require, and it allows you to grow. A vision quest requires you to find your own power and summon ways to use it effectively.

Usually a vision quester returns with a fur, a feather, or a stone in his medicine bag that serves to remind him and be his guide. Sometimes the quester takes on a new name.

Tell It Like It Is

The theme of the holy grail story is that the quest for the grail, the chalice of Christ, is the quest to end the inauthentic life. In the legend, the country has been laid to waste. Mythologist Joseph Campbell defines the wasteland in psychological terms: people who are living lives dictated by others, without the courage to live their own. "The grail," he said, "represents the fulfillment of the highest spiritual potentialities of human consciousness."

Your Own Quest

When you get to the big questions, a vision quest may be the way to get the big answers. You may set up your own vision quest by designing a trek that you take on your own. Maybe it's a camping trip, time spent in a cabin in the mountains, or a week in a deserted oceanside tourist town. Or maybe you do want to go to a Native American sweat lodge. Maybe you want to go to a Buddhist monastery or Catholic retreat center, or perhaps your quest is of the humanitarian kind, such as volunteering with Habitat for Humanity or Amigos de las Americas. Again, your path to the essential questions is up to you.

You can design your own quest, just by choosing a weekend getaway or even an afternoon. Just remember that your vision quest should have these elements:

1. **Set your intention.** *I want to understand more about ….* Make up a list of 10 to 12 questions you want answered.

2. **Choose your place.** The place should be a sacred place for you, one that calms your spirit.

3. **Leave the world behind.** You don't have to shed yourself of all your personal belongings or buy sackcloth and ashes. But it is important to leave the cares of the world behind by disconnecting from e-mail and the phone. It's important to leave your task list behind. Don't worry about whether the lawn is mowed or the sheets are clean. But also leave resentments behind. Take some time to write in your Oracle Journal to clear your head.

4. **Make it a challenge.** It can be a physical challenge, such as a fire walk or rock climbing, but it need not be extreme. If you choose a deserted tourist town by the beach during the off season, you may just choose to walk the beach as far as you can. Or it can be a mental or emotional challenge. Nor should you put yourself in danger—by hitchhiking, for instance. If your style is high energy, you may want to seek a quiet place. If contemplation and solitude are already your natural tendency, you may want to choose a group humanitarian effort. Whatever, the test is whether the quest you choose is set up to jar you out of your complacency.

5. **Go it alone.** It's important to be alone with yourself, without the trappings of your identity as defined by others.

6. **Collect talismans.** As you meet challenges and capture new insights, collect objects along the way that remind you of your victories.

A Check-In

We are focused on getting all the answers, but what we have the most control of is the questions. It's worth it to take the time to walk the inner path and get clearer on the questions you want to pose to oracles.

The Least You Need to Know

- To get a finer point on your questions, take each area and ask what you need, what you want, and what you desire about this area.

- It is just as important to get clear on what you are afraid to ask as it is to know what you do want to ask.

- It's important to keep yourself centered and not let the external influences of the world throw you off track from your essential questions.

- Resentments—holding on to your need for justice to be done—can weigh down your spirit.

- Creating a vision quest for yourself is a way to get clear on your questions and get centered. You will emerge with renewed strength and fresh insights.

Chapter 10

Gifts and Offerings

In This Chapter

- ◆ New and ancient sacrifices
- ◆ Rehearsing the act of giving—to yourself and others
- ◆ All-out generosity
- ◆ Steering clear of nonintentionality

Now you are ready to ask your questions. But is the oracle ready to answer? Traditionally, at least in ancient times, oracles have been prickly about how they are treated, expecting sacrifices or at least some serious servile praise.

The oracle tradition has a colorful history of the gifts and offerings made to those who knew the shape of the future. The ancient oracle seeker would often sacrifice something meaningful or something for the greater good of humanity. In this chapter, we show you how to align with the pure energy of generosity.

Traditional Offerings

Historically, those who beseeched oracles for wisdom showered them with the bounty of the earth. Though they had little to offer, the seekers of wisdom gave great sacrifices in the form of the fatted calf, the lamb, a percentage of the crops, wine—even vestal virgins. The quest for oracle wisdom was not inexpensive. At Delphi, for example, in the fifth and fourth centuries B.C.E., a suggested donation was the equivalent of two days' wages, and of course, there were additional sums to be paid in the form of free-will offerings.

The other trick was that the seeker had to know *what kind* of sacrifice to make. The oracle gods were picky. Many times, the seekers brought animal sacrifices, which were burned on an altar. Pig sacrifices were popular in ancient Greece. Dogs were sacrificed to cleanse oneself of murder.

In other cultures, people brought talismans, such as the Egyptian scarab, or planetary stones and gems. Sometimes they lit lamps in the sepulchers. In some cases, they just brought gold.

Whatever it was, it was important that the sacrifice be meaningful—in the case of the pig, cow, and rooster sacrifices, it was something that could have provided nourishment for the entire family.

The New Generosity

In modern times, an offering to an oracle of wisdom is less likely to be so material. It's more likely to take the form of generosity of the mind and spirit.

Generosity is like a magnet. It draws all good things to you. It draws to you what you want to manifest in your life. But perhaps more importantly, it draws to you the clarity that helps you decide and act in the best and highest way for yourself and for others. Suppose, for instance, that you want to change careers, from business to the arts.

Here are some ground rules about how to prepare yourself to give an offering in hope of receiving oracle wisdom:

- **Give with intention.** Know in your heart why, where, and when you are giving. Know what you are giving and what you are hoping to receive.

◆ **Give something of meaning to you.** It does not necessarily have to be a sacrifice. (We talk about that in a minute.) But it should come from the essence of who you are. It should be something from your active present life. The oracle will not work for you—the real you—if you do not lift up the veil to reveal who you really are. It should not be something from your past that you may already have relinquished or you wish to shed.

◆ **Give something you really needed.** The oracle will know if you gave something you didn't like or didn't need. If your heart is really in this question, your offering should be, too. This matters.

◆ **Be careful not to give to excess.** Yes, you really want it. But oracles are not impressed with grandiosity, not in the least. Your gift must be sincere.

◆ **The gift must stretch you in some way.** It may be something you *wish* you could give but tell yourself you are not ready to give. Do it anyway. It may be that to obtain the item you give as an offering, you have to meet a challenge. Embrace it.

> **Tell It Like It Is**
>
> The idea of karma is that energy does not stop after it's released into the world. It keeps going, and it comes around to you again. So if you give out positive energy, even if you see no immediate effect, it will come back to you. You have just increased the amount of positive energy in the world. Likewise, don't think that negative energy just disappears. It comes back to you, too.

Each time you make an offering, the process becomes easier. Make generosity a practice in your everyday life, and you'll find that oracle wisdom is available to you everywhere. To cultivate the practice of generosity, start by being generous in your thoughts.

Take a good, hard look at your life—trust us, your oracle will already have done this, so you might as well. The oracle will know whereof it speaks when it urges you to change your ways.

Be generous in your thoughts and actions. Are you often disappointed in people? Being disappointed with someone means you had expectations that the person may or may not have been aware of. Don't hold grudges. It's like living life with one piece of the puzzle missing. Don't absorb other people's weaknesses. When you allow yourself to be disappointed in people, you create a slow drain on your energy. Align yourself with people who share your values and support them in their thoughts, deeds, and actions.

Align yourself with people who set an example. Find the joy in being generous in your expectations of others.

Acts of Generosity

True generosity of the spirit is to commit your time and effort to service without any thought of personal reward. We like the concept of "pay it forward," introduced by novelist Catherine Ryan Hyde, and adapted by screenwriter Leslie Dixon in the movie of the same name, and which afterward became a movement. The idea is not to pay back an act of generosity to the person who gave, but rather, express your gratitude by paying it forward—to the next person who needs a helping hand. Give someone else a chance. Give someone else a boost.

Roman orator Cicero said, "Gratitude is not only the greatest of virtues, but the parent of all the others." Or as the spiritual study manual *A Course in Miracles* says, "Gratitude is the first step toward love." Carolyn used this concept in her short story "Detox," which has been published in the literary journal *Ellipsis* and *Wilde Frauen*, an anthology of women writers. The story was about a man and a woman, longtime friends, who turn to each other as they try to detoxify from devastating love affairs. They learn to trust, and to love, again, by taking the first step, gratitude, toward one another.

Generosity opens your heart, and an open heart has a way of opening your ears. It helps you recognize that you have already received a message of wisdom.

A Dress Rehearsal

Gary has found it helpful in his own life and with people he has counseled to encourage them to visualize themselves being generous with other people, especially people with whom they are angry or feel a disconnection. This could mean imagining yourself actually giving them something, or saying something nice to them, or asking them to tell you about what causes them pain and why they behave the way they do. Or you can meditate on their success, or visualize it, or pray for them.

It also can be helpful to rehearse a situation in which you get in touch with someone and actually initiate the reconciliation, writing lines like in a play. Maybe you can't follow up on it for some reason, or don't feel ready to, but all of this can begin to shake some of the rage loose, break up the big iceberg that keeps you focused on the barrier.

Being the one to take the first step, when you are mentally prepared, can mean a lot. We can become so focused on why the other person needs to take the first step that nothing happens. And remember the law of karma. Even taking the first step, even if the other person doesn't return it, is creating positive karma. Your generosity will come around.

Be Generous to Yourself

Just as you begin cultivating the spirit of forgiveness toward others, don't forget to target yourself. We can't prevent people from acting or speaking as they do, but we don't have to let it affect us.

Criticism can really hurt. But know that you have a choice about whether you can integrate it into your psyche. Know that many times, it's a choice you make in how you interpret their actions. And you can change that choice. Know that many times, their words are about their pain, something that is missing in their lives, and not about you. And know that sometimes there is a truth buried in there that you need to heed. The choice, whatever the situation, is to not let it sway you from your commitment to walk through the world with a generous heart. To do otherwise is to do what don Miguel Ruiz calls "taking the poison" in his book *The Four Agreements* (see Appendix B).

Gary encourages people to create their own antidotes to the poison of disapproval from others, in the form of affirmations. The affirmation counters the criticism (or perceived criticism). Here are examples of how Gary turns negative statements into affirmations:

Negative: My boss is always on my back about something. I can never anticipate her needs.

Affirmation: I am resourceful and flexible, and I can anticipate these needs so that I can bring some peace to the office.

Negative: I must be stupid and clueless if I get treated as I am.

Affirmation: I am an intelligent and perceptive person, and every day I am developing my natural abilities.

Negative: I really am plain and ugly.

Affirmation: I possess a beauty that begins on the inside and radiates light to the world around me. Hey world: better put on your shades!

Negative: Yet again I have totally messed up something that people were counting on me to do right.

Affirmation: Every failure teaches me something and I always come back stronger and more competent.

Negative: I will always be second rate.

Affirmation: My self-worth is not dependent upon whether I receive praise from others, but from within.

Negative: I don't ever seem to be in the right place at the right time. I am a loser.

Affirmation: There is a divine purpose guiding my life and I am open to new possibilities and opportunities. I am always in the right place at the right time.

Negative: If she hates everything I do, I must be a failure.

Affirmation: I know there is a grain of truth in it and an opportunity to learn here, and I open myself up to growth.

Negative: The only way I could really feel better in this situation is to break his jaw.

Affirmation: We are all in this world together, doing the best we can, all of us facing the pressures of life. My heart is big enough to forgive him and send him light.

> **Oracle Advice**
>
> Sometimes people let the threat of karma rule their actions, as in, "I couldn't do that, it would be bad karma." But there is no such thing as good karma or bad karma. Karma just is. Like karma attracts like karma. But instead of evaluating your karma, choose instead to put out karma that reflects your values of generosity, mindfulness, and kindness.

True Generosity

What's your giving style? Are you generous with your time? Your words? Your deeds? Your money? There are many ways to show your love. Use this guide to determine your giving style.

Ways in which I give to others:

_____

My favorite way to give a gift:

_____

My least favorite way to give a gift:

_____

The last five people to whom I gave a gift:

_____

What I gave and why:

_____

What was easy about it?

_____

What was hard about it?

_____

What I'd like for them to think about me as a result of giving the gift:

_____

What I want them to give back to me:

_____

Someone I would like to give something to and why:

_____

How I receive gifts from others—with comfort? With discomfort? With expectations? With anticipation?

_____

The best gift I ever received:

_____

The worst gift I ever received:

_____

Recipient Disclosed

One problem, you say. Got an offering, but no address. Who, exactly, do you give the offering to? Your oracle may not be exactly a _who_, and after all, we said the source of the oracle is divine wisdom. So it's not something you _see_ so much as a presence that you _know_.

What you can do is define the evidence of the divine presence in your life. The following exercise will be helpful to you, whether that presence is clearly defined in your life or whether you are just starting to explore the question.

At Your Peril

Sometimes giving a material gift is easier than giving of yourself. It's easier to buy something than to spend time with someone. Make a point to go beyond the easy way out. Block out time for someone. Give that person your full attention. Engage that person, enjoying him or her just for who she is.

How does the presence express itself in your life? What do you receive in your life so that you know the calling card of the Divine? (In the New Testament, it says, "by my works, you will know me ….")

What do you receive from the Divine, "that you may know?" Is it hope? Then give hope to your world. Is it optimism, a belief that all things are working together for the good? Then give good cheer to your world.

Sacrifice

In ancient history, people brought items of great value to oracles, and they carried them from afar.

In Christianity, it is said the greatest gift is love, and the faith centers on the act of Jesus Christ being willing to give his life for humankind. That level of sacrifice is nigh impossible for most of us to attain. But can you think of loved ones for whom you would lay down your life? Can you think of people and situations for which you would be willing to give without regard to whether you are giving too much?

Wise Words

Sacrifice is the act of offering the life of a person or animal as homage to a deity. It is also the act of giving up something of value for the sake of a more pressing concern. Let that be a test as you consider making a sacrifice to an oracle: is this concern you have pressing enough that you would give up something of true value to the oracle?

Sacrifice is often defined by loss. But we choose not to define sacrifice by deprivation, not by what it takes away from the person. Instead, we think sacrifice is a barometer of your intention. The man who gives his kidney to his younger brother says, "I intend for you to survive this." The couple who commits to intensive marriage counseling, even risking great financial strain, says, "It is our intention to prove that this marriage and the love we once had for one another is more important than temporary financial challenges."

The act of sacrifice recognizes that we are all in this together. There is no boundary between giver and recipient, no yours or mine.

Pachamama: What Sustains You

PACHAMAMA
HEALING/WHOLING/HOLY

Pachamama was a goddess of agriculture to the pre-Incan civilizations of Peru and Bolivia. Animals, particularly llamas, were offered to her as sacrifices. Pachamama reminds us to honor the Earth—to honor what sustains us. She reminds us to bless our food. Are you giving back to what sustains you? Or is there more taking than giving? Pachamama reminds us that great wisdom is found in nature. When we open up the conduit—giving and taking, giving and taking—we tap into that great wisdom.

Acts of Love

St. Teresa de Avila wrote that acts of love melt the soul. In this lies the kernel of truth: this is why oracles test us before flooding us with their wisdom. What are the ways that you can melt your soul?

♦ **Practice gratitude.** Every day, make a list in your Oracle Journal of what you feel grateful for.

♦ **Keep a gratitude archive.** Your gratitude quotient increases when you see it coming back to you in the form of thank yous from others.

♦ **Lift the burden of another.**

♦ **Serve.**

♦ **Plant trees.** "One generation plants the trees. Another gets the shade." So goes a Chinese proverb. Even if you don't get the immediate payoff, do something that will enrich someone else's life.

♦ **Love your enemies.**

♦ **Practice empathy.**

♦ **Be kind with your words.** Every word you utter is a choice. You have a choice to be kind, or to be focused on protecting your boundaries, proving you are right and the other person is wrong. It's okay to stand up for what you believe, but you must do this with kindness. The first step to kindness is to acknowledge to yourself that this person may have a viewpoint that conflicts with yours—and to see that as invigorating, not threatening.

♦ **Embrace suffering with compassion.**

♦ **Let yourself lean on others.** Leonardo da Vinci said, "Two weaknesses leaning together constitute a strength. Therefore one half of the world leaning against the other half becomes firm." You become stronger by knowing when you gain strength from joining with others and allowing yourself to open up to them.

♦ **Practice tolerance.**

♦ **Choose truth.** Be honorable in your words.

♦ **Choose peace.**

Take a few minutes to write in your Oracle Journal, strategizing about ways you can be more giving. How will this make your world a better place? How will the recipient benefit from my act of giving?

Every Sunday, Gary gets up early to have breakfast with cancer and HIV patients (and caregivers) who are in New York City for treatment. Gary doesn't call this a huge sacrifice, but it is a minor sacrifice to arise so early and get on the subway—particularly because he likes to sleep in. But he finds it very rewarding to listen to these vital people and to give them directions and insight about getting around New York.

Not only is he helping ease the path for these survivors, Gary gets a whole new perspective on his life in the process. He is reminded that we are all in the world together, all connected in some way. Their troubles are his troubles, their path, his path—indeed our human path, in a way, and Gary feels a sense of responsibility to share their burden and contribute where he can.

Make a list of people you see as generous with their spirit, their time, their words, their money. Bill Gates says he gives away about $10 out of every $60 he makes, for instance. Although you can't match him, you can certainly take inventory of the areas in which you are giving.

And along with that list, make a list of ways in which you could be more giving—time, concern, donations, gifts, daily acts of kindness. Get specific—people you want to have an effect on and why, and how you will do it. Choose people that are easy to give to and those that are not so easy.

Yemaya: Across the Water

Yemaya was an African-Caribbean goddess who was believed to rule the surface of the ocean, where humans sailed. She was the goddess of salt water. Every year at summer solstice, the people (all dressed in white) would traverse the ocean to her shrine, rowing in small boats with offerings and candles. Her worshippers are generous, almost extravagant, in their gifts.

She is inspiring us to fill up our boats with gifts and trinkets to bring to the Divine. In this case, more is better!

YEMAYA
SURRENDER

Oracle Advice

Light a candle for someone who has many burdens. This ritual holds up this person to the Divine, enveloping him or her in light and warmth. When you do, we assure you, the person feels loved, whether that person knew about your candle or not. Sometimes Gary does this in his mind. He lights a candle for that person and holds him or her in a special glow, surrounding the person with positive thoughts and genuine concern.

The Trap of Nonintentionality

As good as your intentions are, an oracle has a way of purging out your imperfections. Oracles work to keep you honest with yourself. And they home in on the places where your intentions are not quite yet pure.

If you have ever pursued something with ardor, thinking you had the best of intentions, but then ended up with a clumsy or unsatisfying result, nonintentionality could be the culprit. Nonintentionality is when your conscious focus was on the good, but you neglected thoughts that might undermine your true aim. The cure for nonintentionality is to become more conscious of your thoughts and actions. It means living with purpose. It means treating everyone you encounter as you would treat yourself. This is the way *A Course in Miracles* puts it: "When you meet anyone, remember it is a holy encounter. As you see him you will see yourself. As you treat him you will treat yourself. As you think of him you will think of yourself. Never forget this, for in him you will find yourself or lose yourself." Remember, the gods often come disguised as angels. And remember that oracles are the conduits for divine wisdom. In other words, they know who butters their bread, and that's where their loyalty lies.

Oracle Advice

Keeping an altar is a good way to keep your focus on purposeful living and avoid the nonintentionality that can undermine your highest goals. Set up an altar in a quiet space in your home. Start with several objects that symbolize the key people who influence your life now. Choose some that symbolize the generosity you want to cultivate.

Affirmations can also keep you on track with intentionality; mantras, too. Affirmations are positive statements about what is. Saying them aloud or writing them or just reading them thoughtfully can cement your best intentions. Mantras are chants that resonate in the body and evoke certain energies.

If you created a sacred space in your home, or found one in the great outdoors, another exercise you can try is to bring that person into your meditations when you are there, mentally creating a space for that person. Visualize that person sharing this sacred space with you. You can nurture them the same way that being in that space nurtures you.

Cultivating Generous Oracles

After cultivating all this generosity, don't you feel good? However, don't overlook the importance of cultivating generous oracles. Take your wisdom from people who express these same values. Don't lament what is lacking in the world. But remember that a better world really does begin with you. Remember the lyric from "The End," one of the last songs The Beatles recorded: "And in the end, the love you take is equal to the love you make." What that means is, you don't get any more than you give. Or as Mahatma Gandhi said, "We must become the change we want to see in the world."

The Least You Need to Know

- Gifts to modern-day oracles take the form of generosity of mind and spirit.

- Visualizing your generosity is a good way to take the first steps in your heart toward reconciliation with someone.

- Be generous with yourself by using affirmations as antidotes to disapproval and criticism.

- Identify your giving style, and you will learn to appreciate your unique gifts to the world.

- Cultivate other people who are generous so that you may bolster your budding generosity habit.

Chapter 11

Start Making Sense

In This Chapter

- ◆ Bold questions, radical honesty
- ◆ Unadulterated prayer
- ◆ Mindfulness: living in the moment
- ◆ Find or create a bliss station
- ◆ Getting proactive

You asked for a kiss, and you got a thimble. You asked for a thimble, and you got a kiss. This doesn't make sense!

In the recent remake of *Peter Pan*, prepubescent Wendy offers to give Peter a kiss, but he doesn't know what one is. "I shall know what it is when you give it to me," he says. Instead, she gives him a thimble. He announces he will give Wendy a kiss, and she closes her eyes and puckers up. Instead, he gives her an acorn.

So in the palm of your hand you hold a kiss—a message of wisdom from the Divine. You know that a kiss is something good. But why does it look like an acorn? You just don't know what it means. You've turned your message over and over in your mind. You've tried to interpret and apply it in your life, but … it's no go. You're starting to lose faith. In this interactive chapter, we will help you sort out this strange, beautiful shiny thing you call an oracle.

Go Deeper

Once Gary had a client who was in a rut. He had interesting work and it paid well, but he was working too hard, exhausting himself during the week. The man used the whole weekend to catch up and get ready to do it again. Every Friday he would work late into the evening, then sleep late on Saturday, catch up on chores, and then have dinner with the same friend on Saturday evening. Sunday brought more work and getting ready for the workweek. Invariably, a severe sense of despair would descend on him Sunday evening.

The man told Gary he was having dreams about catastrophes, such as explosions. Or he would dream he had found himself in a strange place and didn't remember who he was. He would have an intense sensation that he was too big for his own skin. The man recognized it as an intuition—or an oracle, if you will—but he certainly didn't know what it meant.

Gary and his client discussed what it meant to feel lost in a strange place. At first this seemed terrifying, but when they examined it, both saw the possibilities it presented. The idea of being lost meant not being available for work, not being around to fall into the same weekend rut. The explosions, too, offered a possibility: freeing him from his current entanglements. Then there was the strong sensation of bursting out of his skin. The dreams were expressing his deep desire for a change.

Some of the greatest wisdom available to us can come in inscrutable messages. It can be an image from a dream, a strong feeling, or a partially formed intuition. Many times, our intuitions point the way to unlocking the wisdom of oracles. Intuitions don't come to us fully formed and interpreted. Many times they are glimmers or inklings. They can only become crisper and clearer if we allow them to born.

In this case, Gary combined a dream message with talk therapy to go deeper with his client. Other techniques for going deeper include the following:

- Prayer
- Meditation
- Mindfulness
- Nonattachment
- Compassion

Going deeper is just another way of saying "try harder." Press yourself to go further into it, ask bolder questions of your oracle and yourself. Press yourself to get radically honest about why you asked for what you asked for. Go past the superficial reason. Go past the substantial reason. And get to the heart's great truth about it. How is this question good for your soul?

Power Prayer

If you have a regular practice of prayer, more power to you. Taking a closer look at your prayer style—or starting a practice—may be just the thing that deepens your understanding of the oracles you receive.

Although many prayers are petitions—asking for something specific—they can also be a form of communion. They can be a dialogue with your higher source. In just engaging in that dialogue, sharing your day-to-day inner thoughts, you create the fertile ground for deepening your understanding of the messages you receive. You may even find that you have been receiving more messages than you realize.

Prayer Without Strings

Prayer is a way of seeking guidance, but remember the phrase often added to Christian prayer, "Thy will be done"? This phrase is also Zenlike in a way because it means you are letting go of controlling the outcome. When you say this, you are admitting you don't know the answer. You are admitting there is knowledge in the universe—or knowledge that the Divine has—that is much greater than what you possess.

It's easier to practice nonattachment when you can trust that there is a perfect plan for your life and can allow yourself to be open to whatever that path might be.

Tell It Like It Is

In the Grimm Brothers version of Cinderella, she receives her boon *not* at the hands of a fairy godmother, but rather through her own strength. When she is barred from going to the ball, she goes to the courtyard where her mother is buried beneath a hazel tree and calls out to the dove spirit that resides there. In that version, Cinderella knows that what she has wanted has been there all along. "Shiver and quiver little tree, Silver and gold throw down over me," Cinderella says. Nothing comes to us until we are strong enough to ask for it.

Sometimes people use prayer like a magic wand—a wish made to a fairy godmother who will materialize a glittering dress and a stagecoach. (And by the way, fairy tales can serve as oracles, too.) But we haven't let go when we use prayer to control or twist a message into what we hope it means. If we announce to the Divine that we already understand it a certain way and all we need is his support for our strategy, we might get something else entirely. Or we might get what we want and realize that's not what we wanted. It's the old adage, "Be careful what you wish for because you just might get it."

In your Oracle Journal, start keeping a list of prayers. Use your journal to start that dialogue with the Divine. Here is the place where you can be completely honest. You can reveal all of your desires, fears, and weaknesses. It's human nature to shy away from the idea of confession—it's so hard to admit when we fall short of the mark— but this is the place. It's the place where you can be vulnerable enough to voice what you really want, no matter how grandiose or impossible or silly anyone else might think it is. It's safe here. In that dialogue, you will find serenity and wisdom.

Make a point to shift the language from a prayer of petition to a dialogue with the Divine. Remember, a dialogue is two-way street. It involves some listening on your part, too.

A Clean, Well-Lighted Mind

Meditation is a powerful technique for gaining clarity when we are confused and uncertain. The techniques bring us inward. They allow us to relinquish our attachments to the world and go within. Within, we find something truer, a wisdom that is more constant, not so subject to the whims of the external world or the constraints of our own stratagems.

In this meditation, envision holding up your inscrutable message, imagining a bubble around it. Stay with it for a few moments. At first, when you concentrate on your desire at the same time you focus on how it's still just out of reach, you will likely feel tension. But hold your thoughts there in that space between. Allow the paradox of the unanswerable to just be. Thoughts will go through your mind about how you wish to change it. You may want to spin out imagined scenarios of how it will be resolved. Or you may want to rehash the events leading up to this, hoping to sort out some answer. But don't engage those thoughts. Let them pass. Do this for as long as it takes for the tension to soften.

Then release your hold on the bubble. Imagine letting it go and watching it float away. When you release your hold on it, you are acknowledging that the question remains unanswered, but now you are not squeezing the life out of it.

As you practice this, it will get easier. You will grow accustomed to how it feels when your mind lets go. Notice how it feels in your gut—in your solar plexus—when you can truly relinquish. In time, you will find a storehouse of serenity there. You'll get used to the feeling.

Mindful Living

Start practicing *mindfulness* in small amounts during the day. Let the peacefulness of prayer and meditation carry over into your daily life. Mindfulness is something that is possible to achieve every moment of every day. It means simply staying in the present moment. With mindfulness, you do not let the thoughts of the past and the future cloud your experience of the here and now. You train yourself to heighten your awareness, drawing upon all five senses. When you do this, you attract additional truths to you.

Use this next exercise to get yourself back to mindfulness when you catch your thoughts dwelling on what you need to do in the future or what you didn't do in the past.

> **Wise Words**
>
> **Mindfulness** is keeping your mind on what you are experiencing in the present moment. Mindfulness is experiencing life with full awareness, engaging all the senses.

In this moment, I see _____

In this moment, I hear _____

In this moment, I taste _____

In this moment, I smell _____

In this moment, I feel _____

Sometimes we don't want to live in the present moment because it's not all we want it to be. Some of Gary's clients, for instance, have told him that they have received small insights into their relationships just by practicing being more in the present moment. Those insights were about aspects of their partners' characters that made Gary's clients realize the relationship was not a perfect match. By being mindful, we see what we may not have wanted to see before. We cannot live in an imagined world, where we hope for a relationship to be something it will never be. In that respect, the present can be a powerful oracle.

Get Softer

If you are not getting answers, you may start hardening yourself. You may wonder why you believed you could gain wisdom this way in the first place. But the answer is not to get harder—get softer.

Zen Buddhist master Sheng-yen says, "Be soft in your practice. Think of the method as a fine silvery stream, not a raging waterfall. Follow the stream, have faith in its course. It will go its own way, meandering here, trickling there. It will find the grooves, the cracks, the crevices. Just follow it. Never let it out of your sight. It will take you."

Maintaining an altar in your home, as discussed in Chapter 7, is one way to keep your focus on this soft place within. This soft place is defined as simply a place where you can experience who you are and bring forth what you might be. Buddhists call it soft-belly thinking. Mythologist Joseph Campbell calls it the place of "creative incubation." He goes on to say that you may find at first that nothing happens there. But he says, "If you have a sacred place and you use it, something eventually will happen … Your sacred space is where you find yourself again and again."

Your Bliss Station

A bliss station can be something you create, or something you find. Whether it's a sacred space to which you take a pilgrimage, an altar you create in your own home, or a sanctuary you find in a cathedral or a garden, it's a place you can go to again and again and remember your bliss. In that place, you can see the purpose for the events unfolding in your life, and you draw strength. Your burdens are lifted, because you cast aside the things you don't need to do in favor of the things you must do to follow your bliss.

It's important to keep your bliss station pure. If it's a place in your home, keep it free from clutter. Remember Gary's sacred space in his Manhattan apartment? He's got a small space, but he always makes sure to guard this space from clutter. He doesn't place papers or junk on the table for more than a few minutes. This is saying a lot, because he often works in his apartment. But he feels that a part of himself resides in this wall, and he doesn't want clutter to disturb it.

It's also important to keep your bliss station free from entanglements with people or endeavors that diminish you. No matter how love that mint-green chiffon blouse, if it reminds you of the ungraceful way your last boyfriend dumped you, send it away. If your personal growth focus at this moment is to create a very individual, unique identity for yourself, stepping out of the expectations of your family, then objects that remind you of your family will impede that. Likewise, if your focus is on creating community, you will want to furnish your bliss station with objects that connect you to the experiences you have had with people who have great meaning to you.

The same principle works with the food you eat. There's a lot to be said for blessing your food, taking that moment to acknowledge the Source. In our time, we live with new food warnings every week—mercury in tuna, mad cow disease in beef, PCBs in farm-raised salmon, and so on. Take the time to sanctify what you take in. If your food has not been prepared with love—say you and your partner were fighting as you cooked it—then it won't nourish your soul. It's like that line from the movie *Like Water for Chocolate*—every time people ask the character about her recipe, she says, "The secret ingredient is love."

Every object in your world has only the meaning you give to it. If it doesn't bring you bliss, sanctify it or relinquish it. For further reading on how objects can enhance—and not detract—from your happiness, read *Objects of Our Desire* by Dr. Salman Akhtar (see Appendix B).

Candle Gazing

Gary often lights a candle when he is working. It is a really calming, centering feeling to look over at this wall, to contemplate the feeling of simplicity and space (again, this is all relative in New York City), and to think about the candle.

A lighted candle is a link to the most ancient of ways of illuminating our worlds. It almost instantly softens a room. A lighted candle can be an invitation or a vigil, but it can also bring forth the aspiring soul within.

Use this candle-gazing meditation to awaken that and renew yourself. Sit comfortably in an unlighted room with a candle before you, about eye level. Gaze at the flame for three to five minutes, long enough to let your gaze focus on a point beyond the flame. (Be careful, of course, not to get too close.) Now close your eyes and focus on the afterglow of the flame on the inside of your eyelids. Allow the light to fill your mind.

This meditation will soften you and open you to new insights. And it has a cleansing effect on the eyes.

Compassion in Action

Compassion gets us outside of ourselves, another way of detaching when we are hanging on too much to an outcome we want. It also gets us into the flow of life, out of our inner world and beyond those desires that may keep us from understanding truths. Compassion opens us up to the world around us, and not only clears our heads but also opens us up to *passion*. It is in passion that we find the new energy to start new endeavors. We meet new people and we start new activities that may be meaningful in ways we never imagined.

Make a list of ways that you can begin practicing compassion now in your life. If this sounds a little like the Buddhist practice of *metta*, then you are right on! Metta is about lovingkindness, and the practice focuses on embracing all aspects of ourselves, including the difficult ones. Ultimately, metta overcomes the illusion of separateness.

With yourself: _____

_____

With someone to whom you feel grateful, someone who may have shown you kindness or generosity: _____

_____

With someone who is a beloved friend: _____

_____

With someone about whom you feel neutral, someone you may see regularly but do not know well: _____

_____

With someone you have had conflicts with: _____

_____

With all beings on the planet: _____

_____

Just Go!

When the answers aren't coming to you, just get up and go! Get out and exercise; just get the blood pumping. Or get out of town. Take a pilgrimage, as discussed in Chapter 7, or a vision quest, as discussed in Chapter 9. A change of scenery will do you good.

A new place gets you to that place of elsewhere—the place where your imagination runs free.

A funny thing happened to Carolyn when she took her twins to Florida. The trip was for them—Disney World—but Carolyn very badly needed to get away. As someone who never stops, never lets her spirits flag, she was close to having a meltdown on the eve of the trip. A single mom, she was focused on taking care of all the details—arriving at the Orlando airport late at night, getting a rental car, making sure she had a map and all of her travel confirmations, and driving to the villa on the Gulf Coast after midnight. And then she arrived at the villa—and it was clean, beautiful, and relaxing. The space was so nurturing that she found herself slowing down and luxuriating in making the twins meals and washing the dishes—two tasks that one week before she was ready to relinquish *forever!* But she was free of all the other distractions and demands of her life and could just be in the moment.

At Your Peril

Could your bad habits be getting in the way of receiving wisdom? Possibly. When Gary talks to people about breaking bad habits (Gary co-wrote *The Complete Idiot's Guide to Breaking Bad Habits, Second Edition;* see Appendix B), he points out that bad habits are often paired with other activities: Getting bored and overeating. Not getting enough sleep and having obsessive thoughts. Drinking coffee and smoking a cigarette. Gary tells them that to change, they have to shake themselves up by getting rid of the activities they pair with the bad habit.

If you aren't getting the answers to your oracle question just yet, you need to get out of the box. Stay in the box, and you risk not being able to see new truths because you interpret all information through your limited worldview. (Carolyn is a case in point. In her regular life in New Mexico, cooking was defined as bad. In her week in a relaxing Gulf Coast villa, cooking for her twins was heaven. The experience helped her connect with the simple pleasure of being a mom and taking care of her kids, and it helped her realize that she's presented with the opportunity to do that every day. It's her choice whether she chooses to look at making Annie's macaroni and cheese as a burden or a pleasure.)

So take a new route home. Do something completely different this Saturday night. Make a pact with yourself to meet five new people. Leave the house in silence rather than turning on the stereo. Make a list of five aspects of your daily or weekly routine that you will do differently this week.

Get Proactive

At last, now we will go direct. Let's get proactive. Or as a friend of Carolyn used to say, "Let's shake some trees." Let's see what falls out. Maybe a coconut or two.

Nu Kua: Find Your Compass

NU KUA

ORDER

The Chinese goddess Nu Kua was believed to be the creator of the human race. She dipped a rope into yellow mud and trailed the rope around, and the drops of mud formed into men and women. She also is credited with restoring the world when evil giants set it aflame. Another time, she melted stones of five colors to repair a rip in the sky. In some depictions, she holds a pair of compasses.

Nu Kua reminds us to rediscover our purpose, and she presents the picture of protectoress—the one who would restore us and repair us as we venture forth.

Let's take stock of your purpose under your Nine Wise Ways by doing this oracle reading. Using your Goddess Oracle Deck, we will create a nine-card spread. Each card will represent one of the areas in your Nine Wise Ways: love, prosperity, career/calling, family and community, home and hearth, well-being, creativity, learning/self-actualization, and spirituality.

Let the goddess oracle for each Way give you insight into how you might deepen your purpose.

Kuan Yin: Strengthen Your Resolve

KUAN YIN
COMPASSION

Now we turn to the Chinese goddess Kuan Yin to strengthen your resolve. She played many roles in Chinese mythology and Tao theology: protector of women, bringer of rain, savior of sailors, goddess of mercy and knowledge, goddess of fecundity, goddess of compassion. She is sometimes called the All Merciful, Bodatsu, Bodhisattva, Buddha, the Divine Voice of the Soul, Great Bodhisattva, the Melodious Voice, the Merciful Mother, the Mother, of the Hundred Hands, the Prostitute, the Saviouress, the Triple, Wife and Daughter, Goddess of Eternal Life. In one legend, she was an immense peach tree that grew in the Garden of Paradise and sustained the whole universe. She is often depicted with a thousand arms. Certainly, she's someone who can get a job done.

Let's call upon the energy of Kuan Yin to take the purpose of your Nine Wise Ways a step further. For each Way, write an affirmation in your Oracle Journal that seals your commitment to this purpose. The affirmation should affirm your strengths in this area.

As an example, suppose in your first Way, love, you originally wrote something like "create a meaningful relationship in my life." But let's say that when you did your Nine Wise Ways spread, in the previous exercise, you sharpened your definition. Perhaps you got clearer about what is important to you in a meaningful relationship. Maybe you want to be with someone who shares your desire for a harmonious home or shares your values about healthful eating or cultivates his or her spiritual growth. Maybe what you care about is good, honest, clear communication and everyday integrity. Whatever it was, it just got more specific. The more you described it, the more committed you became to that and nothing that falls short of it.

Affirmations for that area could be around the strengths that you bring to a relationship. Or it could be around the belief that you will manifest the kind of relationship you deserve to have.

For some people, affirmations don't seem natural at first, but they are actually easy to write. Affirmations should be simple, declarative statements, and they must always be positive. It's important that you don't use tentative words, such as *hope*, *wish*, or *want*. You must write the affirmation as though it is already true and it has already happened. It's also important to weed out any "fear" words, which can be subtle. *Hope* is a fear word—you don't yet believe it will happen or that it's within your control. *Should* is, too. So is *try*. Instead of "should," say, "I will." Instead of "try," say, "I am."

Successful Outcomes

So you see, it may be a great blessing to receive a puzzling oracle. It may spur you to delve deeper, and you may learn more about yourself. You may in fact find that victory is sweeter for having had to back up and regroup. Or you may find your success is greater because you came back at it more wisely.

The Least You Need to Know

- ◆ When you hit a snag with interpreting an oracle, slow down and go deeper.

- ◆ Go within, with prayer and meditation, but go in with a commitment to radical honesty.

- ◆ Make your prayer about communion, not petition.

- ◆ Create a bliss station to get connected to your desire.

- ◆ Use journaling to rediscover the purpose of your goal and use affirmations to strengthen your resolve.

12

Being in the Know

In This Chapter

- ◆ Got wisdom?
- ◆ An inquiring mind
- ◆ Oracles in action
- ◆ Silent oracles

If you have ever practiced yoga, then you are familiar with "namaste," the gesture that closes a yoga session. In yoga, you say "namaste" with reverence, with your hands in front of you, prayerlike, because it means to honor the light in everyone, holding an awareness of our similarities and differences, our strengths and our weaknesses.

This chapter recognizes that everyone carries the light of wisdom within. Oracle wisdom is composed of collective human consciousness, and each one of us contains that sliver of divine wisdom that we seek from without. In this chapter, we show you how you might become an oracle, tapping into what you already possess within.

What You Know: The Wisdom You Already Have

You may already know you possess a certain brand of wisdom. Your family and friends may reflect that back to you. If you have ever joked that you "could write the book" on something, whether it's failed romance or ornery computers, then you know what we mean.

But do you trust that wisdom? That's the first step to becoming an oracle. In a way, this is what therapists do when they are training. You have to really understand yourself, your values, and your strengths before you can help someone else.

Although we imagine the priestesses of Delphi had to pass some pretty interesting job screening ("do fumes of dead snakes nauseate you?"), your screening may be a little more down to earth.

First, take inventory. What were the turning points of your life? How did you make those key decisions?

Take a minute to list five of them right now.

_____

_____

_____

_____

_____

In one sentence, what did you learn? Self-reliance? Interdependence? Greater compassion? Deeper knowledge? Who was instrumental in that epiphany? How did it alter your course?

Lessons Learned

Were some of the turning points on your list painful? Even if most or all of them were triumphant, it may also be true that you struggled through them. After all, that's what triumph is all about.

Growth hurts. Rejection, disappointment, and suffering certainly get our attention. If your turning point was brought upon by asking "How can this be done differently?" you are not alone. If your turning point came after a significant setback, then you already know how to make lemonade from sour lemons.

Know that the way you respond to setbacks determines whether you are prepared to be your own oracle or be one to others. If you wallow in self-pity, bitterness, and inaction … you're not ready for prime time. If, on the other hand, you are quick to accept the setback, to ask how you might forgive, and to seek out what you need to learn, then you are well on your way to being an oracle.

Take a present-day situation in which you have a continual challenge. Choose something from your Nine Wise Ways list in which you seem to perpetually struggle.

> *How can this be different?*
>
> *How can I choose again—make better choices?*
>
> *What can I learn from what people around me are telling me?*
>
> *What can I learn from what people around me won't tell me?*
>
> *Who do I need to forgive? (It might be yourself. It might be someone in your past.)*
>
> *How can I forgive this person?*

When you respond to setbacks in this way, you become a wisdom magnet, if you will. Your willingness to open up and face your most painful experiences and profound disappointments is a gateway to higher wisdom.

Courage, Replay

In the third Harry Potter movie, *Harry Potter and the Prisoner of Azkaban*, there is a chilling moment when Harry is watching himself in a replay, dying as the Dementors suck the life out of him. He knows what to do. This is a replay, and he knows the ending: to repel them, he must not give in to the fear. He must cast a spell that puts a shield around him by summoning a happy memory. But until this moment, Harry believes his deceased father is going to show up and cast the spell. His friend Hermione says, "He's not coming. Your father is not coming." "He'll come, he'll come," Harry assures her. But Harry sees himself dying across the lake and no one coming. In one swift move, Harry steps forward with his wand and casts the Dementors away. As Hermione and he fly back to the castle at Hogwarts, he tells her, "I knew I could do it, because, well, I'd already done it."

Courage is feeling the fear and doing it anyway, as they say. In Harry's case, the Dementors *used* his fear against him. Courage is when you take a chance even when you're afraid. This is the kind of courage an oracle must have.

Like any feeling, fear is just a feeling and not reality. But we have to acknowledge it—call it by name—until we can move to the other side. When we let it in, we also learn that it doesn't kill us.

Pain and Suffering

But is *suffering* really necessary to achieve growth? First, let's distinguish between pain and suffering. Pain is when you hurt. You're disappointed, sad, or angry. But suffering is when you have pain and you struggle against it.

Wise teachers will tell you that suffering is not necessary, that it is we who make it so. Learn from your suffering. Your suffering is telling you something. What you desired matters. It matters enough to grieve its loss. It matters enough to take the time to learn from it. Either you will try harder, with wiser eyes and a more loving heart, or you will let go and make peace with it.

We are most receptive to insight when we suffer this much. This is where we experience quantum leaps of consciousness.

Carolyn offers this story of the way pain propels us to do what we otherwise would not do. It happened when she was in the darkest times of her divorce. She had the demands of two-year-old twins, mounting financial problems, a looming court date, a big crunch at work—and her car blew a head gasket. Essentially, it was DOA (dead on arrival). It would have to be replaced—immediately—or her barely functioning life would not be able to function. She had to rent a car just to make her court date. The priest who had married Carolyn and her husband had extended the invitation months earlier for one, either, or both of them to come see him. It was this crisis that propelled Carolyn to set up a meeting, even though she didn't have a car to get there. But the insight and compassion of the priest was crucial—exactly what she needed, words that she treasured in her heart and carried forward. The meeting was the turning point for her—one she would not have sought out if not for the pain.

> **Wise Words**
>
> Buddhist monk Thich Nhat Hanh describes **suffering** as the agent of beauty that makes love possible and life meaningful. When you practice *karuna*, or compassion, it helps you suffer less. It transforms the suffering. Suffering is like compost, and karuna is like the flower. If you know how to make use of suffering, the compost, you can bring about the flower and the beauty.

What You Don't Know

Sometimes the wisdom is in the questions. Once Carolyn was taking a demanding new job. She felt confident of her knowledge for most areas of the job, but she was concerned about her knowledge of technology. Her mentor advised her not to worry: she didn't have to have all the answers, just all the right questions. This placed Carolyn in her power center. As a journalist, she felt comfortable with formulating the questions. That proved to be her strength as she took on the new job. One of her biggest allies in her work group had the technical knowledge, and she played complement to him, asking the questions and finding ways to use the technology creatively and effectively for her department.

Take inventory of your natural strengths and your personal style. In those you will find your power centers. You may not possess all knowledge. But when you are coming from your power center, you can be confident in what you don't know, as well as what you do know. In Gary's field of psychology, therapists and counselors strive to be aware of how they can impart wisdom to others. Is it by asking the right questions? By pointing out patterns or contradictions? By providing examples?

Tell It Like It Is

A lifelong commitment to discipline is often what sets an oracle apart. Consider the discipline of seven-time Tour de France winner Lance Armstrong. It was because he was so strong through determined physical training that doctors treated his cancer aggressively—so aggressively that some say anyone else would have died just from the treatment. Consider, too, the disciplined diet and exercise regimen of Nelson Mandela during 26 years in prison. Because of that discipline, he had the stamina to be president of South Africa in his late 70s. Make this quote from Armstrong your mantra: *Pain is temporary. Quitting is forever.*

The Unlived Life

Writer Anya Achtenberg teaches a workshop called "An Unlived Life." She says that most powerful moments in fiction come from the life that the character did not choose. That is where regret, shame, fear, sorrow—the most powerful emotions—lie.

It's true in life as well as in fiction. What life did you not choose? Could you have gone to medical school and provided health care to third-world countries? Do you have a movie screenplay in you? Do you regret not having children? Is there someone in your past that you wish you had married? How would your life be if you had chosen that path?

It can also be helpful to formulate your biggest questions about life. What do you most want to know about? What personal attributes do you wish you had? What question is left unsolved for you? This is not only about your limitations but also your values. What aspects of life do you question and wish you could have explained to you?

We think it's important to take the time and ask these questions of yourself. The areas of life that you yearn to explore may drive your thinking. When you don't know the answer to a question, that question draws you to it like a magnet. We mean questions such as "What was it really like for Mom after Dad left?" or "What would it be like to be a strong athlete?" Even when you are not conscious of them, these questions steer your thoughts and form your orientation.

At Your Peril

Oh, but aren't oracles mysterious? Aren't they confounding? Maybe you certainly don't speak in iambic hexameter, but you are perfectly capable of confusing people. But if your aim in being an oracle is to mess with people's heads, then we need to talk. Like a Zen teacher giving a koan, an oracle sometimes leaves the work to the student—but with kindness. You know the receiver needs not to be handed wisdom, but to experience it for himself or herself.

Getting Ready

Now if you are ready to be an oracle, there are a few more practical steps. There is the matter of finding people who want to hear what you have to say. Of course, the Buddhist saying goes, "When the student is ready, the teacher will appear," but you may put forth a little more preparation than that. And the truth is, even Buddhist teachers do print up cards and put out shingles.

You may not do this formally—set yourself up to do oracle readings, send yourself out on a lecture tour, or set up in private practice as a psychologist. But we can take a cue from people who do. Make a list of groups that might benefit from your wisdom. Why? What is it they need? What can you offer them? In what situations might you encounter them?

Even with a license to practice counseling, Gary finds being helpful to people requires knowing not only what to say but when and how. That means keeping your mouth shut when it is not the right time to speak. Being tapped into the wisdom of the universe, if you want to look at it that way, is about timing and patience and sensitivity. It's like the beginning of this Tao poem:

> *The highest good is like water.*
> *Water gives life to the ten thousand things and does not strive.*
> *It flows in places men reject and so is like the Tao.*

—Lao Tsu, *Tao Te Ching*, Chapter 8

We will return to this poem as we examine two principles for getting ready to be an oracle: living mindfully and living kindfully. But we compare the practice of right timing to planting seeds versus planting a forest. It's how we know when to speak and spur someone to action and when to wait for further wisdom.

Gary has made suggestions to clients that seemed to fall on deaf ears. Later he realized that he was so worried about being right or about dealing with the helplessness he felt upon hearing about their situation that he was acting more out of his needs than theirs. He needed to be right about his advice and know he was right by seeing the person take it. Sometimes he has had to apologize because the person also realized what he was doing and called him on it. So they both learned. Gary has learned by being patient, he can better sense the timing of when the person is ready to hear and ready to act (two different things!). And he has learned to trust that without an immediate response, he is still being helpful.

Living Mindfully

We have talked a lot about living mindfully, but another way of looking at it is that it allows us to increase our own wisdom. By staying in the moment, we have opportunities to learn and grow, to glean bits of wisdom simply by observing people and situations around us. Gary learns a lot by watching people interact on the subways of New York City. He sees how parents behave with children or how words or behaviors affect other people. Being mindful—aware of the here and now—teaches him a lot.

> ### Oracle Advice
>
> Part of living mindfully is to control your input. This means the media—books, magazines, television, movies, newspapers, websites. But it also includes friends in your inner circle and people you see day in and day out. Take a good look at how this affects you. You may think, "I'm wiser than that mindless sitcom or fluff magazine," but the point is, you're consuming it and not some healthy mind food that enriches your soul and edifies your thoughts.

Living Kindfully

We can get caught up in being oracles and let our egos run wild. This is not useful. But it is a danger of calling yourself an oracle. And it is also something Gary sees with people who are in the position of helping other people.

Is this about you, making you look smart, wise, important, otherworldly, or is this about reaching out to someone else by sharing something you have learned? When we forget ourselves, our egos, we can speak from the soul instead of from our needy side.

We must remember to be empathetic, not sympathetic. Sympathy is great—certainly it comes from a caring place—but sympathy still has the overlay of our own experience on the situation. Empathy means really putting yourself in the other person's head and experiencing their unique situation.

Once Gary had a client who was dealing with a really abusive boss. At first Gary had to remind himself that to be helpful he had to focus on what his client needed and not get caught up in thinking he had to fix everything for her. She did not need him to do that, nor did she want him to. She was stressed but not helpless. When Gary was able to put himself in *her* situation, he was able to help her articulate how she was feeling and how frustrated she was. Together they explored different ways of coping with the situation.

Universal Acts of Kindness

The bumper sticker "Practice Random Acts of Kindness" has proliferated on the planet. But we encourage you, as an oracle-in-waiting, to practice universal acts of kindness. This is taking random acts one step further. Strive to practice kindness universally, in every facet of life, every moment of the day. We all have a light within, and you can open people up to their own light when you show that you recognize theirs.

Maeve: Taking Charge

MAEVE
RESPONSIBILITY

Maeve, the Irish goddess of war from our Goddess Oracle Deck, was a woman who knew what she wanted. Legend says she was a fearless warrior and a courageous lover, sleeping with many kings. She was said to run faster than horses, and she is sometimes depicted carrying birds and animals across her shoulders. One day she learned that her consort, King Aillil, had a magic bull that she did not have. She decided she wanted it. She ordered her army to steal it, but she got into a great battle with Cuchulain. She finally prevailed, taking the bull, but she had to turn around and fight the bull. They tore each other to pieces.

Maeve wanted that magic bull with a fierceness. Do you allow yourself to feel that fierce about what you desire? Has it been a long time since you have pursued what you want with that kind of desire? It can be frightening to want something in your life that much. It can tear you in pieces. Or not. Is there something in your life that you are not pursuing out of fear there will be a battle for it? If so, recognize that its fierceness still exists, unexpressed within you. This card encourages us to look full on at that fierceness. How bad do you want it?

Write in your Oracle Journal about how you can take responsibility for living the life you want. Write about how you may practice mindfulness and kindness to attain the life you want. Explore the ways you might be tested to act with less than full mindfulness or kindness.

Being the Oracle

In the last book published before his death, *Where Do We Go from Here: Chaos or Community?* Martin Luther King Jr. wrote, "We are now faced with the fact that tomorrow is today. We are confronted with the fierce urgency of *now*. In this unfolding conundrum of life and history there is such a thing as being too late. Procrastination is still the thief of time." As Dr. King saw, so must we: we must take activism to the universal level. It's not just about forming groups and public awareness campaigns. It's not about T-shirts and campaign buttons. It's about becoming the embodiment of the change. You practice what you preach. If you believe in staying calm and not fighting, then you must live a life free from conflict. You become the agent of peace that changes the world.

You can be an oracle simply by living as an example. Go ahead, live the life you envision. Live with integrity. Be your word. Commit to mindfulness and don't compromise. Commit to self-care and hold to the discipline of that. Do it time and time again, each time it's tested. Commit to compassion, and practice it even when it's tested.

And now, here's the rest of that Tao poem:

> *In dwelling, be close to the land.*
> *In meditation, go deep in the heart.*
> *In dealing with others, be gentle and kind.*
> *In speech, be true.*
> *In ruling, be just.*

In business, be competent.
In action, watch the timing.
No fight; No blame.

—Lao Tsu, *Tao Te Ching*, Chapter 8

When you live this way, you will not necessarily have to give voice to the wisdom. It will be apparent. Gary has had clients tell him about situations in which observing someone caused discomfort because they realized what they were missing in their own lives. It was like a confrontation that didn't actually involve any interaction. People with anger problems, for example, spent time with someone who was calm and didn't overreact to everything. Or a client with a negative, glass-half-empty attitude was around people who were really positive and coping with the challenges of life without throwing in the towel. Simply observing these people made Gary's clients realize what they were missing in their own lives. So in a way, these people were silent oracles for them.

Gary admits he has learned the most from people who didn't tell him but showed him by being an example. Before he was self-employed, he really respected and envied people who were self-employed. He felt like they had control in their life that he did not have. It wasn't what they told him, but it was a self-confidence that they seemed to possess. As Gary got closer to making that decision himself, he kept encountering more of those people. It was really exciting!

Be a Mirror

You'll know you're an oracle when you hold up the mirror to others, and you hold them up to the light. It will be because you have already allowed the same to happen to you; you have allowed others to hold up the mirror to you, to show you who you really are and how you come across, to show you the ways in which you must grow. It comes when you can accept the criticism and learn and grow, when you can see yourself wholly, good and bad, and still be centered.

It will come when you treat others with the same compassion, and this is natural and effortless to you.

Amaterasu: Pure Light

AMATERASU

BEAUTY

Amaterasu is the sun goddess in the Buddhist and Shinto tradition. She is vital as the founder of sericulture, the guardian of agriculture, the deity of peace and order. She rules the realm of light on *ama* (heaven), Earth, and the plain of heaven.

But her brother, Susanowo, committed atrocities against her, and she retreated into a cave, withdrawing all the light from heaven and Earth. All the other deities implored her to come out, but to no avail. Finally, they hung a mirror named Kagami and a necklace in a tree outside the cave. Still, no action. A goddess named Ame-no-uzume-no-mikoto performed a sexy little dance, stripping off her clothes and drawing glee and laughter from her audience. Amaterasu was curious. She poked her head out to see what all the hoopla was about. The deities said they had found another goddess to take her place, and she was beautiful. Amaterasu saw her reflection in the mirror and moved closer. The deities apprehended her and brought light back to the earth.

Maybe this is something we need to do, at least temporarily. We have to be able to retreat into ourselves to get in touch with what is important to us, and to assess our strengths. We have to step back from the world and grow, to be introspective and not always extroverted. Siddhartha, for example, went out on his own, and Jesus went into the wilderness. Retreating for a while may help us decide what we want to fight for—and risk everything—and what we don't want to fight for. Those decisions, notwithstanding all of the oracular advice we come into contact with, have to be made on our own.

Shining Oracle

A final image: in many depictions, Amaterasu is depicted with the necklace, a symbol of spiritual power and fertility, and a mirror, the sacred symbol of purity.

Let Amaterasu remind us to see our own beauty reflected back in the mirror, and to do the same for others. Let that mirror capture the divine light in you that desires to be an oracle. Let it be reflected back so that you may see what you must do and be.

The Least You Need to Know

- Take inventory of your areas of wisdom.

- Oracles use their personal setbacks to gain wisdom and share it with others.

- Being an effective oracle is as much about what you don't know as what you *do* know.

- Living mindfully and practicing universal kindness make you a wisdom magnet.

- Allow others to hold up the mirror to you so that you may learn and grow.

- Being an oracle is about capturing the divine light that is in us all.

Part 4

Wise Oracle Tells All

Oracles have many ways of teaching us. Some are practical and direct—the yes or no, either-or type. Others, such as the Mouth of Truth in Rome, featured in the classic Audrey Hepburn film *Roman Holiday*, like to test your worthiness. And oracles come in the most unlikely of forms, as the ancients knew, in the rustling of trees, in mysterious words, or in the movements of the sun, moon, and stars. Some touch us in our dreams, whereas some come in movie-screen visions. In this part, we explore all the wild and woolly ways oracles try to get our attention.

Yes or No?

In This Chapter

- Egyptian oracles: on the move
- At a crossroads: the career question
- The I Ching
- Love and changes

Want wisdom that is pragmatic and sensible? The Egyptians may be what you're looking for, with their simple yes-or-no brand of oracles. Want wisdom that is beautiful in its simplicity but recognizes that we are all in a state of flux? The Chinese may have the method that works for you, with the I Ching.

In this chapter, we explore these two practical and straightforward styles of oracle giving, both of which are constructed on a binary model. Egyptians received their oracles through a string of yes or no questions. The I Ching system is based on combinations of six different aspects of yin and yang, called hexagrams. The result, we think you'll find, is an intelligent, effective, and shrewd brand of wisdom.

A Tour of Ancient Egypt

The oracle tradition of ancient Egypt was much more pragmatic than the Greek oracles. Egyptian oracles were mobile, and they were more direct. Oracles were transported through the streets in processionals, and people could come up and ask their question. Usually the answers were a simple yes or no.

One of the most famous Egyptian oracles is that which Alexander the Great received at the Siwa Oasis. Alexander went to this oracle to legitimize his rule of Egypt, and he got a big payoff. The oracle there was believed to be the voice of the god Amun, or Amun-Ra, a god who was worshipped from the eleventh dynasty on (2134 to 1991 B.C.E.). Upon entering the temple, Alexander was declared the son of Amun, or the son of God. Siwa Oasis is a most inaccessible place, about 60 feet below sea level and very remote. So you must go there with great intention.

To bring oracle wisdom to the masses, priests would load a statue of a god on a barque, or royal boat, which was a canopied pallet, carried on poles. You see a lot of depictions of this in Egyptian art. The priests would announce when the oracles would parade through the streets, and people would line up along the edges of the street to wait to ask their questions. Usually, these processionals occurred during festivals.

The answers were delivered very simply. If the barque resumed forward motion, the answer was yes.

All oracles were written in those times. They were either written on papyrus or engraved on temple walls. (Usually these engraved oracles were instructions about the passage into the afterlife.) When you asked a question of the oracle in the street, you received a written papyrus in a scroll, and you could wear it like an amulet. (Papyrus was a sedge plant that grew in the Nile Valley. The Egyptians would make it into paper by cutting it in strips and pressing it flat.) Many of the documents were preserved with the question, too, as we know from the many preserved from the Ramesside period (nineteenth and twentieth dynasties, 1295 to 1070 B.C.E.), carved into limestone flakes and written in hieratic.

Gods and Goddesses

Amun was premium among the oracle gods of ancient Egypt. He was known as the Hidden One, the soul of all things. He was known as a supreme creative god, a god of war, and the force behind the wind. He was elevated to Amun-Ra (or Amen-Ra) by the priests, who wanted to associate him with the sun god, Ra. He is shown as a bearded, blue man with the tail of a lion or bull, wearing a headdress with two plumes, usually red and green or sometimes red and blue. In his right hand, he holds an ankh (the Egyptian symbol of life), and in his left hand he holds a scepter.

Other oracular gods of Egypt included Horus of the camp, Horus-Khau at Hiba, Seth at Dakhla, Isis at Koptos, Ahmose at Abydos, and Sobek. Probably one of the most influential was Isis, the sister-wife of Osiris and mother of Horus, goddess of the earth and patroness of loving wives and mothers. Isis is represented in many of the symbols of ancient Egypt, from the buckle, which came from her belt, to the vulture, which brought her protection. (More about these in Chapter 20, and you can turn back to Chapter 1 to see the Isis Goddess Oracle card.)

Symbols of Life

The average person receiving an oracle might literally wear the words of the oracle, rolled in a papyrus. Or the user might carry a symbol of the oracle god or a symbol of protection.

Ankhs and other symbols figure prominently in Egyptian oracles. Often they were representations of what the oracle had revealed to the listener—a reminder of the message. They were worn as amulets, a remembrance and a protection. (We discuss amulets in more detail in Chapter 20.)

Ankhs are the symbol of life, and they are believed to be a precursor to the Christian symbol of the cross. They evolved from the Egyptian glyph for magical protection. Some have theorized that the ankh symbolized the sunrise, that the loop resembled the path of the sun from east to west. Others believe that the ankh was a stylized womb. Mummy cases often depicted the figure with arms crossed over the chest, holding an ankh in each hand. Depictions of processionals of the gods often showed them carrying ankhs.

Tell It Like It Is

A symbol similar to the ankh was used to symbolize the Roman goddess Venus. The symbol is known benignly as Venus's hand mirror but probably was a representation of the womb. In alchemy, the symbol represented the element of copper. In biology, it represents woman. The symbol was adopted by the early Egyptian Christian church and may have been the precursor to the Christian symbol of the cross.

North, South, East, or West: New Directions

So how could we learn from the practicality of Egyptian oracles? Let's take an example from real modern life—the question of what you want to be when you grow up. Baby Boomers, more than any other generation before them, have really put their stamp on this issue. They have put a premium on personal fulfillment as integral to a career. Following quickly along behind them are the Generation Xers, who not only expect personal fulfillment but work-life balance. With so many of us living longer, we not only have the opportunity for a fulfilling career—we might have the opportunity for two, even three. If you count yourself among the fulfilled, more power to you. If you wonder sometimes if you are doing it right, then this exercise is for you.

Yes and No to Your Career

We have composed a list of simple yes or no questions to help you get a handle on improving the career you have or making a career transition. Remember in ancient Egypt, the barque would move forward if the answer was yes. Instead, it might be helpful to think about it like the needle that measures audience applause. More applause—more noise, more enthusiasm—and the needle rises. As you ask yourself each question, pay attention to whether the needle rises or falls. Really pay attention if it's off the scale.

First, we start with five questions that Suzy and Jack Welch use in their book *Winning* (see Appendix B):

- Does this job allow you to work with "your people"—individuals who share your sensibility about life? Or do you have to put on a persona to get through the day?

- Does this job challenge, stretch, change, and otherwise make you smarter? Or does it leave your brain in neutral?

- Does this job, because of the company's "brand," or your level of responsibility, open the door to future jobs?

- Does this job represent a considerable compromise for the sake of your family, and if so, do you sincerely accept that deal with all of its consequences?

- Does this job—the stuff you actually do day to day—touch your heart and feed your soul in meaningful ways?

And now, a few more beyond those from *Winning*:

- Is your career leading you somewhere?

- Is your career emotionally rewarding?

- Does your salary cover your essential needs?

- Does your career give you a good, balanced sense of your personal power? Do you feel your views are respected?

- Do you have a sense of pride in ownership, either in the work that you do or in the brand of your company? Can you say you are proud of the quality?

- Do you believe your knowledge is being tapped in your job—that the company values your expertise and talents?

- Do you believe you are learning and growing? Do you have a mentor, someone who shows you the ropes, someone who strengthens your strengths and strengthens your weaknesses?

- Does your job allow you to make a contribution to the world?

- Are you following your bliss?

- Do you know what your bliss is?

If "no" dominated this list, then it's probably time to listen to that and make a big change. Now we have two big questions: What should you change *to*, and *how* should you change it?

To answer the first one—what should you change to?—take the previous questions and evaluate how important those factors are to you in a job. Write in your Oracle Journal about *why* they are important to you. What does it look like and feel like to work with an *esprit de corps* of like-minded people? What do you envision as a career that *does* tap into your unique talents? It's important also to evaluate your successes— what have you enjoyed doing in the past? To answer the second one—how to go about it—make a list of action steps. Some of them might be broad, such as "go to medical school," but make sure to put some things on the list that you can start on tomorrow, such as "call friend who is in medical school to pick her brain."

> **Oracle Advice**
>
> In your Oracle Journal, free associate words that describe your ideal work, work environment, and work community. Fill the page with as many as you can think of: rewarding. creative. friendly. supportive. challenging. Distill this list to the most essential 10 to 12 words. As you move forward, and opportunities are presented to you, use your list of words as a test. Is this job challenging? Is this job creative? Remember, no job is perfect, so don't idealize your definition of creative. Creativity can be found in just the approach you take to your career, even if you're manufacturing computer chips.

Taking the Leap

Maybe you know what your bliss would be. You just don't know how to take the leap. Usually behind this question is, "How will I make a decent living?" But sometimes it's about establishing yourself as a legitimate player—it's about getting an education, developing the qualities an employer would seek, learning how to talk the talk and walk the walk.

It's good to do this next exercise with a partner, with both of you answering each question about you. (Then switch off, returning the favor for your friend, answering the same questions for him or her.) The reason a partner is valuable is that your partner will have perspective on you. For instance, your partner may say that although you don't know where the money will come from, he (or she) knows you are the kind who will work hard and create money-making opportunities for yourself. So *he* doesn't worry about whether you will accomplish this. He knows you. He's seen you do this a million times.

Another way a partner can help is she can steer you back to your core values. If you have shared your vision with your partner—if she knows why this is your bliss—then she can be a counterbalance to you, keeping you in balance with your goal. She can remind you why this goal is important to you. She can tell you when it's not a good fit for you.

Ask the following yes or no questions. After going through the list, follow up each question with "why" or "why not." Be specific. If you got a big *yes* to "worried about making enough money," then write down in your Oracle Journal how much you think you need to make. Then ask: What would it take to accomplish this in the next five years? What is the one thing you could do tomorrow that could further that goal?

Who is the person who has the resources, power, and knowledge to help you meet that goal?

- Should I be worried about making enough money?

- Should I be worried I don't know enough about doing this?

- Should I go back to school?

- Should I stay at the same company and work toward a promotion?

- Will I be happy if I stay the course?

- Will things get better if I stay the course?

- Will I be happy if I make big changes?

- Will my health/my family/my partner be able to withstand a transition?

- Is it a time for a radical change or incremental change?

- Should I relocate, or should I stay close to home?

- If I have less money for six months (a year/two years), will I live?

- If I have less money temporarily but achieve this goal, will it be worth it?

And now for some hard questions:

- Does this change mean realistically that I may never make the kind of money I could make in my current career?

- Am I willing to live with the tradeoff of more job fulfillment for less money (for instance, moving from the private sector to nonprofit, from technology to the arts)?

- What will I realistically need to give up?

- Is there stability in my current field in terms of job security that is not a characteristic of the new career (e.g., computer professional to fundraiser or freelancer)?

- Have I really considered the kind of work environment I will be facing in the new career?

- Am I viewing it without rose-colored glasses (e.g., giving up an office staffed with personal assistants to one in which professionals must be self-sufficient, or moving from an office to cubicles)?

You get the idea. With your friend, develop more questions. Keep going until you get to the heart of the matter. Keep exploring it until you know the whole shape of your vision—like a blind man placing his hands on an elephant. Keep delving into the questions until you have broken down your goal into steps—until you have something you can do tomorrow to further your goal.

There is something pretty shrewd about this method. Yes or no makes it pretty simple. You may want to make it more complex, but you have to come down on one side or the other. There's just no two ways about it. It also puts you in control, step by step. You get accustomed to paying attention when the needle rises … or doesn't. If it doesn't feel right, the needle won't rise. Your head may say yes, but your gut is saying no. This method can be very empowering.

Hecate: At a Crossroads

HECATE

CROSSROADS

Hecate wasn't Egyptian; she was a Thracian (or Greek) goddess who completed the goddess triumvirate with Persephone (maid) and Demeter (mother). Hecate represents the crone, the wise woman at the end of her life. This is the woman who has nothing to prove. She shines in the glory of her wisdom. (Indeed, in many depictions, she has a torch, and she was only worshipped at night by torchlight.) She emanates serenity and quiet power.

Hecate was worshipped in the places where three roads crossed. She is the convergence of wisdom, the place where various sets of wisdom come together. She reminds us that sometimes events converge in just the right way to make it happen for us. She is the woman who has found her place in this world, who knows her own brand of magic. She also reminds us, because she has inhabited her realm for so many years, that we play many roles in life. In fact—talk about wearing many hats—she sometimes is depicted with three heads, that of a dog, a horse, and a lion. Hecate reminds us that we have many talents, and that life calls upon us in different capacities at different times. She encourages us to accept that a fulfilled life has many mutations.

At Your Peril

When using oracles, it's important to avoid falling into preconceived notions about whether associations are good or bad. Hecate, for instance, was the name of one of the witches in *Macbeth*, so you might resist the idea of turning to a witch for wisdom. The number 13—the number of this chapter—is considered unlucky. Like the elevator that skips the thirteenth floor, this chapter didn't really exist for a long time, as Gary and Carolyn both kept putting it off. But try another interpretation: transcendent 13, the number of transformation and rebirth. The 13 colonies of the United States declared independence from Britain. There are 13 ranges on a pyramid. At the Last Supper, there were 12 disciples plus Jesus. Thirteen is the number of resurrection, rebirth, and new life. It reduces to the number 4; in numerology, 4 is the number of the master builder.

I Ching: In Tune with Nature

The I Ching, an ancient Chinese form of divination, is based on the balancing of the male and female energies of the universe. We include a segment explaining them here because, like the Egyptian yes/no oracles, they are pragmatic, clear, and effective. Both systems are binary—like a computer chip—with each question or transaction drawing one answer or another, forming an infinite chain of wisdom.

The I Ching, also known as the Book of Changes, is an intuitive decision-making system. Drawing from numbers and nature, the system examines the intricate balance of yin and yang, the two primary energies of the universe. Yin is what we think of as feminine energy; yang is male energy. Yin is a cloud, embracing moisture, holding what will become rain; yang is the rain.

The I Ching is intricate, yet simple. Confucius was fascinated with it; so was psychologist Carl Jung, who studied it for many years, and identified its 64 main readings as archetypes.

How do we use archetypes as oracles? Let's take one of Jung's archetypes, the wise old man. He can be interpreted as a kindly higher power to help guide our path. Or he can represent a father figure that we have had difficulty accepting, and encountering this archetype may signify the need to accept and forgive before we can move forward in our path. Or this archetype could signify a quality that we want to develop in ourselves.

Tell It Like It Is

The other aspect Jung identified in the I Ching was that of interconnectedness. All things are connected in time as well as space, not by cause and effect, but simply by occurring simultaneously. Jung called this synchronicity, which reflects a higher logic, a more elegant hand orchestrating the music of life.

The I Ching reinforces the concept of interconnectedness, and so when we encounter an archetype, our task is to understand how we are connected with it. It can represent something that we seek outside of ourselves, something we need to develop internally, or something we have to come to terms with. Or it can connect us with the idea that aspects of others that bother us the most are aspects of ourselves that we don't want to accept. Aspects of others that we admire are also qualities that we want to nurture in ourselves, or that we perceive as necessary for our completion.

How the I Ching Works

The I Ching is constructed in hexagrams, or two groups of three lines that are stacked. A broken line is yin; a solid line is yang. Hexagrams are always constructed from the bottom to the top. Each group of three lines is a trigram; there are eight trigrams, and they are connected to nature:

1. Three solid lines = heaven (force).

2. A solid line, two broken lines = thunder (arousing).

3. Broken line, solid line, broken line = water (difficulty).

4. Broken line, broken line, solid line = mountain (stopping).

5. Three broken lines = earth (yielding).

6. Broken line, two solid lines = wind (entering).

7. Solid line, broken line, solid line = fire (intelligence).

8. Two solid lines, broken line = lake (openness).

The I Ching can give 64 times 64 possible readings, or 4,096 readings. A reading usually has three parts: the first hexagram, the changing lines, and the second hexagram. The first hexagram defines the current situation, and the changing lines, quite obviously, identify the dynamic features of the situation. The second hexagram indicates the way the situation might develop. If you have no changing lines, there is no second hexagram. That indicates your situation is fixed or static.

Connecting to the One You Love

Because the I Ching is about the interconnectedness of all things, we think it is a good place to turn for insight into a relationship, particularly one that is stuck. (We discuss more ways oracles can help you with your relationships in Chapter 21.) The I Ching looks for significant patterns of change. The goal of a relationship is to keep it in balance. When yin and yang are in a balanced relationship, the world is in harmony. The I Ching can provide insight into what's out of balance in your relationship. Knowing where there is too much yin or too much yang can bring you back into harmony. We offer some good sources for the I Ching in Appendixes A and B.

Perspective and Harmony

If you need to break down a big goal, you might want to "walk like an Egyptian" and use the yes-or-no method. And if you seek harmony amid the flux of life, you might turn to the I Ching to remind yourself that we exist in a dynamic state of constant change—and it's natural. Achieving harmony in and of itself will bring you more wisdom than you will know.

The Least You Need to Know

♦ Egyptian priests brought their oracles into the streets, transporting a statue of the god on a barque.

♦ Egyptian oracles were answered with a yes or a no. If the barque resumed forward motion, the answer was yes.

♦ A yes-no sequence of questions is a good way to sort out a major life-change question, such as a career move.

♦ The I Ching is an ancient Chinese system of making intuitive decisions.

♦ The hexagrams of the I Ching are based on yin, the female energy, and yang, the male energy. Harmony is found in balancing these energies.

♦ The I Ching maps changes and identifies patterns of significance. It also indicates the underlying interconnectedness of all things.

Mouth of Truth

In This Chapter

- Being authentic
- No more illusions
- Mandalas: the central truth
- Ways to power think

The Mouth of Truth is a stone sculpture in the courtyard of the Santa Maria in Cosmedin church in Rome. If you know it, it's probably because you remember it from the 1953 movie *Roman Holiday* with Audrey Hepburn and Gregory Peck. The Bocca della Verita, as it is called in Italian, was said to cut off the hands of liars who put their hands in its mouth. Just so the Mouth of Truth could live up to legend, the priest caretaker sometimes would put a scorpion in the back of the mouth to sting prevaricators. While filming the movie, Peck stuck his hand in the mouth and slipped his hand up his sleeve so that when he pulled his hand out, it was missing, causing Audrey Hepburn to gasp. The scene wasn't in the script, but it worked so well, they kept it in the movie.

The Mouth of Truth tests your honesty. And other oracles do, too, if they are worth their salt. Historically, the seeker of oracle wisdom was required to prove his or her authenticity. In this chapter, we show you how to prove you are true, and we show you how you can know what is the truth for yourself.

Authenticity and Integrity

Mythologist Joseph Campbell discusses the role that writers play in revealing the truth in the book *The Power of Myth* with Bill Moyers (see Appendix B). In the interview, he is discussing the way novels can illuminate and enlighten us. Authors that he loved were James Joyce and Thomas Mann. He quotes Mann as saying, "The writer must be true to the truth."

Campbell says that means we must tell the truth even when we describe the imperfections of another. "The only way you can describe a human being truly is by describing his imperfections." But he says, "It is the imperfections of life that are lovable. And when the writer sends a dart of the true word, it hurts. But it goes with love."

Wise Words

Integrity is the quality or state of being complete; unbroken condition; wholeness; entirely. It means to be unimpaired. When you live with integrity, you live in harmony. All facets of you coexist without friction—perhaps some dynamic tension, but not out-and-out friction. You are able to integrate your conscious and subconscious beliefs and function at optimum levels.

The key to being authentic is being able to accept the imperfections of the truth. When you can do that with love, with love for your own imperfections, then you are ready to be authentic. It is only when you embrace all of you—even the dark side—that you can truly act with *integrity*.

Oracles require us to be truthful with ourselves. They test our authenticity and our integrity. Oracles work like karma—like energy attracts like energy. When your heart is true, you attract the truth. When your purpose is noble, you attract noble followers and the means to do noble deeds. When it's not the truth, the complete truth, you are bound to attract experiences to yourself that reveal that to you. This is especially true when you have committed to the higher path of authenticity.

What is the difference between authenticity and integrity? Our read on it is that authenticity is how you relate to yourself, whether you are honest with yourself, through and through. Integrity is how you relate to others and to the world. Authenticity means you are not compartmentalized. Being compartmentalized means you act one way in one area of your life, but you have a different set of ethics in other areas. In other words, you don't hide things from yourself, like credit card debt or a sweet tooth or too many glasses of wine. You know what you believe, and you are that way on every layer of your existence. Authenticity is when you act as you say you believe.

Acting with integrity means that your ethics are transparent to others. You don't act one way with one person or one situation. People can trust you. You are reliable. You are good to your word.

Here are some guidelines:

- Treat others as you wish to be treated.

- Be true to your word. If you say you'll be there, you're there. If you say you'll do it, you will.

- Honor those who are absent. Speak of people out of their presence in the same way you would speak if they could hear you.

- Ask yourself if your actions will contribute to a better world.

- Always believe that the other person wants to do his or her best and is doing the best he or she can.

Integrity means to be whole, unbroken. There are not parts of you floating off to act as their own free agent. You don't have one set of ethics for one situation and another for others. Realistically, though, sometimes one area of life fails to catch up with the others unless we are conscious of our development. We may have updated our belief system in one area but not in another. Life circumstances have changed, but maybe not so dramatically that we thought to update the files.

Sometimes Gary meditates on the idea of wholeness. He imagines himself as various pieces and he visualizes them coming together, coexisting with each other, welcoming each other, supporting each other. It is about having compassion for yourself, even the parts of yourself that you wish would grow up and go away.

Relinquishing Illusion

The next step to take before you approach the Mouth of Truth for wisdom is to learn to distinguish between truth and illusion. This sounds really obvious—of course, rational, thinking people distinguish between truth and illusion. But this step is one of the most vital to effectively using the power of oracle wisdom in your life.

Oracles require us to relinquish our illusions. Their loyalty is only to the truth. The spiritual belief system A Course in Miracles says, "When a situation has been dedicated wholly to truth, peace is inevitable." If Croesus had only cared more about the truth than victory when he received the Oracle of Delphi, he might not have sent his soldiers into a massacre. To find that peace, though, you must be willing to see the imperfections of something, to ask the hard questions that shatter the illusion.

This is so easy to say, but it can be quite a challenge when you are talking about a dream you have nurtured for years. You may have expended a lot of time and effort glamorizing this dream. You may have nursed it so long you forget why you gave birth to it. You may have lost any sense of the pleasure the dream once brought you.

It's ever so vital that you start to notice early on when you are glamorizing a dream. Glamorizing a dream only leads to betrayal. There, we said it. Glamorizing is fun—don't get us wrong—but inevitably the glamour exceeds reality. The sweetness turns sour.

We hate to be the ones to burst your bubble, but illusion leads to defeat and power-lessness. That's because you just can't stay in the illusion. Clinging to illusion means that some outside force will have to disillusion you. It may be okay to glamorize your dream, but you will have to be the first to bust that myth and bring yourself down to reality. So yes, we want you to dream. We want your imagination to flourish. But we want you to know that you need to be in the driver's seat. You need to bring it home. You need to bring your dreams back down to Earth.

Allure is the most dazzling form of glamorizing, and it's dangerous. Allure is just this side of addiction. It's intoxicating. Sex, money, and fame are such powerful intoxicants that they can undo the best of us. How many times have you read about the movie star or athlete with the perfect marriage only to read months later that he has left her for a rock star? It's a cliché, we know, but clichés have their basis in a reality that is repeated so often that it becomes … well, a cliché.

Of course, it's easy to say *you* are not susceptible to the temptations of money, sex, or fame. If you are like us, you don't have to worry about anyone tempting you. No one is offering! Most of us would not describe ourselves as materialistic or narcissistic, not in any way that announces itself like a made-for-television movie. Our challenge is to recognize the small temptations that present themselves every day. They creep into our lives when we least suspect it and dazzle us. It's like the line from the rock group U2's song, "Vertigo," "All of this could be yours." It echoes the words of Satan when he's tempting Jesus in the desert, laying the kingdoms of the earth at his feet. Or Buddha's temptations when he was sitting under the bodhi tree.

But buying into temptation is not buying into power, but powerlessness. Believing the illusion only leads to betrayal. Inevitably, the illusion wears off like a bad spell.

Coming to Terms

Gary often helps people make career transitions and face the changes they make in their lives. One example is a woman who was a paralegal in a law firm and wanted to leave. She was tired of her boss, who she thought was demanding and unappreciative of her creative side.

After a taste of volunteer work, she developed the dream of writing grant proposals for nonprofits. She sought guidance from self-help books that talked about following your passion, stepping out in faith, and being true to yourself. She devoted time to meditating on her ideal career, using creative visualization. She poured her thoughts into a journal.

In a way, she created an oracle. The oracle told her that if her motive was really to help other people and make a difference in the world, the universe would be behind her 100 percent. So she decided to write grant proposals as a freelancer. She could get involved in a variety of causes, plus have the autonomy that she didn't have in the regimented atmosphere of the law firm. A few phone calls yielded some interest, and that was enough of a sign for her. She couldn't wait to drop the news on her boss.

But when she did, he was not only disappointed, he was concerned about her plan. He wondered if it was a wise idea, and he wasn't sure she knew what was involved in writing proposals full time. "Do you have work lined up?" he asked her. This conversation only served to remind her of the reasons she wanted to get out.

But her boss called her back in his office that afternoon and made her an offer: work half time, at home. She still got to keep her benefits. He suggested she could do it as a transition. Though she was annoyed, she consented.

The first two weeks were rough. None of the agencies had any work. Finally one called. They promised to give her background material in a few days. But a few days passed, and she called back. *They certainly aren't as organized as a law firm*, she thought to herself. Later, when she turned in her work, the agency director scorched it, asking her if she had ever written a proposal.

This went on for a while, as she was living on half of her previous salary, and she began to question her decision. Who was this oracle who had been guiding her? Was it real, or created out of her own restlessness and frustration? Was this about making a contribution or about escaping a job she was tired of? Was it the structure of her job she hated? Where were the idealized passionate people who would cherish and love her and take her into their family?

So she was able to see she had created an oracle who was really her own neediness—for expression, for connection with other people, for a direction in life. And the *real* oracle was her boss, the boss she was dying to get away from, who saw through her decision and not only advised her but rescued her. She also saw that she had projected her internal dissatisfaction on the world, perceiving that her boss placed limitations on her instead of understanding these were limitations she had placed on herself. After that, she was more open to growth and she was able to see a more authentic path for herself.

This story reminds us that sometimes it is painful to be truthful to ourselves. We would rather soothe ourselves and tell ourselves what we want to hear. Our ego steps in and takes over but wears the robes of the wise oracle.

Gary finds that when we have an image of contributing to the world, we need to be mindful of our motivations. It's not that we don't want to help make the world a better place. But this can also be a lie we tell ourselves, and the universe, to get what we want. We have to ask ourselves hard questions:

◆ What am I missing in life? What is the need here?

◆ What am I getting?

◆ What would I need to give up to gain what I think it is I want? And just exactly what is that I am gaining?

This can require asking the following:

◆ What is the new direction going to get me?

◆ And what does it mean to get that?

◆ And what does that mean to me?

It is kind of like thinking of your new life as a big onion but before you slice into it, you want to make sure it is not rotten at the core. So you peel each layer away, one by one, to get at what is *really* at the center.

Rhiannon: Redemption

Rhiannon's story is about waiting for the truth to come out. She was a Gaul and Celtic moon goddess, believed to be the deity over horses. One night otherworld forces kidnapped her son, Pryderi. The nannies who were watching him were terrified they would be blamed, so they killed puppies and smeared blood on Rhiannon's face while she slept. She was found guilty of devouring her son. Her sentence was to carry every visitor to the court on her back, on all fours like a horse. Each time, she must tell them of her wicked ways. This was Rhiannon's fate for many years, until her son was returned from the otherworld, and Rhiannon was acquitted.

Rhiannon's story is encouragement that all will be restored and the truth will win the day. When she comes up in a reading, she bodes that the future will bring about that day. When you need an injustice revealed, use Rhiannon to build a meditation on redemption. Dedicate your situation to the truth, and let it be revealed to you.

> **At Your Peril**
>
> Beware of your own ego and desire for seeing the world, or a situation, as you want to see it, which can masquerade in the robes of an oracle. Peel away the layers of what it is you think you are being promised and you will see a little version of yourself as a child, blowing out the candles on a cake and telling yourself that you will get your wish!

Circles

The truth is easy to find. It's in the center of everything. The Greek writer Empedocles, often credited with inventing the study of rhetoric, said: "The nature of God is a circle in which the center is everywhere and the circumference is nowhere." The circle as a powerful center of truth appears as an image in many belief systems and mythologies. Jung, of course, saw the journey to the center as the journey of individuation. In the center the self meets the Divine. American poet Robert Frost wrote, "We dance round in a ring and suppose/But the secret sits in the middle and knows."

The center plays a strong role in Native American spiritual beliefs. The center is where the Great Spirit resides, central to the four directions. Oglala Lakota Sioux Black Elk wrote, "Everything the Power of the World does is done in a circle. The sky is round, and I have heard that the earth is round like a ball, and so are all the stars. The wind, in its greatest power, whirls. Birds make their nests in circles, for theirs is the same religion as ours. The sun comes forth and goes down again in a circle. The moon does the same, and both are round. Even the seasons form a great circle in their changing, and always come back again to where they were. The life of a man is a circle from childhood to childhood, and so it is in everything where power moves."

The circle, or mandala, shows up in nature in countless ways, from spider webs to flowers to snowflakes to mineral crystals, the solar system, the nucleus of an atom.

Mandalas

Many cultures use mandalas for meditation and healing. They are most commonly associated with Tibetan Buddhism, but they show up in the rose stained glass windows of Christian cathedrals and in the intricate patterns of Islamic art. They are present in the Celtic knots and in the sand paintings of Native Americans and Tibetans.

Coloring a mandala can be an excellent way to get back to the truth. It's an active meditation. After you have created it, you can return to it for contemplation.

Some good sources for mandala ideas are abgoodwin.com/mandala and mandalaproject. org, and some of the books listed in Appendix B. Before you begin, though, it's a good idea to spend some time looking at mandalas, just to get the visual side of your brain stimulated. Before you begin to draw your pattern and color it in, set your intention. Close your eyes and take three deep, cleansing breaths. Visualize the area in your life where you are seeking the truth. Picture a setting. Picture the people who are vital to it. Now feel the energy of that scene. Notice the areas of your body that are tight, and send your breath to that area. Now picture the energy you want to feel. Imagine bringing it in with each breath. Hold that energy in your mind's eye for three deep breaths.

Here's what you'll need:

- Paper, of course

- Paint, colored pencils, colored markers, pastels

- Drawing tools, such as stencils, or a compass and ruler

Trace a circle on your paper. Use a compass, or turn a bowl upside down and trace around it.

Start your drawing at the center, filling in the circle with forms and patterns.

Fill in your pattern with colors, working from the outside in.

Remember, there is no right or wrong way to do this. And it's okay if your idea evolves as you draw it.

Here's an example of what the numbers in your mandala might symbolize:

Oracle Advice

As you design your mandala, be mindful of the symbolism of the colors, shapes, and numbers. You may find as you start out that you did not consciously set out to use the symbols of red or one, but take note. Creating a mandala is a good way to reveal your subconscious mind.

1   Creation, origin, God, self

2   Equilibrium, duality, symmetry, pairing, synergy, partnership

3   Expression, creativity, synthesis, harmony, discovery

4 Foundation, solid, stable, balance, Earth, form

5 Action, movement, integration

6 Home, hearth, comfort, family, union

7 Solitude, mysticism, spiritual nature of things, redemption, compassion, forgiveness

8 Renewal, transformation, mastery

9 Completion, essential truth

Take this list of shapes and define what these symbols mean to you:

Circle _____

_____

Cross _____

_____

Spiral _____

_____

Square _____

_____

Star _____

_____

Triangle _____

_____

And what do these colors symbolize to you?

Red _____

_____

Blue _____

_____

Yellow _____

_____

Green _____

_____

Orange _____

_____

Purple _____

_____

White _____

_____

Black _____

_____

The Labyrinth Way

Walking a labyrinth is an act of committing to the truth. But walking a labyrinth is full of illusions. A labyrinth is distinguished from a maze in that there are no blind paths—no paths that dead end. There is only one path in a labyrinth, and it leads to the center. When you walk a labyrinth, you walk the whole path—there is no part of the path that is not taken. The path of a labyrinth doubles back on itself so that as you are walking, sometimes you are walking toward the center—the truth—and sometimes you are walking away. If you walk the labyrinth with another person, sometimes it will seem that the person is far away from you, on a different path, when he is only a few steps ahead.

Tell It Like It Is

Theseus, king of Athens, was sure he could defeat the Minotaur, a part-human, part-cow creature who lived in a labyrinth on Crete. An oracle had advised the Athenians that in order to repel famine and disease, they must send seven young men and seven young women to be sacrificed to the Minotaur. But Theseus defeated the Minotaur through the love of Ariadne, daughter of the king of Crete, who advised him to unwind a thread attached to the entrance of the maze, which allowed him to find his way out after he killed the Minotaur.

A labyrinth can be a metaphor for the way we approach the truth. It's never full on. It's a gentle unfolding of truth, and many times, it's a mystery. A guide to labyrinths of the world can be found at gracecathedral.org/labyrinth. You may also put a labyrinth in your backyard. There also are tabletop labyrinths or ones you can print out from the Internet. With those, you trace your finger over the pattern, moving toward the center.

So is a labyrinth an oracle? You bet!

Power Thinking

You have probably heard the saying, "What a tangled web we weave when first we practice to deceive," written by Scottish scholar Sir Walter Scott.

When we deceive ourselves about our strengths and weaknesses, or our true desires, we create a lie that begins within. We force ourselves into a box by creating an image that we have to then live up to, no matter how uncomfortably it fits. And it may be an image that is much more limited than it would be if we allowed ourselves expression. Or forces us to go in a direction that is totally unnatural. It is like the guy who tells himself he is an accountant because it seems practical and feels like what he should do instead of letting himself be the creative person that he is.

Being honest about ourselves also keeps us from imprisoning ourselves in the eyes of other people. Gary had been in work situations where he encountered people who had lied about their professional credentials or had allowed misperceptions to remain unclarified. For example, Gary had a co-worker who let the company represent him as a college grad to clients, even though he had not attended college. He was then forced to participate in lies that made him uncomfortable, like discussions about his supposed alma mater. And when he couldn't change jobs easily because a new company would require proof of a college degree, he was stuck deeper in that lie. He had to pretend he wanted to stay where he was rather than develop his career. And he would have to go to college in secret to obtain his degree. He had allowed himself to be placed in a box.

Being truthful allows you to speak what you think and feel, and to be who you really are. That can set you free. In truth lies power.

Lilith: Taking Back Your Power

LILITH
POWER

Lilith, from the Goddess Oracle Deck, inspires us to take back our power. In Hebrew mythology, she was the first woman created, the first wife of Adam. Some say he rejected her because she would not submit to him; other myths say he rejected her because she was part divinity, part human. Now banished and powerless, Lilith found herself with the curse that every child she gave birth to would die in infancy. Not good, you say. But when the Lilith card turns up for you, it's not the irrevocable truth. It's a signal that you must reclaim your power.

New Sources

Look at your Nine Wise Ways. In what area have you relinquished your power? Let's draw three cards from the oracle deck. The three cards represent the natural cycle of life, the natural cycle of power. Let the goddesses that come up in these areas guide you in claiming new power for yourself in this area of your life.

The first card represents Birth—what you must allow to come into your life to regain your power. This card might point you to how you must soften, or it might open you up to new people in your life who will teach you about new sources of power.

The second represents Vitality—the strengths and wisdom you already possess, in full bloom. Let this card encourage you.

The third represents Relinquishment—what you must let go of. This card will point you to power centers in your life that no longer give you power. They might have been strengths for you once, but now they are holding you back from taking the next step.

Looking No Further

"If you cannot find the truth right where you are, where else do you expect to find it?" said Dogen, a thirteenth-century Zen Buddhist monk. The truth is right here—here and now. It's just a matter of lifting your eyes to see. This is why you should never give up looking for the truth. *Never give up.*

The Least You Need to Know

- ◆ To be authentic, accept the imperfections of the truth.
- ◆ Let go of any illusions you have about your dream.
- ◆ Use the practice of coloring mandalas or walking labyrinths to awaken central truths in your life.
- ◆ Know that your power is in the truth, and you can take back that power.

Chapter 15

A Rustling of Leaves

In This Chapter

- ◆ Nature's wisdom
- ◆ Ancient ways of nature
- ◆ Modern-day paths
- ◆ Rituals and observances

In a sacred grove in Dodona in Greece, the trees are said to rustle with the voice of Zeus, speaking in human voices and imparting divine wisdom. Alexander the Great consulted the "most hallowed trees of the sun and moon" at the top of a mountain in India, receiving a prophecy that was fulfilled.

The Oracle of Zeus at Dodona honors Gaia, the Earth Mother, through a holy tree in that sacred grove. It is one of the many examples of ways the ancients sought divine wisdom through nature. Oracle wisdom has always been conveyed to us through the divine conduit of nature. Wisdom is all around you, embedded in the workings of the natural world.

Nature's Wisdom

Let's take a closer look at the brand of wisdom we find in nature. In nature, we find the blueprint for all life. We discover the intention of creation, the plan for all living beings. Examine any living thing—a maple leaf, a sunflower seed, a bird's nest—and you will observe the intention for life and regeneration. A green maple leaf in the height of summer is a snapshot of photosynthesis; a red maple leaf in autumn, fallen to the ground, is a snapshot of regeneration, as it decomposes and nourishes the soil.

In his book *Creativity: Where the Divine and Human Meet* (see Appendix B), Matthew Fox writes that a bird's nest is a sign of optimism, a show of confidence in creation. He says that when we observe a bird's nest, we "place ourselves at the origin of confidence in the world. We receive the beginning of confidence, an urge toward cosmic confidence."

The bird that builds a nest is showing an instinct for the principle of intention—that we will create what we can imagine, that we trust in the plan of the universe to assist us in the unfolding of that creation.

But nature's wisdom lies not just in creation. It lies in its very character. Nature is both gentle and harsh, sometimes soothing, sometimes tumultuous. Serenity comes from a quiet walk in a pine needle–carpeted forest or taking in the view of an azure mountain lake. But nature is also violent as it regenerates, transforming one thing to another, as when a Gulf Coast hurricane rips palm trees from the earth and destroys homes, or when a volcano erupts with fiery lava that changes the very face of the earth.

Gary and Carolyn each have experienced both sides of nature, getting sunburned at the beach. Gary was at a barbecue at the beach, and he was reminded of how we live with nature but get lulled to thinking we are in charge. The beach was calm, and the sound of the waves added to the sense of peace, almost lulling him to sleep, making him want to take a nap on the beach. But the crashing waves can be a threat if you are not a strong swimmer, a challenge if you are a surfer, or a menace if you own beachfront property and you worry about erosion. Gary enjoyed that day at the beach, but took home a sunburn to remind him who's really in charge.

Carolyn took her twins to the south Florida Gulf Coast, where the waves were wild and wonderful after a tropical storm had passed through. It was exhilarating to jump the waves, but they did not realize how much the ocean was splashing off their sunscreen, leaving the fair skin of her son and herself exposed to ultraviolet rays (but giving her daughter a nice copper glow). She and her son ended up with a serious sunburn, and her son got blisters, requiring a creative strategy for their expedition to Disney World. Again, who's really in charge?

At Your Peril

Because nature abides by certain laws, nature keeps us honest. Think of nature as an integrity meter. Did you wear sunscreen? Well, no, the evidence is right there, in the blisters on your shoulder. Nature also occasionally has to remind us that we are taking a risk when we build a resort on the shoreline or a house on a fault line. Nature humbles us—sometimes your life plans are disrupted because you have to wait for the hurricane to pass through. It reminds us that things happen in their own due time. Or sometimes, that you have to rebuild or regroup.

Why is nature both kind and harsh? Soothing nature gives us solace, strengthens us, refortifies, gets us back in touch with our souls, points us inward to explore our inner life, hear our inner voice, get it in tune with the Divine. Nature, literally and figuratively, nourishes us. Harsh nature reveals the truth, is always honest, expects more of us, spurs us to change. Nature teaches us.

Nature gives to us but constantly reminds that we don't control it. It reminds us we are just passing through. Nature is constant change, regenerating and perpetuating itself, moving and shifting to its own rhythm. We are here a short time. Eighty years means a lot to us, but nothing to nature. Our beach houses tempt us to believe we have tamed nature, but in the big picture, it is nothing.

Nature's oracle wisdom reminds us of the cycle of life, of birth, growth, death, and regeneration. These cycles are represented in the triple goddess, so let's take a look at three goddesses who represent the three stages in the cycle.

Corn Woman, Demeter, and Pele: Mapping the Landscape

From the Goddess Oracle Deck, we choose three different goddesses of nature to represent the cycle of life. The Corn Woman, from the Native American tradition, represents birth; Demeter, the Greek goddess of agriculture, represents growth; Pele, the Hawaiian goddess of fire and the Kilauea volcano, brings about death, destruction, and regeneration.

CORN WOMAN
NOURISHMENT

DEMETER
FEELINGS/EMOTIONS

PELE
AWAKENING

The Corn Woman teaches us what needs to be done to plant the seeds of sustenance. She helps us give birth to new things. She shows us how. She's practical. She taught the Native Americans how to plant corn. She's smart and savvy. The Corn Woman is about empowerment.

Demeter serves as a reminder of what we need for growth. She reminds us to nurture ourselves and our emotions. Demeter went into mourning when her daughter, Persephone, was kidnapped into the underworld, sending the world into a drought. She reminds us to take care of our emotional well-being. She reminds us that our connection to the earth—and to those we love—must never be severed. It's vital for life.

Pele is the make-it-happen goddess. She demands that we bring forth what we want to create. She requires that we multitask or die. She expects us to keep up, to change with the times, to stay one step ahead of the molten lava. She expects that you will be strong, that you are up for the task. She says not to fear change, but to delight in the new face of the landscape that the change will create.

Again, take a look at the goals in your Nine Wise Ways. Where do they fall? Are you at a time of birthing, of learning the ways to sustain your dream? This is Corn Maiden time. Then focus your efforts on discovery—finding the resources to achieve your dream and finding the power within.

On the other hand, have you lost sight of your dream? Are you exhausted from the effort? Are your spirits flagging? This is Demeter time. You must reconnect. Cherish yourself, cherish those you love, cherish your talents and gifts. Take care of yourself.

Or maybe you are in action on your dream, but too much is changing around you. Keep focused on your dream, and step up your efforts. Feel the fear you have about the changes, but do it anyway. This is Pele time.

If you look at your Nine Wise Ways, you'll find you are at different junctures on the path with each one. Knowing where you are is a key step to understanding where you will go next and how you will get there.

The Ancient Way

Many early cultures believed that the physical surface of the Earth *was* the body of the mother goddess. Some nomadic tribes believed stones protruding from the surface were quite literally the mother goddess's bones. They believed, as the Greeks at Delphi believed, that the gods spoke to them through cracks in the earth or the wind in the trees. The cave at the Oracle of Trophinius is an example of their belief that the features of the earth were conduits for wisdom.

Mountains have often been believed to be the home of the gods. In ancient times, as now, the mountains were a place to go in quest for the Divine. Mountains figure in many belief systems as places of vision and higher consciousness. Alexander the Great climbed to the top of a mountain in India to receive the oracle of the talking trees. Moses climbed to the top of Mount Sinai to receive the Ten Commandments.

In ancient times, all the features of the landscape—rivers, springs, waterfalls—were believed to be the dwelling place of spirits, gods, or ancestors—people of wisdom. Cultures such as the Maoris of New Zealand, the Aboriginals of Australia, and the inhabitants of Papua New Guinea study the landscape for signs of their ancestors' presence.

Water in particular is a symbol of the renewal of the soul. In Christianity, water is consecrated to give believers healing, cleansing or spiritual awakening, performing baptisms and other rites. In Hindu India, believers gather at the shores of the Ganges River to drink the water and wash in it because it is believed to be the personification of the Hindu goddess Ganga. Natural springs have long been associated with creativity, purification, fertility. They are thought to be openings to sacred realms beneath the earth.

Trees of wisdom are revered in many cultures. In Angola, the Herero people believe the Omu-mboro-mbonga tree is the place of the origin of the first humans. In Nepal, shamans perform a ritual around the Life Tree. Hindus revere the banyan tree, often placing shrines at its base, believing it has the power of longevity and regeneration. In Greek mythology, nymphs who inhabit rivers and trees figure heavily; the Greeks saw the lives of nymphs and their trees as intertwined, giving rise to the concept of *hamadryad*, which meant that when a nymph dies, the tree withers, and the souls of both go together. Nature spirits such as nymphs, satyrs, or sprites were held in highest esteem, believed to dwell in nature's finer realms, only rarely visible.

Wise Words

Hamadryad is one of many concepts in the ancient Gaia mythology, the belief that the earth *was* the mother goddess, that nature and spirit are intertwined. With hamadryad, it is believed that a nature spirit's life is linked to a feature of nature. When a tree nymph dies, the soul of her tree accompanies her, and the tree withers. Remember Amaterasu, the Shinto sun goddess from Chapter 12? When her brother betrayed her, she retreated into a cave, taking all the light with her. And then there is Demeter, who plunged the world into drought when she grieved her daughter.

Creatures—from the bee to the scorpion to the serpent of wisdom to the self-renewing phoenix to the Egyptian scarab beetle—are prominent players in oracle wisdom. In early Christianity, three fishes symbolized the trinity, and the fish remains a symbol of modern Christianity. The fish is also one of the eight sacred symbols of Buddha.

The bee is a symbol of wisdom because it collects pollen from flowers, representing the wisdom that we extract from daily life.

And it wasn't just at Delphi that snakes figured heavily. There are the hooded cobras of India, the snakes carved in the stones of Mayan and Aztec shrines, the Midgard snake of Scandinavia, the mystic serpent of Orpheus, the serpent mounds of Native Americans, the sacred serpents preserved in Egyptian temples, and even the serpent entwining the staff of the physician, the caduceus.

Behind all of this fascination with bees, fish, snakes, and creatures of all ilks is the realization that the best way to understand the Creator is to study His (or Her) handiwork. Every existing creature is a manifestation of the intelligence and power of the Divine.

Then ... and Now: Wisdom in Nature

But it wasn't just the ancients who turned to nature for wisdom. We still do. Bioneers is an organization that promotes the idea that biology will take center stage in the twenty-first century as we develop a deeper understanding of our connectedness with the environment. The thrust of their ideas is that nature gives us the best operating instructions we can find. Their mantra: "It's all alive. It's all intelligent. It's all connected. It's all relatives." On the Bioneers radio show (check your local public radio station or go to bioneers.org), the hosts highlight scientists and engineers who turn to the natural world for inventive solutions to large- and small-scale problems. For instance, to design an environmentally friendly storm-drainage system in Chicago, scientists studied earthworms. Birds inspired us to manufacture airplanes; hummingbirds pointed the way to helicopters. An intelligent intention is built in to nature, and we see it in an acorn.

We also turn to nature for rejuvenation and replenishment. Writers and artists go on retreats. Pulitzer-winning author Michael Cunningham (*The Hours*, Picador, 2002; *Land's End: A Walk in Provincetown*, Crown Publishers, 2002) often retreats to his home in Provincetown, Massachusetts, to write. Provincetown holds an artist's retreat in the winter—which allows writers and artists to come with the intention of working *with* nature's harsh side. Writers and artists let nature "trap" them there so they can hole up and work. Occasionally, writer and teacher Natalie Goldberg (*Writing Down the Bones*, Shambhala, 1986) holds a silent winter walking and writing retreat in Taos,

New Mexico, which allows writers to cocoon in a soundless world and explore the realm of their own imaginations.

Nature-based meditation retreats are everywhere, from Thich Nhat Hanh's Plum Village in France (www.plumvillage.org) to the Findhorn Institute in Scotland (www.findhorn.org). Serenity in nature was the urge behind Teddy Roosevelt's vision of the national park system, to make that available to everyone.

> ### Oracle Advice
>
> Make a plan for a mini nature retreat. In your own garden, plant some seeds. Hang wind chimes. Take a day trip to an orchard or berry farm to pick fruit. Fill a bowl with dried herbs or seedpods, shells from the beach, or semiprecious stones, and place it on your desk. Or buy flowers and put them in a vase on your desk. After they fade, put them in a flower press. Marvel at a design of nature: an artichoke, a fig, a jellyfish, the yet-to-be-named deep-sea fish that hunts with a red light.

Right Before Your Eyes

Begin to raise your awareness of nature, just by being more mindful of nature in your daily life. Notice the position of the sun in the sky as it rises each morning; notice as it moves north along the eastern horizon as summer solstice approaches. Notice the days growing shorter and the nights becoming darker as winter solstice approaches. (We talk more about the calendar in Chapter 17.)

In our daily lives, we tend to pay attention first to what shouts for our attention. That means the bright, loud, and colorful. If you are like us, that means the cell phone, the billboard, the beeping signal of earth-moving equipment, or the traffic light. Instead, listen for the buzz of a bumblebee's wings in the courtyard garden. Look up from the highway and notice the hawk on the cliff. Take a moment to lift a ladybug from a grass blade and let her tiny legs tickle the back of your hand—then let her fly.

The ancient Egyptians, like the Mayans, Native Americans, and many other cultures, mapped the heavens in great detail, not just for agriculture but for insight into the influence of the motion of heavenly bodies on the destinies of humans. Some of these systems were so ingenious that they are still in operation. An observatory of immense stone sundials in Jaipur, Rajputana, India, is one example. It was that vital to them, yet could you really tell us, today, what phase the moon is in? How many constellations could you point out in the night sky—other than the Big Dipper?

Elemental Wisdom

The ancients of the Occidental world believed that four primary elements composed the universe: air, fire, water, and earth. In the Orient, however, there were five elements: air, fire, water, metal, and wood.

Both worldviews used these elements to define life. Furthermore, these ancient cultures believed that each element was inhabited by divine wisdom in the form of gods, goddesses, and other spirits. Let's take a closer look at how the Divine expresses itself through these elements.

- **Air.** Air animates all living things. It fills the expanse between heaven and Earth, the divide between the Divine and the human. Air is *chi*, the life force energy in the traditional Chinese belief systems; you may know about chi from feng shui, the ancient Chinese art of arranging your living space. Air is *prana*, the vital life force that animates our bodies through breath, central to the belief system in India and integral to the practice of yoga.

  The Divine aspect represented in the air element shows up in depictions of winged creatures in the Bible (in Ezekiel, for instance)—as manifestations of God's spirit. Air also shows up in the depictions of the Egyptian goddess Isis, who is sometimes shown with wings. The thunderbird and the eagle are prominent symbols in Native American culture. Tibetan Buddhists invite the spirit of the divine to their temples through prayer flags that are borne in the wind.

- **Fire.** Fire is the source of light and warmth, so it has long been associated with the Divine. It is the source of Divine illumination. Christians light candles at Christmas and Easter or to say prayers. Jews light menorahs at Hanukkah, the Festival of Light. Fire is also the force of creation.

- **Water.** Water represents renewal and enlightenment. The lotus blossom, which is a type of waterlily, is a symbol for the unfolding of an enlightened soul. The Islamic view of paradise depicts four rivers radiating from the center of all things, irrigating four glorious gardens.

- **Earth.** As mentioned earlier, the earth itself is believed by many to be Divine. Earth represents the womb of the soul. Earth is the element that reminds us to get real. It grounds us when we want to think loftier thoughts. The Persian poet Rumi wrote of the beauty of the mundane and its role in illumining our pursuit of spiritual union with the Divine. For him, the mundane was vital—not as a counterbalance to thinking spiritual thoughts all day, but as a conduit to the Divine, finding the natural rhythms of the universe to be the study of the mind of the Divine.

Bringing It All Together: A Collage

Let's get in touch with how these elements can point you to your inner oracle wisdom. You will be making a collage, and each element must be represented in it. Choose one of your Nine Wise Ways—maybe one that, before now, you have been hesitant to delve into because it seems like a big goal or the goal is too near and dear to your heart.

As you collect images and objects for your collage, choose something meaningful to you—something that defines who you are, exemplifies a lesson well learned, or depicts an aspiration. When you choose a water element, take care to find an example of both sides of nature—gentle and harsh. It could be a calm lake and a raging flood, a campfire or a towering inferno, a spring garden or a freshly dug grave, a hammock in the trees or a black tornado. Also bear in mind the three stages in the cycle of life: birth, growth, and regeneration. You may want to choose a water element that represents each stage. Do this for all of the elements.

After you have compiled your collage, take a step back and examine it. What do these images mean for this path on your Nine Wise Ways list? What images did you include that surprised you?

Another approach is to create a collage that represents your relationship to nature—where you stand. Are you in harmony with nature? Do you wish to be? How do you relate to it? Do you practice reciprocity—giving back as much as you take from nature? If nature were your spouse, would nature say the relationship is in balance? How do you work *with* nature, not against it? How does nature soothe you? What do you fear about nature?

Harmony and Feng Shui

Feng shui's principles of arranging your space for harmony are a good way to remind you to stay in touch with the elements. For instance, in feng shui, it matters how your house is oriented to the sun. Windows and doors are the way chi enters your home and flow through it. You do not want to block the flow.

In feng shui, a space is divided into nine areas, called *guas*. The central area, the center of your house, is health, surrounded by the other eight guas in an octagon. The front door, or the door through which you regularly enter, determines how the eight areas that encircle your health gua fall. At the entrance is the career gua. Then, moving clockwise, are skills and knowledge; family; and prosperity, forming the left side of the octagon. At the top is fame and reputation. Then, going clockwise down the right side are relationship; children and creativity; and travel and helpful people. Each gua is governed by one or two elements, so that if you want to bring more helpful people into your life, you place metal (a silver photo frame or a mirror) in that gua. If you want to enhance your career, you might place a fountain or a painting of a waterfall in that gua.

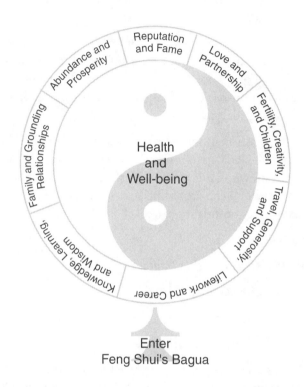

Enter
Feng Shui's Bagua

Whether you believe there is something to this or not, the act of hanging wind chimes or placing a pot of marigolds on your kitchen window sill brings you back to mindfulness. It makes you aware of the natural world around you and how you are connected to all other living beings, to something larger than yourself.

Metamorphosis: From Caterpillar to Butterfly

Perhaps one burning question you have as you read this book is how you can, quite simply, make something happen in your life. Maybe it's a creative work that you have been nurturing in your mind for quite some time. But you haven't done it. You don't have time. You don't have the energy. Too much of your real life is in the way. You're not even sure the world wants this creative work. Some days you're not sure you are talented enough. Maybe you don't have it in you.

This exercise turns to nature to give you a step-by-step plan.

1. **Caterpillar.** Right now you are a caterpillar, ignorant and unenlightened, munching on leaves in the forest. You start out pretty helpless. You have to taste like poison just to keep everyone else from eating you. But you have this idea: Someday you'll be beautiful. Someday you will fly.

   First, let yourself have this idea. It's not impossible, and it's not stupid. Go ahead and write about your idea in your Oracle Journal. Envision the final product: a stack of novels at your book signing, a standing-room-only theatre for your premiere, a lovely flower or vegetable garden to grace your home, a Friday-night opening at an art gallery.

   Now write some affirmations, being as specific as possible. For instance, when you say, "I am talented," go on to say what your talents are. Make it believable to yourself. Keep up with your affirmations, and as your vision for the project becomes more vivid, keep recording it in your journal. Commit to spending 10 to 12 minutes a day on this for 3 weeks.

   Here some others:

   I have something to say that only I can say.

   I have the discipline to do this project.

   I believe in this project because _____.

   Someone wants to hear what I have say.

2. **Cocoon.** One thing caterpillars do before they go into the cocoon is they get fat. They eat everything in sight, just like *The Very Hungry Caterpillar* in the children's story by Eric Carle. What this means for you is to be a sponge. Soak up all the knowledge you can about the area in which you are pursuing your creative work. Become a high consumer. Become a disciple. Become an eager initiate.

   Some of this is outer work—seeking out books, lectures, classes, articles, or just all-out networking—but some of this is inner work, too. Some of this is finding out who you are and what you really want.

   Make a list of your time obligations now. In what ways do these support your creative project? Rate each on a scale of 1 to 5, with 5 being "strongly support" and 1 being "strongly detract." Rank them. Which of these time obligations can you ditch immediately? Which of these are harder to get your arms around—perhaps obligations to your family or relationships that are emotionally draining. In the case of family, you aren't going to be able to ditch them. (Sorry!) But you will need to put boundaries around them, which takes time and effort, requiring changes on your part—and theirs. Trust us, though, they are probably more readily able to change than you.

If one of them was your full-time job, the answer is probably no, you can't do that right now. So here's a big juncture: do you stay or do you go? Here is where you get pragmatic. Maybe you want to design a yes/no oracle list of questions, as we did in Chapter 13. Or maybe you want to make a pro and con list.

Now follow this pragmatism with a long walk, a mindful walking meditation. Use all five senses to notice your surroundings. Ask the Divine for insight into this. Does it feel like a "not now"? Or does it feel unmovable? If the answer you got was to leave, go back to caterpillar stage and start visioning again, envisioning *that*. If the answer you got was to stay, modify the timeline for your project.

In the chrysalis stage, you are a disciple. That means two things: you are seeking knowledge, and you are disciplined. Your focus is primarily inward, focusing on the work and focusing on the truth.

3. **Butterfly.** The butterfly stage is the unfolding of your dream. In real life, this isn't just one moment of emerging from the cocoon. When it comes to creative work—or creating anything in your life—you may climb back into the cocoon again and again. But each time you emerge to fly away, you are smarter.

Tell It Like It Is

The butterfly is a symbol of Psyche, the Greek nymph who personifies the human soul and immortality. The Oracle of Delphi prophesied that Psyche would not marry an ordinary man, and indeed, she married Eros, the god of love, who was in disguise. He visited her nightly, but he concealed his features. He would always leave before dawn. One night, she shone her lamp upon him, and she was enraptured by his beauty. But a drop of oil from the lamp fell on his face, and he awoke and fled. She wandered in search of him. Zeus granted her immortality, and Psyche was able to join Eros on Mount Olympus. She is often depicted with wings of opalescent light.

In Good Time

Nature offers millions of little clues about the natural rhythm of our lives and our aspirations. It teaches us there is a time to grow, a time to gestate, a time to retreat and regenerate. It teaches us there is a time to sow and a time to reap.

Nature's wisdom is easy to access, and it is eternally wise. It always stands at the ready to teach us. Nature will always lead you to the truth within—and without.

The Least You Need to Know

- In nature, we find the blueprint for the unfolding of all life.

- Nature is both harsh and nurturing. It both creates and destroys.

- Begin to notice the influence of the elements of nature—air, fire, earth, and water—on the rhythms of your daily life.

- Bringing yourself into harmony with nature through mini retreats or practicing feng shui for your home is a way of bringing forth your inner oracle wisdom.

- Nature provides operating instructions for a metamorphosis in the oracle of a butterfly.

Chapter 16

Oracular Utterances

In This Chapter

♦ Sounds of wisdom: chimes and chants

♦ Words of wisdom: metaphors, verse, rhyme

♦ Contemporary examples

♦ All the right words

It was quite the scene at Delphi. The priestess bathed herself in a Castelian spring, chewed laurel leaves, inhaled the fumes—and began uttering strange and impenetrable sounds that only the initiated could interpret. Priests took these sounds and translated them into verse for petitioners.

Oracle wisdom is often embedded in words and sounds. You can find it in chimes, chants, rhymes, verse, and nonsensical words. Or you can find it in poetry, plays, novels, or song lyrics. Often you may tap into this oracle wisdom through techniques such as meditation—or just simply getting into the flow.

Wisdom That Resonates

We like this brand of oracle wisdom found in words and sounds because of its simplicity. On the surface, it seems just as mystical and confounding as ever. It's almost never as direct as a voice saying, "Buy Berkshire Hathaway stock."

But this kind of wisdom touches you on the heart level. It goes straight to your heart chakra, the energy center in the body that unites all the chakras, upper and lower.

This kind of wisdom resonates with your inner wisdom, and that is how you know it is true. There's no questioning that it is true. It just is. There is almost no thinking about it. Wisdom comes, and you act.

The sound "om," used in Eastern-influenced meditation, is an example. It is considered a supreme and most sacred syllable, believed to be the spoken essence of the universe. The sound itself is make up of the sounds "a," "u," "m," and a pause. Something incredible happens when a group of people chants this sound together. Their voices join in a single vibration. "Om" is the sound of life. It is all the complexity of life distilled into simplicity. At one moment, all voices in a room blend together. The differences of the individuals come together as one, and we see they are not vast differences after all. We honor those differences, yet we do not stumble over them. Integrating those differences into one whole makes us better individuals.

Another sound with this level of simplicity is that of Tibetan chimes. Carolyn has Tibetan chimes that she uses to begin her regular writing practice. The sound of these chimes is so pure that it's like a full moon clearing out all the stars from the sky. The sound clears her head. She will hold the chimes at her heart chakra and sound them, lifting the chimes so the sound travels up through her upper three chakras. It has the effect of calming and centering her.

Gary is a big fan of the Gregorian chant. He finds that when he listens to chants, they put him in an open, centered frame of mind. He will often put the chants on the CD player when he wants to relax or meditate. But he also uses them when he needs to concentrate. He has found that when he has to do something tedious, something he may not really want to do, the chants help him overcome his resistance to the task. He gains a sense of peace about his responsibilities. He's assured that he can meet them.

The therapeutic qualities of music have been known since the times of the Greeks and Egyptians. It was the Greek mathematician and philosopher Pythagoras who defined many of the laws of consonance and dissonance, demonstrating the mathematical foundation of music. Pythagoras applied his law of harmonic intervals to nature, identifying harmonic relationships between planets, constellations, and elements. In modern science, this theory is corroborated in the chemistry, in the law of octaves, which is that every eighth element in the periodic table represents a distinct repetition of properties. Pythagoras and his disciples are said to have cured many ailments of the body, mind, and spirit through music or verse.

No doubt you have heard of the concept of the "music of the spheres," the idea that the heavenly bodies join in a cosmic chant as they move through the sky. Pythagoras says he heard it, and others, such as the Chaldeans, describe it, too. In the Bible, Job mentions a time "when the stars of the morning sang to-gether," and of course, the shepherds describe the choirs of angels singing on the night that Christ was born. William Shakespeare refers to it, too, in *The Merchant of Venice:* "There's not the smallest orb which thou behold'st but in his motion like an angel sings."

This stems from the Pythagorean idea that everything that exists has a voice and all voices are eternally singing in praise of the creator.

The Greeks, famed for their architecture, believed in an analogous relationship between sound and form, considering the elements of architecture comparable to musical notes. So the whole of a structure was likened to a musical chord, with all elements harmoniz-ing. The German poet Johann Wolfgang von Goethe saw this analogy, too, writing that "architecture is crystallized music."

Tell It Like It Is

One legend has it that Pythagoras was meditating one day on the problem of harmony. Passing by a bra-zier's shop, he took note of the variances in pitch as the work-ers pounded out a piece of metal on an anvil, using various sizes of hammers. He duplicated the weights of the hammers in his shop, playing with the sounds until he identified various harmonic intervals.

There is also the idea that every being has a keynote that, if sounded, will destroy him. One example of this idea in action is in the Old Testament, when the Israelites sounded trumpets, bringing down the walls of Jericho. A contemporary reference to this is in a song by British recording artist Kate Bush about someone who is in a military lab under orders to create "a sound that would kill someone," on her CD *Hounds of Love.*

So we have come full circle, from "om," the sound that joins, to the keynote sound that destroys. Sounds, when you listen to them with an ear turned to the Divine, can have this kind of power, to unite you or to be your undoing. Or, rather, as we look at it, breaking apart the way that isn't working and pointing you to a wiser way. Tune in to the sounds that can be heard in the undercurrents of your life—the bells that sound every dusk at the church on the hill that you pass on your evening walk, the roar of the ocean as you sun yourself on the beach. How do these sounds connect you? To whom and what do they connect you?

Rhythm of the Universe

Drumming is another way to connect with the wisdom of the Divine. Sounding out the rhythm on a drum is like connecting with the heartbeat of the universe. Every day, we experience the rhythms of the universe in our own heartbeats. Each season, we experience the rhythms of nature as leaves fall to the ground, snow falls to the ground, crocuses shoot up through the soil.

Drumming is primeval. It reminds us that every entity in the universe vibrates—every galaxy, star, planet, ocean, tree, molecule, atom.

Throughout time, drumming has been used to mark passages: births, weddings, funerals. In Shintoism, a Japanese religion, drums are used to speak to the spirits. In many civilizations, drums are used to ward off evil spirits—or to invite rain.

So there are cultural benefits, but scientists have discovered physiological benefits. Drumming can produce an alpha state in your brain that is associated with relaxation, creative flow, and euphoria. (For more about this, read *The Healing Power of the Drum* by Robert Lawrence Friedman; see Appendix B for details.) Drumming also helps to synchronize the left (rational) and right (creative) sides of your brain, making them work together. This produces a transcendent state of relaxation and heightened awareness.

Euphoria? Transcendence? This sounds a lot like the Pythias at Delphi. Could you use drumming to induce this state where you free your mind and connect with the Divine? Absolutely.

UZUME
LAUGHTER

Uzume: Movement and Laughter

Remember Amaterasu from Chapter 12? Well, Uzume was the Japanese goddess of laughter who was sent to coax Amaterasu, the sun goddess, out of the cave. She danced erotically to the drums of the gods, and she was so bawdy and so unabashed that all the gods laughed, creating the uproar that piqued Amaterasu's curiosity.

Uzume's wisdom is in laughter, movement, and rhythm. She reminds us to break the rules, to just let loose, to not care what people think. Are you just too serious? Do you need to lighten up?

It's one thing to be the spectator, as Amaterasu was. But it's quite another to be the one dancing, the one who brings it forth for herself. More than likely, Uzume was not dancing for everyone else—she was dancing for herself. Uzume is a reminder of how movement—dance, exercise—can shake out all that old, stiffened thinking and awaken us to new, more supple ways of thinking.

Uzume is about looking at life from different angles. Carolyn has something she says during a crisis that helps her regain perspective: "Ten years from now, I'll think this is funny." She's been saying it so long now that sometimes she adds, "I think I'm just going to go ahead and laugh now."

To Gary, Uzume doesn't mean turning everything into a joke but using humor to realize not everything is a tragedy. One day, Gary had a really crazy day, and he decided to amuse himself by restaging the day's events as a comedy. When he did, it was really quite funny. He reminded himself that he was really living the life he wanted and all the competing demands meant he was part of the world, not hiding away (like Amaterasu) while it passes by.

Comedy, like dancing and drumming, reconnects us with the essential joy of life. It reminds us that we are part of something much larger than ourselves and our daily hassles.

Words of Wisdom

The right words, chosen at the right time, can change our lives. We know the power of words, even in our contemporary times, in the information age, when words are flying back and forth in bits and bytes through cyberspace, when there are so many trillions of them. Still, when they are such a rife commodity, there are some words that we hold sacred. They are worth treasuring because they point us this way or that way. Or they keep us on the path.

"Have faith" or "It's going to be all right" are just two examples of simple statements that can ring true—and be the difference between persevering or quitting.

Oracle Advice

In your Oracle Journal, begin to collect quotes from people you admire. Carolyn collects these on little Post-it Notes that she keeps on her computer screen. When it's time for a new quote, she adds it to her permanent collection. Some books have quotes on a certain theme, such as dreams or wisdom. You may also find spiritual and personal growth quotes on the Internet, at such sites as ThinkExist or BrainyQuotes.

Words of wisdom can come from anywhere in your life. What determines whether you will receive them, then? Because we know the intention of the Divine is always that you *will*, if you are ready. The key, then, is your intention to be open. How do you know if you are receiving the *right* message? After all, you can't just let yourself be open to it all—it would overwhelm you. The answer lies in being authentic to yourself and your true purpose in life. As country music singer Dolly Parton says, "Find out who you are, and do it on purpose."

Sacred Words

There are many ways to find sacred words in your everyday life, but to really tune in to the sacred, let's take a look at the ways sacred words have come to us through the ages.

In ancient times, the most sacred of all words were preserved in religious texts such as the Christian Bible, the Jewish Torah, the Koran, the *Bhagavad Gita*. Because of the fragility of political kingdoms and the whims of nature, these texts required devoted protection from their believers. Believers consecrated sacred texts as they were discovered and had strict laws about who could read them and who could copy them. For many centuries, monks copied text painstakingly within the walls of monasteries under the scrutiny of the church. Because in those times so many different sects of belief existed, it was important that believers authorize their sacred texts so that fellow believers would not be led astray.

One of the most sacred rituals in ancient times was reserved for death. In many different traditions, death is the passage from the material world into the spiritual world, and therefore it's a holy experience. Thin pieces of gold leaf have been found in graves in southern Italy and Thessaly with brief text. Archeologists believe they were instructions for the dead about their passage into the afterlife—sort of operating instructions for the spiritual realm.

Other famous inscriptions include the Ten Commandments, the Rosetta Stone, and the Immortal Emerald, believed to have been written by Hermes, father of the Egyptian arts and sciences. Sacred messages were inscribed into mountains or etched into stones, as with the petroglyphs of the Anasazi Indians of the American Southwest. Messages also were inscribed into columns of temples.

Some common themes emerge about these sacred writings that can help us understand what makes a writing an oracle:

- Sacred texts are protected from being harmed or altered.

- Sacred texts are guarded from theft.

- Sacred texts are often written on precious substances, such as emeralds and gold leaf.

- Sacred texts are sometimes disguised as ciphers or puzzles.

- Sacred texts require some effort on the part of the reader to "decode" them. If the reader is worthy, the message is readily available.

- Sacred texts can contain information necessary for personal, political, or political success.

Ten Commandments: Your Personal Mission Statement

What are *your* operating instructions? That is, for life, not death. (We're trying to keep this light!) To what texts do you turn for wisdom? Don't feel the pressure to be noble, altruistic, or faithful here. You might want to include the Bible or the Koran on your list, but you also might want to include contemporary literature or a self-help book. Make a list of books that sparked turning points in your life. Include books that blew your mind—opened up a whole new intellectual and spiritual terrain. Include books to which you continually turn for solace, comfort, and wisdom. Include books and authors that you quote regularly.

From those books, you may be able to compile your Ten Commandments of Life—personal guidelines about how you treat people, what matters to you, and the kind of person you want to be.

Here are some examples to get you started thinking:

- Be honest, be open, be clear.

- Honor those who are absent.

- Do your best. And always remember, we are all doing the best we can.

- Do unto others as you would have them do unto you.

Maat: Weighing Your Soul

MAAT

JUSTICE

Maat is the Egyptian goddess of justice. It was her job to weigh the souls of the dead as they entered the Hall of Judgment, appearing before Osiris. There were 42 judges in the Hall of Judgment, each representing a misdeed, and a dead person had to convince *each* one that he or she had not committed any one of those acts. Maat could be your best friend, or she could set you on the course for eternal doom. The judges would take into account her assessment of whether you were innocent or guilty. She would use a feather (in some depictions, an ostrich plume) on her scales of justice to counterbalance the weight of your heart, which would be burdened with any infractions you may have committed—that is, if she liked you. If you were guilty, a terrible fate awaited you. The monster Amit stood at the ready to gobble up the hearts of the guilty.

After you survived that ordeal, the dead had to name the parts of the door that open into the realm of the blessed.

So much of ancient mythology is about preparing for the afterlife so you can enter the realm you want to enter. But what about now? What about preparing yourself to enter the life you want to inhabit? What are your personal Ten Commandments? How would you assess yourself? Would you stand up to 42 judges? Kind of bewildering to think about it, right? What would counterbalance your imperfections and little misdeeds? Commit to being more aware of any tendencies you have to undermine your best intentions. How does this happen?

Beautiful Words: Poetry and Literature

Wise words can keep you on track. They can take the form of poetry, a novel, a theatrical play, or a movie. They can take the form of a time-honored aphorism. Or they can be affirmations, simple positive statements that underpin our efforts to move forward on a goal.

What makes these words so wise? To answer that, and to give you some tools for deepening your understanding of why the poetry and literature you love has great meaning for you, let's take a look at a few examples—"The Second Coming" by William Butler Yeats; Mona Simpson's novel *Anywhere but Here*, which was a movie with Susan Sarandon; and the Harry Potter books by J. K. Rowling.

- ◆ "The Second Coming." This poem was inspired by Yeats's belief that we were living in the last years of a Christian cycle. "Turning and turning in the widening gyre/The falcon cannot hear the falconer;/Things fall apart; the centre cannot hold;/Mere anarchy is loosed upon the world,/The blood-dimmed tide is loosed, and everywhere/The ceremony of innocence is drowned." Yeats is talking about the sense that the end of an era approaches, that life will regenerate. But what does the falcon mean, and who is the falconer? If Yeats had just said "man has forgotten God and lost his way," would we remember this poem so well? *Metaphor* has the power to create something memorable, something that helps us understand more deeply and we can't erase from our minds. A metaphor, then, can work as an oracle, just as the lines of iambic hexameter in the Delphic oracles did.

- ◆ *Anywhere but Here.* This is a poetic, poignant story of a young girl's aspirations for a real father, a peaceful home, and a chance at being a Hollywood star. The story touches the reader on an emotional level, as the character sees lack in every detail (including the steaks, not tuna casseroles, that appear nightly on the dinner time after her mother remarries). In this case, the story is so poignant because hope is mingled with a growing despair, a perpetual yearning that will never be fulfilled. The pain of the character is evident on every page. This is what Carolyn identifies as the "live wire" in her Live Wire writing workshops, the electrical current of emotion that courses through engaging writing. The character is vulnerable, and we connect with her desire and despair. We have all known what it is like to hope and hope, only to confront the realization that we will never get there.

◆ *Harry Potter and the Sorcerer's Stone.* In J. K. Rowling's Harry Potter books, what's at work here is simple mythology. The characters are archetypes: Harry the hero, the young initiate into magic who must confront his inner fears; Lord Voldemort, the force of evil; Dumbledore, the wise wizard who shares his knowledge with Harry and ushers in his rite of passage.

Archetypes tap into the universality of human experience. Although we don't get to be wizards and learn about magic at an enchanted school, we do, each of us, receive a calling for what our lives must be. We do receive lessons for a curriculum, and if we accept them, we pass into a role that is our unique role to play in the world. We are tested, and if we succeed, if we gain the knowledge and courage, we find our destiny. It is not until the sixth book in the Harry Potter series that he accepts his fate to be "the chosen one" to fight the battle of good and evil. Harry Potter sees that he can fight his role, trying to evade Voldemort and have a normal life as a teenager just trying to get past the death of his parents—or he can know this is his chosen role and enter into the halls of adulthood, knowing this is his experience, he is equipped for it, his head held high. And that is indeed what he chooses.

> **Wise Words**
>
> A **metaphor** is a figure of speech that implies a comparison between an image or symbol and a situation. "All the world's a stage" is an example. Metaphor has the power to illumine a situation in a way that direct language does not.

In short, metaphor helps us *see*. Vulnerability helps us *feel*. Archetypes help us *connect*. That's what words can do.

The Power of Words

One simple word, or a few well-chosen words, can resonate for us. It can bring everything into focus. Here's a look at why:

◆ **Symbols.** An apple, for instance, is a powerful image, because it has many religious and cultural associations: Adam and Eve and the apple from the tree of knowledge. Hesperides' golden apples that Heracles had to find. Paris's golden apple inscribed "To the most beautiful one," which led to the Trojan War. In

Norse mythology, the apples of immortality. The symbol of love and sexuality and the goddess Venus. The Russian political party Yabloko, which means apple. Apple computers.

◆ **Patterns.** Rhymes in poetry or lyrics provide us with patterns that quicken our understanding and increase our capacity for memory. The meter of a poem or the rhythmic dynamic of a heartfelt sermon or speech—these start to work on a much deeper level than the mere words. They start to vibrate so that we are awakened to the message of the words.

◆ **Passion.** Behind all great words is emotion. There is nothing more powerful than the passion of the speaker of great words. Think Martin Luther King Jr. on the steps of the Washington Monument and "I have a dream." The person who believes wholeheartedly in his cause is irresistible to listen to and memorable in her passion. That person can be pretty convincing.

Free Association

From the following list of words, we want you to free associate words that come to mind. It will give you insight into how your mind works—how you make the connections that give meaning to your world. It will help you understand which images might be positively or negatively charged. For each word, write 10 other words that flood into your mind.

Apple _____

_____

_____

Palm tree _____

_____

_____

Dove _____

_____

_____

Willow _____

_____

_____

Red _____

_____

_____

Lily _____

_____

_____

White stallion _____

_____

_____

Moon _____

_____

_____

Grecian urn _____

_____

_____

Diamond _____

_____

_____

Mahogany _____

_____

_____

At Your Peril

In our modern world, words can come in just as many disguises as ancient words. They can be diluted, or just buried in the onslaught of messages. Therein lies the danger in looking everywhere for wisdom. You want to be open, but you don't want to be a sponge, soaking up everything that smacks of wisdom. You must remain centered, with your eyes and heart focused on the true purpose of your Nine Wise Ways. You have to stay centered—and remember that oracles are not always here to tell you what you want to hear.

The Realm Beyond

In previous chapters, we have given you techniques to free your mind from the literal, rational-minded material world and seek the information you can get through life's undercurrents of intuition and universal patterns. We have alerted you to notice synchronicities as a way of detecting larger messages for your life. We also have discussed meditation and relaxation techniques that prepare the fertile ground of your mind and imagination for receiving greater wisdom.

But we have yet to discuss doing deeper into relaxation, into that same trancelike state that the Pythia at Delphi was able to achieve (we know now) through a narcotic gas. We are not suggesting that you alter your state through substances—please don't get us wrong—but we can suggest that through more natural, timeless means, you can achieve such a state of relaxation that you lower all barriers to universal wisdom. Even in our busy lives, simple techniques can get us to a state of relaxation where we allow our minds to be open. Yoga, breathwork, massage—any of these are pathways in. (For more about ways to use massage to open your mind to empowerment, see *Empowering Your Life with Massage* by Carolyn Flynn and Erica Tismer; details in Appendix B.) Prayer and meditation can produce almost a state of hypnosis in us, under the right master teacher. But you can try it yourself, by shutting off all stimuli one day when you are home—no TV, no computer, no phone, no stereo. Just silence. You would be surprised what 10 minutes of complete quiet can do.

The Least You Need to Know

◆ Oracles embedded in words, music, poetry, and percussion speak directly to the heart.

◆ Music contains within it the structure of the harmony of all creation.

◆ Drumming connects us with our own heartbeat—and that of the universe.

◆ Metaphors and archetypes help us gain a deeper understanding of the complex meaning of life.

◆ Words can bring our desires, dreams, and action into a crystallized focus.

Chapter 17

Written in the Days

In This Chapter

- The Mayan calendars and the progression of time
- The Sun: oracle of light
- Celestial rhythms
- A time to reap, a time to sow

Timing is everything. In our ultra-busy, high-speed world, we believe we have to hit the day running, with a thermal coffee-to-go mug and making all the green lights. With little margin for error, knowing which way the day is going to flow is vital to making it all happen.

Now we rely on electronic calendars we park on our laptops or Palm Pilots, but in ancient times the Mayans developed a calendar that calculated, with uncanny accuracy, the positions of heavenly bodies. From that calendar, they divined oracular truths to make their lives run smoothly—a Long Count calendar that was the ultimate Day Planner.

All in all, using the heavens to map out your days is about going with the natural flow of the universe. In this chapter, we show you how to take on your day with divine inspiration.

What the Mayans Knew

The Mayan calendar represents the idea that time was cyclical, not linear, like our Western concept of the calendar. They believed that time repeated itself, which means that the past could predict the future. Time and space existed in a single entity represented in a spiral, which was called *najt*. Through this, they believed they could gain power over their worlds.

The Mayans developed a series of calendars—not just one—to explain the progression of time. One was the sacred 260-day calendar called the Tzolkin; another was a 365-day calendar called the Haab. To synchronize these two cycles, the Mayans used a 52-Haab cycle called the *calendar round*.

In the Tzolkin calendar, each day has a unique name, which shows a reverence for the splendor of each day we live. The calendar combined 20 day names with 13 numbers. Their system reversed our Western system of a month followed by a date. In the Tzolkin calendar, the number is followed by the day name. For instance, the day names are listed as follows, along with their meanings:

- Imix (Waterlily)
- Ik (Wind)
- Akbal (Night)
- Kan (Corn)
- Chicchan (Snake)
- Cimi (Death head)
- Manik (Hand)
- Lamat (Venus)
- Muluc (Water)
- Oc (Dog)
- Chuen (Frog)
- Eb (Skull)
- Ben (Corn stalk)
- Ix (Jaguar)
- Men (Eagle)
- Cib (Shell)
- Caban (Earth)
- Etznab (Flint)
- Caunac (Storm cloud)
- Ahau (Lord)

So the first day of the year was 1 Imix, followed by 2 Ik, 3 Akbal, and so on to 13 Ben. Then the numbers started again, but continued through the rest of the day names, with 1 Ix, 2 Men, 3 Cib, and so on.

Tell It Like It Is

In Mayan time, time is not linear in the sense of a beginning, middle, and distinct end; instead, time moves in cycles in which the beginning of something new has its origin in the end of something old. Picture a date on the calendar as a point on a spiral. In a year's time, you circle back to that point, only at a point further up on the spiral. As you learn and grow, you will advance up the spiral, but each time you return to that point, you are more enlightened.

There are various theories about the origin of the Tzolkin calendar. One is that 13 symbolized the number of levels in the Upper World, where the gods lived, while 20 was the basis of the Mayan counting system (based on fingers and toes). Another theory is that the 260-day period is the length of human gestation—that perhaps midwives developed it to keep track of when a baby would be born.

The Haab calendar was based on the sun, with 18 months of 20 days and a 5-day month at the end of the year, which was called the "nameless days." The starting point was the winter solstice, when the light returned to the northern hemisphere. The Haab was the foundation of the agrarian calendar, and the month names derive from crops and weather. For instance, the thirteenth month is Mac, which refers to the rainy season, and the fourteenth month is Kankin, which refers to the rice crops.

The calendar round coordinated all of this, coinciding every 52 Haab years. (By the way, neither system numbered the years.) The end of a calendar round cycle was a time of high anxiety, as the Mayans waited to see if the gods would grant them another 52-year cycle. If you want to see our calendar integrated with the Mayan calendar, go to www.sacredroad.org, which is a website supporting Mayan and indigenous spiritual study.

At Your Peril

Does the Mayan calendar foretell the end of the world in 2012? Predictions of just that are based on the Long Count calendar, a cycle of about 1,872,000 days, which started on August 11, 3114 B.C.E. and ends on winter solstice in 2012. A sacred book of the Mayans, the Popul Vuh, says we are living in the fourth world—the world in which the gods created humans. Mayans believed that at the end of the fourth world, the gods would create a fifth and final world, which would signal the end of humankind. Most people, though, believe that if the Long Count calendar predicts anything, it's a new cycle of deeper cosmic awareness.

The Truth in the Sky

A reverence for the sun shows up in the earliest and most natural forms of religion. Tracking the movements of the sun is one of the first attempts to understand the divine workings of the universe. The sun represents life-giving light and warmth. Sun represents birth, fecundity, plenty; it represents rejuvenation and regeneration. In many religions, the central deity is the sun itself, rules the sun (Osiris in Egypt, Apollo in Greece), or is symbolized by the sun (Jesus Christ).

The zodiac was one of the first attempts to map the journey of the sun through the sky over the course of a year. It was important to know how this life-giving orb was moving, and how it was influencing day-to-day life. In the pagan era, stars were living things, exerting their pull on the destinies of people and nations. And in the early Jewish times, the stars *participated* in our lives, as mentioned in the Old Testament book of Judges: "They fought from heaven, even the stars in their courses fought against Sisera."

We have science to explain the position and movement of the sun, moon, and stars—the way mass and gravitational pull define an orbit. We also know the world is not geocentric—that is, the sun and stars do not revolve around us, but rather Earth revolves around the sun.

But we also know, as the ancients sensed, that there is a natural rhythm to the energy of the universe. The movement of the earth in relationship to the sun creates the seasons, and we mark the arrival of spring, not by the brightly colored Easter egg candy in the stores, but by the vernal equinox. And we do understand that spring has a rejuvenating energy that summer, fall, or winter do not have.

Astrology isn't scientific in the sense that someone has proved that the stars that make up the constellation Libra, for example, exert a pull on us to find balance and beauty in our lives. But what astrology can do is remind us of a connection to nature, especially with our modern artificial demarcations of time. The sun enters the constellation Libra at the autumnal equinox, a date when the length of the day and the night are equal. The earth is equally balanced on its axis. Sunlight and darkness are equal. The very planet on which we travel is reminding us to get in balance.

Lore has it that the constellations of the zodiac came from imaginations of shepherds in the fields, who connected the shimmering dots in the sky to make figures. But the Greek zodiac has its origin in the Babylonian calendar, which divided the sky into 36 sections and identified 12 constellations. The word *zodiac* originates from the Greek word *zodiakos*, which means "circle of animals." Most scholars believe that the 12 houses of the zodiac use animals as metaphors to describe the intensity of the sun's energy as it moves through the constellations of little animals.

So the zodiac can be understood on a metaphorical level, as a way of describing the energy of a time, personifying the sun's energy as a bull (Taurus) or a crab (Cancer). The creatures of the zodiac, then, are archetypes. And we can understand that sometimes we assume the energy of that time. Caroline Myss, author of *Sacred Contracts: Awakening Your Divine Potential* (see Appendix B), has a nice way of putting it: she calls the archetypes of the zodiac "a united cosmic support system." (We discuss archetypes more in Chapter 18.)

The Machine of Time

Although not everyone is open to using astrology for insight into personalities or the rhythms of the universe, most of us do know that it's important to wait until the time is just right. Sure, you can force it sometimes, and no doubt you have, but generally, that's doing it the hard way. Gary, a double Gemini, describes himself as an "incredibly impatient person" and says he has to learn this one over and over again. In his case, meditation really helps, because when he visualizes his dream and focuses on it, he finds a greater good behind the situation. When he visualizes himself as part of something bigger, he reminds himself that other events must happen before what he wants can come about. That's what understanding the rhythm of life is all about.

In a nutshell, it's about relinquishing your will, recognizing that you are not the boss of the universe. Although both Gary and Carolyn use creative visualization—and Carolyn has written, with Shari Just, *The Complete Idiot's Guide to Creative Visualization* (see Appendix B)—there is the danger of becoming too self-absorbed when you *only* visualize yourself getting what *you* want. You can become so focused on *your* desires that you lose sight of the world around you. Tuning in to the rhythms of the Universe gives you a healthy respect for the natural timing of things. You understand there is a bigger picture, and you understand you are just a part of it.

In the Christian Lord's Prayer, there is a line that says, "Thy will be done." When we turn to the calendar—to the celestial world that defines the calendar—we must remember this one thing: We are studying the divine order, and we must acknowledge the Divine, by whatever name we define it.

Oracle Advice

As you practice using oracles to deepen your understanding of the timing of reaching your goals, try this affirmation. State your intention—the vision you have for your Wise Way goal—and then add, "I am at the right time and in the right place." This will remind you that everything is going to be fine, that right now you can't know what you don't know. All you can do is do your best and appreciate what the present moment has to teach you.

Tunnel Vision

When you started this chapter, did you think we were going to tell you that if the sun was in Gemini when you were born or the moon was in Capricorn when you had a big meeting, that your desire was going to be fulfilled next Tuesday at precisely 11 A.M.? We wish it were that simple.

What we think it's all about is this: our vision can be very limited. We think we have the full picture, but our awareness is limited, and it's colored by our perceptions and our experiences. When we focus simply on getting in tune with the universe, with our perfect plan, then things come together in a much more exciting and fulfilling way. Gary and Carolyn admit they are still learning that. Sometimes we are presented with ideas and opportunities that we would have missed otherwise. To stay totally focused on getting what we want when we think we should get it can lead to anger, bitterness, and disappointment.

So focusing on the wisdom of oracles in the calendar is really about staying focused on the greater good, the perfect rhythm, and less focused on our own plan, which we only think is perfect.

In Zen, there is a concept that when you grasp and grab at something, you end up repelling it. If you state an intention and then relax, it is more likely to come to you.

Gary often works with people who have dreams such as becoming a writer or an actor. They audition, they send out stories, and they hope to connect with a high-powered agent. Maybe they make it big; maybe they don't. Gary has often seen people who seem to have no life beyond what they want in the future. The big dreams dominate their existence, and what's around them in the present is only tolerated. It's a tough situation, because you do have to focus and work hard to get what you want. But you also need to be open to the life you have and see the happiness around you.

How do you know when to let go? That question may at first sound like "giving up," but that's definitely not what we mean. Letting go is not one distinct moment—surrendering because you have failed. Letting go is an ongoing practice. Even as you desire your goal and you work hard at it, you should be letting go.

What you are letting go of is your attachment to the future—an attachment that blocks you up. Let go of the big-picture outcome, and let the outcome that brings you joy be the here and now—the process itself. Although writing is not always fun, for example, if there is not an intrinsic joy, why do it? In other words, if you are thinking, "This will only be fun if I hit the big payoff three years from now," think again. It's fun now!

So that's the key—ask your oracle for help connecting with the intrinsic joy of the moment. Ask for that joy, and if it's forthcoming, it's validation that the direction you are taking is right. If not, that's a bit of oracle wisdom, too. It may not be the right direction. As for the timing of it all, all we can do is be comforted that there is a perfect time, and it will occur when it occurs.

Gary's Perfect Timing

As we have mentioned in earlier chapters, Gary always had the dream of working for himself. At one point, he forced it—he went out on his own when he wasn't ready. He got by, but he was unhappy and ultimately landed back in the workplace. But the desire began to gnaw at him again, and he started exploring his options. This time was harder. He was scared because he could remember his first failure, as well as the reality. He had no illusions.

This time, Gary researched sources for clients. He formulated a budget. He consulted oracles around him—other self-employed people, financial advisers. They addressed his concerns and reassured him. This time, he did due diligence and consulted all of them.

Gary was ready to take the plunge but knew the timing was not quite right. As much as he didn't want to hear it, he listened to his intuition to wait another six months. That left an achy, scary feeling inside. He examined it, and he realized it was *not* about the decision but about telling his boss and co-workers he was leaving. After he made that discernment, he felt empowered to face that discomfort and move forward.

This time he had done it right, and the oracles in his life were the key. The timing was split-second perfect. He was successful from the first instant. He listened to his oracles without filtering out what he didn't want to hear. He listened to his intuition to interpret what their words meant to him, and he did his homework. It all came together.

Seasons of Your Life

The ancient peoples of Mayan and Egyptian civilizations had a basic survival need for keeping track of the season. They needed to grow crops for food. But even though those of us who live in cities and suburbs and make our living in other ways are many steps removed from that time, it's still vital to us to know the seasons. It's like the line Solomon wrote in Ecclesiastes, "There is a time to sow, a time to reap."

In many ways, September is Gary's January—his new year. That comes from all of those years in school. It feels like there is a chance to start things anew in September. Carolyn also gets an invigorating rush of energy at this time of year, often teaching writing workshops, starting new book projects, or taking classes.

But there are other times when we can begin anew. The Jewish New Year begins with Rosh Hashanah. The Chinese New Year begins on the first full moon into the calendar year.

Tell It Like It Is

The ancient Celts believed that during the period of days at the turn of a season, the boundary between worlds was more permeable. They celebrated the Celtic New Year at Samhain, which is now our Halloween. On that day, they believed, the doorway to the spirit world was open—and anything could happen. They put out the fires in the hearths of their homes and went to the mountaintops, where they lit bonfires. They used the flames from these sacred fires to rekindle their hearth fires, restoring light and protecting them against evil spirits.

Another cycle that shapes our lives is the lunar cycle, which begins anew with the new moon. Many rituals and festivals are tied to the moon: Passover, Easter, Holi, and the Islamic fasting month of Ramadan. Because of that, they fall on different dates every year.

Our personal cycles exist underneath the overlays of these cultural and celestial influences. Let's turn to our goddess oracles for three takes on how to navigate these cycles of time in our lives.

Nut: Inner and Outer Time

NUT

MYSTERY

Nut is the Egyptian goddess of the sky, the mother of Osiris and Isis. Nut was caught being unfaithful to her husband, who cursed her to only be able to give birth on the days that weren't on the calendar. She appealed her sentence to Thoth, the moon god. He made her play a board game and won back five days during which Nut could give birth. This story is the mythological origin of the five days the Egyptians added into the calendar to make up the difference between lunar time and the standard calendar.

Nut reminds us to resolve the tension between inner time and outer time. She invites you to make peace with your inner world and the world around you. She encourages you to hold strong to your inner sense of what is right for you, even amid others' expectations.

What we like about Nut is that she reminds us to be open to mystery—to paradoxes. If we are open to mystery, we can say we don't have to have the answer to everything. And if we don't have to have the answer, then we can stop being disappointed and angry that things are not happening as we plan, or as we demand. Life is a mystery. Get over it and enjoy it. The truth unfolds slowly. Stay focused on today, what's around you, so that as it unfolds you won't be so buried in your narrow path that you miss it.

Changing Woman: A Changing You

CHANGING WOMAN
CYCLES

Changing Woman, a Navajo goddess, honors the cycles of your life. She respects her own personal rhythms, just as she respects those of nature. In Navajo culture, nature's rhythms trump the rhythms of the artificial calendar. Changing Woman reminds you that it's okay to stay with your natural energy flow and not get caught up in someone else's. She also reminds us to honor our personal changes, to embrace all cycles of life, not just youth.

Eostre: Ushering in the Gifts of Spring

EOSTRE

GROWTH

Eostre is the Anglo-Saxon goddess who ushers in spring. She is the goddess who brought us Easter egg hunts. She protected fertility, and she was a friend to all children. She wanted to entertain the children, so she transformed a bird into a rabbit, which brought brightly colored eggs. She gave the eggs as gifts to the children.

Eostre is an excellent oracle to meditate on when we really, really want something. She is a breath of fresh air, a chance for renewal. Breathe out the toxins of disappointment and obsession and desire. Breathe in fresh energy and new ideas and alternate directions. Maybe some of our desires will be aired out and cleansed and we will welcome them back in. But the cobwebs of outdated wants and needs will be blown away into the wind.

Let Eostre spur you to welcome personal growth in your life. If you constantly affirm this desire, you will stay open to new ideas and opportunities. You can stay connected with your true self, and not your false, ego-driven self. Eostre helps us replace stagnation with growth, without being afraid of change.

Gary is 51 years old, and he is always asking himself, "What's new?" He looks for ways to modify his career, cultivate new interests, ponder new ideas, and hang out with invigorating people. He expects to keep this level of growth all of his life.

The Flow of Success

We think the wisdom in the days is about knowing *where* to put your energy *when*. There is great oracle wisdom in letting the universe define the *quality* of energy with which you apply yourself to your goals and your endeavors. (In truth, the universe will always define the quality of your energy, but with oracle wisdom, you will know what it is!)

So, as you see, the secret is to stay in the flow of success. State your intention, do the work, and then release it all to the greater good for all of us. Have hopes and dreams, but also take time to stay in the moment and enjoy life as it unfolds. Then, assuredly, you will find the source of perpetual wisdom.

The Least You Need to Know

- Mayan time was cyclical, nature-based, and uncannily accurate for predicting what Mayans needed to know.

- The urge to track the movements of the sun and stars was born of the desire to understand the inner workings of the universe.

- The zodiac as we know it is based on the ancient concept of little, benevolent animals who watched over us. Today, we can use these figures as archetypes to gain insight into our personal characteristics and the workings of the universe.

- Use oracles to pay closer attention to the natural rhythm of time, and you will deepen your intuitive sense of the quality of your energy.

- Use oracles to know where to put your energy when—to practice perfect timing.

Chapter 18

A Vision in a Dream

In This Chapter

- Myths, dreams, archetypes, and symbols
- Cultivating your dreams
- Dreams and destiny
- Visions and altered states

Such dreams the prophets of the ages had! Chariots of fire that descended from the sky. Glittering staircases that led to heaven. The face of God surrounded by white woolly hair, wearing white robes and holding seven stars and seven golden lampstands. How glorious! Dreams predicted famines, droughts, floods, wars—even the end of the world. Dreams predicted prophetic meetings and prophetic births.

Our own dreams and visions provide opportunities for inner exploration and oracular wisdom. In this chapter, we explore techniques for nighttime dreaming, lucid dreaming, and even trances to help you discover the power of the subconscious mind.

The Nighttime Voyage

The Babylonians and Assyrians may have been the first to keep track of their dreams, carving them into clay tablets and collecting the interpretations in books. The Greeks built more than 300 shrines to serve as dream oracles. When Egyptians sought divine guidance on their nocturnal journey, they would drink an herbal concoction before sleeping. When they awoke, they would tell their dreams to a priest, who would interpret them.

In the East, particularly in Buddhist and Hindu thought, the dream state was a consciousness similar to what we might experience after death. Many cultures believe that when we sleep, we enter a parallel world. Dreams are often depicted in ancient art as a voyage across the water, from the shores of the material world to the realm of the soul.

Dreams provide a map of our subconscious minds. Psychologist Carl Jung believed that dreams were filled with ancient symbols—many of them universal to the human experience. He called these archetypes. Jung believed that these symbols were the subconscious mind summoning us to heal our psyches. Our dreams were trying to tell us something.

Myths and Dreams

When we dream, it is as if we are fishing in a vast ocean of myths. Jung called this ocean the collective unconscious. Ancient cultures believed dreams were divine revelation, and many modern psychologists see dreams as a way to establish divine contact.

Mythological symbols populate our dreams. Mythologist Joseph Campbell said dreams and myths come from the same place. He said "dream is personalized myth, myth the depersonalized dream." Both are symbolic; both depict the dynamics of the psyche. Dreams are individual; myths are about humankind. The particular details of our daily lives shape our dreams. The obstacles we face in our dreams reflect our unique challenges. The challenges for myths, though, are valid for all of humankind. Campbell put it this way: "Myth is the secret opening through which the inexhaustible energies of the cosmos pour into human cultural manifestation."

Jung wrote about archetypes—symbols or motifs that are universal—that is, they transcend culture or time. The symbols are ancient in their origin, and they populate our dreams.

Dreams that include the archetype referred to as the shadow are especially important because the shadow is unconscious, and repressed or "disowned." It is our dark side.

A Jungian analyst would be looking for the evidence of the shadow archetype in client dreams because this is material that needs to be discussed, owned, and integrated for the client to begin to achieve full self-knowledge. We can't open up to ourselves until we open up to the shadow.

So we share these archetypes, but the *way* in which they appear in our dreams—that is unique to us and only us. That part requires the interpretation. Through examining and analyzing our dreams, we find our own mythic journey.

How to Activate Your Dream World

We all dream. Some of us remember our dreams in vivid detail, whereas others wake up with the vague sensation that they must have dreamed but don't remember them. This vast resource of information is available to you, if only you cultivate it.

Start recording your dreams, even if they are fragments or just vague feelings. You might keep a dream journal on your nightstand, or Gary often recommends purchasing a mini tape recorder that you can keep on your nightstand. You can quickly record your dream and go back to sleep. Sometimes this is easier, because then you don't have to turn on the light and boot up your brain to write it all down. Some people find it easier to get back to sleep.

Tell It Like It Is

Gary lost a good friend years ago, and it had lingered with him that he could have been a better friend. Before his friend died, Gary had blown off an evening meeting to drive out to New Jersey and hang out with him at the shopping mall (a rare treat when you live in New York City). After his friend died, Gary dreamed that he was walking around alone in that shopping mall. Somehow they had gotten separated. Gary felt panic. Suddenly he walked into the food court and saw his friend in the distance. He was holding a Diet Coke in one hand, cradling a bouquet of yellow roses. He was talking and laughing with friends. He looked up, smiled, and waved at Gary. After that, Gary had a sense of peace that he had done the right thing by his friend.

As you prepare for bed each night, state your intention to *allow* yourself to remember your dreams. Our creative dream life doesn't like the direct approach, so we don't tell it what to do. In many ways, it's like a willful child, and will not be ordered about. So instead of imposing authority, you leave your dream life to act on its own. Meditating just before bedtime helps your mind relax and release the stranglehold you have on your thoughts. So take the time to release those thoughts about the day, and let your dreams take the direction they will take.

The Raw Material

Now you are on your way to a richer, more vivid dream life. As you begin to record your dreams, you will undoubtedly notice that they arise from questions you have about what your life will be. Take the classic college test dream, for instance. This one has variations—innumerable variations, from what we can tell—but it might go something like this: you are in the middle of a *really good dream*, but then you enter a college lecture hall and you find out there is a test today, one that you had forgotten or possibly didn't even know about. But you are definitely not ready for this test!

What question formed this dream? Simple: Will I pass this test? Maybe the test is a performance challenge that is playing out in your life right now. But somewhere, deep in your subconscious, you had that question of whether you were prepared, whether you were smart enough.

Dreams are often formed from the very same types of questions you would pose to an oracle. Should I marry this person? Should I take this job? Am I prepared? Am I worthy? Have I done enough? Will I have a child?

MORGAN LE FAYE
RHYTHMS

Morgan le Faye: Making Friends

Our dreams are a way of making friends with our subconscious minds. They help us get acquainted with our innermost thoughts and desires. They help you unlock your own wisdom.

Turning to our Goddess Oracle Deck, let's meet Morgan le Faye, the goddess who dwells in Avalon with King Arthur. In Arthurian legend, Avalon is a land beyond the mists that can only be seen at certain times by certain people. You have to get it just exactly right to make the passage to Avalon.

Morgan le Faye invites us to open to the subconscious mind and trust the information we receive from our intuitive side. Morgan le Faye, like many of the goddesses in this deck, is a triple goddess, the composite of a trio of goddesses called Morrigu—Badb, Macha, and Nemain—representing past, present, and future.

Morgan le Faye mirrors the process of therapy, in which a therapist tries to illuminate the past and gain insight into how it affects the current reality and how to carry learning into the future. She reminds us that the past, present, and future must work together. We are all of these, all at once. She invites us to give the subconscious mind free rein so that we may integrate past, present, and future. Perhaps this is the alignment that allows us to enter Avalon.

The Nature of Dreams

Dreams have made heroes. Take Mohammad, for instance, and his dreams of messages from Allah in the desert. Take Jacob, who wrestled with angels in his dreams and became a changed man. Jacob received an injury in that dream that caused him to limp for the rest of his life, marking him forever by his personal spiritual struggle. After he saw the dream of the angels ascending the staircase to heaven, he changed his name to Israel, and he fathered a nation—the twelve tribes of Israel.

In *Aeneid*, the poet Virgil says Aeneas went down into the underworld, crossing the mythic river of the dead, threw a sop to the three-headed watchdog Cerberus (an offering to placate him) and conversed with his dead father. (If this reminds you of Harry Potter, well … myths are universal!) There, Aeneas had a vision that all things were unfolded to him. He saw his destiny, the destiny of all souls, and the destiny of Rome, which he founded. But mainly, he received great wisdom, gaining a map to all challenges and burdens he might face. According to Virgil, he returned to do his work, passing through an ivory gate.

Our dreams often parallel the hero's journey—the universal mythological formula of a soul's adventure. Even ordinary people have dreams with these qualities: the call to adventure, the refusal of the call, supernatural assistance, crossing the first threshold, falling into the belly of the whale, further initiation, temptations, encounters with benevolent forces, triumph and return. They are everlasting, recurring themes in many dreams, no matter the time or the culture.

We love stories of heroes because we find in them a mirror of our own personal mythic journeys, many of which unfold in our subconscious. The hero is defined as a person who overcomes his personal, local, and historical limitations. Harry Potter, for instance, overcomes being an orphan raised in the cruel household of his aunt and uncle. He overcomes being the target of the evil wizard, Lord Voldemort. Because heroes transcend their limitations, their visions, ideas, and inspirations "come pristine from the primary springs of human life and thought," according to Campbell. That is, they fish in deeper waters. Their dreams and visions arise from original experiences—experiences that have not yet been interpreted.

That is why heroes' journeys often involve images of unknown territory—the dark forest, the world of fire, the endless ocean, Dante's dark wood. When your dreams carry these images, this is a signal that you are unearthing new soil. Let that be exhilarating. Know that you are receiving a call to an adventure. Know that your subconscious is wise: it knows you are ready.

> **Oracle Advice**
>
> As you record your dreams in your Oracle Journal, notice the animals that inhabit them. Sometimes an animal just passes through a dream, but sometimes it figures prominently, giving instructions or even intervening—Lassie style—to steer you away from doom. Take note, too, of the images of nature—forests, rivers, mountains. When you have a collection, examine your dreams for recurring images and symbols, such as an apple. Note recurring themes. Carolyn's sister, for instance, always loses her shoes. Carolyn always dreams of an extra room in her house.

Little Creatures

Dreams are full of disguises, as are myths. In dreams, we are not bound to take the shape of humans, but we can often take the shape of animals.

In one Hindu depiction of dreaming, the god Vishnu is shown lying sleeping on the back of the serpent Ananta, which is shaped like a boat, taking him on a voyage across a river. The painting shows him dreaming as he crosses the water between the destruction of one world and the creation of the next. All manner of creatures inhabit the picture—elephants, fish, dogs, birds.

In one of Mohammad's visions, the angel Jibreel (Gabriel) brought him a winged mule with the face of a woman. Together Jibreel and Mohammad rode the mule into the heavens, where Mohammad heard the voice of Allah, imparting wisdom.

Shamans often assume the shape of animals when they travel into the spirit world. Amazonian shamans often become jaguars when they pursue vision quests. Inuit shamans often take the form of seals or walruses.

In the Morgan le Faye myth, she changes shapes several times in her campaign to charm the hero Cuchulain. When he spurns her affections, she assumes the form of an eel, a wolf, and a red-eared heifer—and attacks him, choosing to do so when he was already vulnerable from injuries received in battle. Both Cuchulain and Morgan le Faye were badly wounded in these repeated encounters. But the story has a happy ending. Later, when he was walking down a road, he encountered an old woman milking a cow. He begged her for a drink, and she did. He bestowed blessings on her, healing her.

Have you ever become an animal in your dreams? Where did the animal take you? Have you ever become an old man or woman—or someone else? Your dreams are trying to take you to new territory—places you could not go otherwise.

> **Wise Words**
>
> A **shaman** is a priest, magician, medicine man, or spiritual healer who has the capacity to influence the spirits of the spirit world. Shamans have the ability to go to the spiritual realm, as well as to change into other beings and take other forms.

Cerridwen: Potion for Inspiration

Cerridwen is a shape changer or shaman, an early British fertility goddess who came to be the goddess of poets, inspiration, and knowledge. She developed a magic potion for her son that would ensure inspiration, conjuring it up in a cauldron named Amen. She used six plants in the potion.

Cerridwen entrusted Gwion Bach to stir the potion, which took one year and a day to make. One day, three drops splashed on his fingers. He sucked his fingers to stop the pain and immediately became possessed of all knowledge. *This is good stuff*, he must have said to himself, so he stole the cauldron and ran away.

CERRIDWEN
DEATH AND REBIRTH

Cerridwen was in hot pursuit, and he changed into a hare. She became a greyhound. He shape-shifted into a fish. So she became an otter. *Oh-oh*, he must have said, *how about I become a bird?* Cerridwen became a hawk. *Finally*, he said, *I will really hide. I will become something small.* He became a kernel of corn. Cerridwen promptly became a hen and swallowed him. The kernel of corn became a fetus in her womb, and she gave birth to the bard Taliesin.

How can you put Cerridwen's story into action? First, make a list of six things that inspire you. What renews you? What invigorates you? Where does your knowledge come from? From where can you seek new knowledge? Who inspires you? What frees your mind? Keep your notes about your recipe for inspiration close at hand so that you may refer to it when you need to enliven your spirits.

Now, let's take a closer look at the shapes Cerridwen takes. Notice that she is tested on land, water, and sky—all realms. When she needs to be fast, she is fast. When she needs to switch gears—from land to water—she does. When she needs to see a great distance—to have vision—she becomes a hawk. When she needs to be clever, she is clever. Her final triumph is consumption—she swallows Gwion Bach whole. Then she becomes pregnant, allowing inspiration to infuse her, to inhabit her very flesh. In giving birth to a poet, she gives generously to the world.

So the qualities she has are as follows:

- Speed
- Versatility
- Vision
- Cleverness
- Sacrifice
- Generosity

Perhaps these were the six ingredients of inspiration, after all! Take a few moments to record in your Oracle Journal the ways in which you have these qualities. In what ways could you cultivate them more?

Visions Across Time

A vision is a dreamlike state you experience when you are awake. Ezekiel's dream of the chariot fire or Paul's encounter with the blinding flash of light on the road to

Damascus are examples of visions. A vision can be the product of a deep state of meditation, hypnosis, or a trance. In some way, you have altered your state of awareness by shutting out other stimuli and going deeper within.

In a vision quest from the Native American tradition, you achieve the altered state of awareness through sensory deprivation such as fasting. Then there is the Toltec tradition, which most people know through the writings of Carlos Castaneda.

Going it alone, going within are common themes to vision quests. After he was baptized, Christ spent 40 days in the desert, during which he was tested—tempted by the devil—and he returned with a new vision. Mohammad also went into the hills, where he received a message from the archangel Jibreel (Gabriel), who told him he was to be Allah's messenger.

What Does It All Mean?

Gary has had clients who report very specific visions or dreams. They have had dreams in which they clearly saw a situation for what it was and were presented a solution. They woke up knowing exactly what to do.

More than likely, the answer was in there anyway. But in the dream state, they got out of their own way and let their minds present the perfect solution. Here's what dreams can do:

- **Provide fresh insights.** Dreams often juxtapose images from your life that can be interpreted in new ways. They often come off as fresh and original because of these odd juxtapositions—which gets our attention. Because they are filled with symbols, and the symbols are often presented quite prominently, they require us to ponder the interpretation.

- **Provide a glimpse of the future.** Dreams lift the veil of time by showing us the seeds of the future in our past. By reorganizing past events in our minds, they allow us to sift back through those events, searching out events that may have meaning in the future. Dreams are full of "day residue," little bits and pieces of your daily life that didn't seem to be significant at the time. But when they bubble up through your subconscious and manifest in your dreams, they are presenting themselves to you in a new way.

- **Provide a wiser discernment.** In dreams, we often react intuitively to the people and figures presented. Said more directly: we easily sense who is friend and who is foe. Dreams present the truth about someone's intentions for us. They also reveal allies and supporters we may have overlooked because they didn't fit our cognitive picture of someone who is here to help. In dreams, we gain the true picture of what is comforting and what is challenging about the present situation.

At Your Peril

It's important to have someone you trust help you work through your dreams, especially if you are facing big life changes or emotional turmoil. That person may be a friend who knows you well and has your best interests at heart, or it may be a trained therapist. Dreams can present our subconscious fears in powerful ways, and it's helpful to have someone at your side to put it into perspective.

Gary is often left with really strong feelings, but no specific images, after having a dream. He has awakened with a strong sense of concern, or compassion, for someone. Or perhaps he has had new insights into what the person is experiencing—insights that he had not had previously. Sometimes he has insights into clients' problems. He may forget the symbolism and may not even remember what happened, but he is left with what was intended for him to be left with: an intuition. It can be that simple: an intuition that is so strong we know it is safe to act.

Here are three examples of how dreams have worked in the lives of Gary's clients.

Coming Home

A man was traveling a lot in his job, leaving his wife home with their son and daughter. One night while he was on a long trip, he dreamed he was walking toward a beautiful young woman. As he got closer, he realized it was his daughter—all grown up! He recognized her, but she didn't recognize him. She was polite, but she insisted they had never met. After this dream, he adjusted his work schedule so he didn't have to travel so much.

Wish Come True

A woman was facing a business decision that involved moving to a larger city. She had a dream in which she saw herself making the decision and it all working out fine. She asked Gary if the dream was wish fulfillment. Gary wondered the same thing. He asked her to talk about what the situation looked like and felt like in the dream. How did the new space look? What was she doing in the space? Did she seem productive and happy? Were her employees there? When the two of them examined the dream from all angles, there was a sense of authenticity that was beyond fantasy. The woman went ahead with the move—and it worked!

Making It Right

A woman was unhappy in a close friendship but didn't know that. But she had a dream about her relationship with the friend in which she was essentially watching her friend talk to her. She saw the friend criticizing her and discouraging her, and she realized how unhappy she was. She hadn't even realized this friend was doing that. But when she thought about the dream the next day, it was clear that the relationship was having a major impact on her life. She began to set new boundaries in this friendship and experienced a change in her own outlook.

> ### Tell It Like It Is
>
> Gary has had married friends tell him they often wake up and realize they had the same dream. Carolyn has noticed that she and her boyfriend often have mirror-image dreams. Once her boyfriend dreamed about his children floating away on a hot-air balloon. Carolyn dreamed that a grandmotherly figure asked her if she would take her boyfriend's children to a safe place. We wonder if there is something about sleeping next to someone that allows your subconscious minds to intertwine in the form of dreams!

Open Lines of Communication

The Divine really works through our subconscious minds. It's possible that our subconscious may be in constant, active communication with the Divine. When we don't pay attention to our intuition or listen to our dreams, we may miss what the Divine is trying to say to us. So open up to your dream oracles.

The Least You Need to Know

- Our dreams are the place where myths and archetypes converge with our subconscious minds.

- To cultivate your dream life, hold on loosely. It's not about dictating or censoring your dreams; it's about allowing the information from your subconscious to bubble up.

- Visions, which are received in a more wakeful state, often produce dramatic, life-changing action.

♦ Dreams provide a glimpse of the future or allow fresh insights about your future because they often juxtapose unrelated information, presenting it in surprising ways.

♦ Though dreams can be murky and the details can elude us the next morning, they more often than not leave us with strong feelings that hearken us to the call of the subconscious.

♦ Because dreams alert us to our feelings and our concerns, we can use that information to be more mindful of taking care of ourselves and our relationships.

Part 5

Everyday Oracles

Let's get practical. In this part, we take oracles out of your quiet place and into your everyday world. You can use oracles on-the-fly, accessing flashes of wisdom just when you need them. We show you how to use oracle decks and other on-the-go tools. We also show you how you can try oracles in real life, applying them to heal and deepen your relationships. Then we look ahead to the next horizon: in what ways will oracles help us meet our challenges? How will they shape our future?

Chapter 19

Using Oracle Decks

In This Chapter

- Choose the deck that's right for you
- Oracles as role models; oracles as journeys
- Setting up your reading
- Understand the questions, understand the answers

Decks of oracle cards such as the Goddess Oracle Deck published by U.S. Games Systems, Inc., which we have used to illustrate this book, can be a fun and clever way to get snippets of insight into your life. There are many oracle decks out there, ranging from the mystic to the mythic, from contemporary pop psychology to ancient wisdom.

Oracle decks can be a way to gain daily insight. You may use them for readings to ponder deeper questions. You may use them for instant inspiration and encouragement. Or you may use them as tools for meditation. All in all, you may find your cards a handy, compact dose of insight.

Just for You

With so many to choose from, you are bound to find the one that's just right for you. To find any of the decks in this chapter, turn to Appendix A.

Many of them accompany books, and any books to which we refer in this chapter are listed in Appendix B. Here's a sampling of what's out there, beyond the Goddess Oracle Deck:

- **Celtic Tree Oracle.** The 25 cards in this deck represent the Celtic tree alphabet called Ogham. This deck is for you if nature resonates for you. Each card represents the spirit of a tree or plant.

- **The Phoenix Cards.** The emphasis of these 28 cards is on past lives. The images on each card depict past world cultures, using symbols to trigger awareness of past live consciousness.

- **Archangel Oracle.** This deck of 45 cards represents 15 angels from various traditions, and it's written by Doreen Virtue, author of *Angel Medicine: How to Heal the Body and Mind with the Help of the Angels* and many other books about angels. This oracle deck is for you if you like the gentle wisdom of angels. Virtue also has these oracle decks: Healing with the Angels, Saints and Angels, and Magical Unicorns.

- **Healing with the Fairies.** Also from Virtue, this 44-card deck draws upon the sweet and gentle power of fairies to help you with self-confidence, relationships, health, and career.

- **Archetype Cards.** This set comes from Caroline Myss, author of *Sacred Contracts: Awakening Your Divine Potential* and other books. She uses the concept of archetypes in her writings, as a way to gain insight in the stories that shape our lives. In recognizing which archetypes influence the agreements you make, she says, you are liberated from the limitations that hold you back from your most sacred path.

- **Tarot Cards.** A good source of insight about how to use tarot cards is Angeles Arrien's book *The Tarot Handbook: Practical Applications of Ancient Visual Symbols*, or Arlene Tognetti's books, including *The Complete Idiot's Guide to Tarot*. Arrien takes a psychological, mythological, and cross-cultural perspective on the classic tarot archetypes.

- **Cards of Alchemy.** This deck of 50 cards uses the ancient art and science of transmuting base metals into gold.

- **The Druid Animal Oracle.** This deck contains 33 cards and lots of background on sacred animals.

- **Lord of the Rings.** If you liked the books and movies, this oracle set is for you!

♦ **Moon Oracle.** This deck of 72 cards is a way to get in touch with your inner currents of wisdom through lunar astrology. The cards represent eight phases of the moon with 28 moon mansions and 12 goddesses.

This is just a start. You can get as esoteric as you want to get, delving into anything from water crystals to tea leaves.

Tell It Like It Is

"Angels help you retrace your steps to heaven," Karen Goldman writes in *Angel Voices: The Advanced Handbook for Aspiring Angels*. Angels appear as oracle messengers throughout history—most often for some highly important tasks. Think about the archangel Gabriel appearing to Mary to tell her she would give birth to the Christ child. Talk about casting someone on the path to heaven! Goldman describes angels as lighting new paths and "closing the distance between that which you are and that which you can be."

A Message from Your Contemporaries

Another kind of oracle deck is the cards that accompany self-help books. If you have read a book that provided great insight for you, this kind of deck is an excellent way to continue to access the wisdom. These decks take bits and pieces of the writings of the author and put them in succinct form on a deck of cards. Here's a guide to some of our favorites.

♦ **The Four Agreements.** This deck of 48 cards from don Miguel Ruiz derives from the book of the same name. The book provides a powerful code of conduct based on four agreements: 1. Be impeccable with your word. 2. Don't take anything personally. 3. Don't make assumptions. 4. Always do your best.

♦ **Inner Peace.** This deck of 50 cards is from Wayne W. Dyer, author of *The Power of Intention* (which also has a companion deck). Each card contains an affirmation.

♦ **Power Thought.** This deck of beautifully illustrated cards comes from Louise L. Hay, author of *You Can Heal Your Life*. Each card contains an affirmation on one side and a visualization on the other. Hay encourages positive self-talk as a way of healing yourself physically and emotionally. She emphasizes being on guard against thought patterns that can cause illness.

- **Self-Care.** This 52-card deck comes from Cheryl Richardson, author of *Take Time for Your Life* and *Life Makeovers*. Each card is oriented to an assignment in self-care.

- **The Power of Now.** Eckhart Tolle, author of *The Power of Now* and *Stillness Speaks*, emphasizes staying in the present moment in this deck.

At Your Peril

Don't let your oracle card readings become an excuse not to pursue your goal. If you find yourself asking the same question again and again, each time with a different oracle, let that tell you something. Are you stuck? Are you seeking resources of knowledge outside of yourself? Remember that the intuitive wisdom you access through oracles is just part of the picture.

Beyond decks, many meditation books include a thought for each day. Many religious traditions have 365-day devotionals that provide a prayer or meditation for the day. There are many writings that come from the recovery community that provide daily meditations to keep you on track. Melody Beattie, who has written quite a lot about co-dependence, has a book of meditations.

Likewise, creative artists offer daily meditation books. Ones we like: Julia Cameron, *The Artist's Way*; *Walking on Alligators*, a collection of thoughts from various writers; or Judy Reeves, *The Writer's Retreat Handbook*.

Your Personal Path

Choosing the deck that's right for you can be about logic, intuition, or a little bit of both. You may want to choose archetypes because you have liked working with the archetypal figures in the Goddess Oracle Deck, and you are intrigued by our discussion of archetypes. But maybe you want to try something different—angels, fairies, or the archetypal figures in the tarot (which closely mirror the Jungian archetypes of the trickster, the wise man, and others).

You may also have a specific application. Maybe you are interested in improving your romantic partnership. So the Soulmate Oracle may be exactly what you need. Or if you are interested in activating your creativity, you may turn to The Artist's Way. If you seek physical healing, you may find the best fit in Louise L. Hay's deck. If you are charting a new career path, Caroline Myss's archetypes may be just right.

Ancient and modern-day oracles can give us guidance. Ancient oracles can provide inspiration and awaken us to aspects of ourselves that we have been unaware of or kept hidden: compassion, creativity, personal power. Counselors and therapists and inspirational authors can help us sort out our feelings and fears, and help us open to what's next. Business and career experts can help us develop practical strategies. Spiritual advisers can help us make a deeper connection with the universe, so that we can move ahead fearlessly.

Creating an Oracle Experience

Oracle decks can be used in many ways. We'll get you started with three methods we have used, but we encourage you to develop some of your own. Experiment and find out what works for you.

Here are three basic methods:

- Oracles as anchors
- Oracles as role models
- Oracles as journeys

Anchors: Daily Insight

A one-card reading can provide daily insight. You pull a card at random from your deck and use it for encouragement. Take a few minutes in the morning to read your card and meditate on what it means for you. Or write about it in your journal.

You might want to carry your daily card with you to work, keeping it in your top drawer or next to your keyboard. Reading a thought or a quote before bedtime can also be helpful. It provides a way to rest our mind and release it from the frustrations of the day. And it can lead to work in the subconscious to integrate it while we sleep. It might even lead to a dream.

Role Models: Life Path

In what ways, exactly, do oracles as archetypes help us? Archetypes point us to our mission in life. On the highest level, they act as spiritual messengers, extending the call.

Caroline Myss describes them as energy companions, the figures that accompany us through life, helping us understand ourselves. She says they shape our lives, calling them the "architects" of our lives. She says that understanding which archetypal energies you most identify with helps you understand the roles of other people in your life.

They can help you understand why you have pursued careers and relationships. They can help you understand the choices you have made that have enriched you or burdened you.

Because all archetypes are part of the universal collective consciousness, you are connected to all other individuals through your archetypes. They are part of our shared experience. So your experience of the Sage archetype connects you with the wise guide archetype in everyone else. Recognizing that there is a little piece of the same archetype in everyone else helps you expand your capacity for empathy and understanding in the people you know.

Wise Words

Transformation is an ongoing process of psychological and spiritual growth, an alchemy of sorts. If life were smooth sailing, it is only human nature that we would stay in place and tread water. It is the challenges of life—the curveballs— that provoke us enough to change. There are oracles all around us—ancient and modern, spiritual, psychological, practical— that can help us turn lead into gold.

Journeys

An oracle reading can reveal to you the steps of a journey. You can set up a progression in time that reveals the growth you may face along the path of *transformation*.

One of the many things that we can thank Carl Jung for is his approach to personality development. Unlike Freud and others, Jung viewed personality development as an ongoing process. Jung believed we face development challenges throughout our lives, and he was the first to identify the midlife change.

A good book on the subject is *Awakening at Midlife: A Guide to Reviving Your Spirit, Recreating Your Life, and Returning to Your Truest Self* by Kathleen A. Brehony (see Appendix B). She is a psychologist and a Jungian analyst, and she uses Jung's archetypes to discuss the midlife transition.

And Away We Go ...

Here are some oracle readings that can get you started. For these readings, you will lay out your cards in certain positions. There are two levels of interpretation: the meaning of the card itself and the position. Cards are dealt at random. As you shuffle your deck, focus on the question you would like to ask your oracle.

Past, Present, Future

Use this reading for a specific situation, something that you are immediately facing. You can use it to define a next step.

Draw three cards. The first card represents the past—the events that have shaped the current situation. It reveals to you your tendencies. How did you create this situation? What was your role in it?

The second card reveals the present and provides insight into defining it. This card will help you see the situation for what it is. Perhaps it is only temporary. Perhaps it is a significant change. This card gives you insight by putting it into perspective.

The third card reveals what is shaping up for the future. Again, you have free will. This future is not a locked-in destiny. You have the chance to shape the future if you take the oracle advice you receive.

A Deeper Look

This reading parallels tarot's 10-card Celtic Cross spread, one of the oldest spreads in history. It allows you to take a really good look at a situation by exploring all the aspects of it. Angeles Arrien does it with 11 cards and calls it the Whole Person spread because it's like a full scan of your consciousness. It collects information about you on all levels—physical, emotional, intellectual, and spiritual.

Generally, there is a horizontal axis of five cards that forms a cross with a vertical axis of three cards (the middle card of the vertical axis is the same card as the middle card of the horizontal axis). To the right of those cards is a vertical column of four cards, sometimes called the staff.

The horizontal cross represents the events working in your life, flowing chronologically from left to right. The vertical axis focuses on who you are and your Higher Power.

Read the Staff cards from bottom to top. This column is sometimes called the Ladder because each card represents a rung on the ladder to higher consciousness.

After you lay out your 11 cards, you begin in the center of the cross, reading it in a spiral. Here are the positions and their meanings:

1. Self—Who you are

2. Situation—Your current situation

3. Challenges—Your challenges

4. Background—Ways your family and background play into your current situation

5. Recent Past—Ways that recent events have influenced your current situation

6. Higher Power—Your Higher Power and how to access it

7. Near Future—A glimpse of what might happen next

8. Issues—Ways that your personal tendencies create issues for you

9. Objective—The goal itself

10. Advice—Recommendations for wise action

11. Long-Term Potential—Possible outcomes if you are more mindful and take advice to heart

Cycles of Transformation

The three cards in this reading reveal three steps toward your goal. They parallel the cycle of nature: birth, growth, decay. Decay sounds dreadful—as though you might lose out on your goal or as though you may attain it and find it not so fresh and lovely. But what it means here is the natural process of your goal reaching maturity and making way for the next big something. This reading shows you how to continue to enrich this aspect of your life through a constant cycle of growth.

Oracle Advice

Continue to take personal notes in your Oracle Journal of all your readings. At this point, you may want to expand your notebook, dividing it by topics paralleling your Nine Wise Ways. Doing so means that you can collect all of your reading relating to one topic—say, love and relationships or personal development—in one place, and you can see your progress. Over time, it's good to see if any of the same cards are popping up frequently. If you keep getting the goddess of laughter or the trickster, you might want to lighten up!

Getting in Balance

This spread of seven cards is based on the chakras, the seven energy centers in the body. It can help you see which of these are spinning strongly and which are weak. It can provide insights into your health, pinpointing certain areas of your body, but it also provides insights on all planes—emotional, intellectual, and spiritual, too. You lay out the cards in a vertical column, moving from bottom to top.

Each card matches a chakra:

- **First chakra: survival and security.** This is the root chakra, centered in the body at the anus. This card reveals information about your roots, your family, your background. It provides insight into your basic survival needs. Some strong fears reside here. You must be assured that your needs are taken care of to achieve balance here. It's often called the allowance chakra because if you do not feel secure in life, you may hold on tightly—and you may not be able to allow change and growth in your life—at least not in dramatic ways.

- **Second chakra: creativity, children, and sexuality.** This is often called the allegiance chakra because it's all about making choices about where your allegiance lies. Whom do you choose for a lover? Where do you pour your creative talents? What are your gifts to the world? This chakra resides in your lower abdomen.

- **Third chakra: power.** This card reveals your sense of where your personal power lies. This is where you establish your will, your self-esteem, your center. When this chakra is healthy, you set good boundaries for yourself. People know where you stand. In the body, the chakra is located in your solar plexus.

- **Fourth chakra: love and compassion.** This card reveals your ability to love. Because love heals all, and love unites, many people believe this chakra is key to achieving balance in all the chakras. Quite naturally, the chakra is centered in the heart.

- **Fifth chakra: expression.** This chakra is centered on your throat, and it's all about how you express your needs. This card reveals your "voice." Are you being heard? Can you say what you mean to say? Do people understand you?

- **Sixth chakra: knowledge.** This card reveals the nature of your knowledge—intellectual and intuitive. It's often called the third eye. The chakra is located in your forehead, about an inch above the eyebrows.

- **Seventh chakra: enlightenment.** This card charts the path to the heavens. The chakra is located at the crown of the head.

A Life Path

This reading is useful if you'd like to look back at your path and see what it all means. It's useful when you are embarking on a new venture and it feels fraught with uncertainty. It parallels the hero's journey.

Draw 12 cards, arranging them in a circle, like a clock, going clockwise. Here are the meanings of the positions of the cards:

1. Call to Adventure

2. Refusal of the Call

3. Inspirational Figure

4. Heeding the Call

5. Crossing the Threshold

6. Belly of the Whale

7. Initiation: Trials and Temptations

8. Renaming: Your New Identity

9. Assignments

10. Triumph

11. Return

12. Mastery or Attainment

Who Are You?

This reading parallels astrology, in which three key signs—sun, moon, and rising—determine your core makeup. Draw three cards to represent each. To know your moon and rising sign, you must know your birth time. You may go to an astrologer for a chart, or you may find a calculator on the Internet that will at least tell you these three key signs:

◆ **Sun.** Your self, your will

◆ **Moon.** Your emotions, your intuitions

◆ **Rising.** Who you are becoming, attributes you present to the world

A Deeper Look: Four Directions and a Center

In the Native American tradition, the world is defined by a center and four directions. The center is where Great Spirit resides. The four directions represent the four key aspects that form your world. In the case of this reading, we will use the four directions to define you—these are the four aspects of you that are what you are really all about. These are what you really need in your life to thrive.

A good oracle deck for this reading is one of the Native American decks, such as a Medicine Wheel Deck.

Draw five cards, one to represent each direction, laying them out to correspond with each direction, with Great Spirit in the center.

1. **East. The Eagle.** Its element is fire, and its celestial spirit is the sun. The direction is manifested in art and writing. The card reveals your creativity.

2. **South. The Mouse.** Its element is water, and it is ruled by the moon. The direction is manifested in music. This direction soothes your heart.

3. **West. The Bear.** Its element is Earth, and the celestial body that influences it is Earth. The direction is manifested in magic. This card reveals your ability to manifest.

4. **North. The Buffalo.** Its element is air, and it is ruled by the stars, particularly the North Star, the star of guidance. This direction manifests itself in philosophy, religion, and science. The card reveals how you define your Higher Being.

5. **Center. The spiritual center.** The element is ether—the cosmic void from which all time and all life began. Its manifestation is spirituality.

Let's turn to the Goddess Oracle Deck for five goddesses who might deepen our understanding of these five concepts. They may give you added dimension to your understanding of creativity or manifestation or just give you images on which to meditate.

- North. Sheila Na Gig was the Celtic goddess of birth and death. She often is depicted in the throes of childbirth. She is about allowing great and higher knowledge to move through you.

- East. Freya, the Teutonic goddess of fertility, had a magic robe of feathers that allowed her to fly. When you think of the eagle, flying into the sun, think of yourself in harmony with the sun that brings you light, that creativity within you that allows you to soar.

SHEILA NA GIG
OPENING

LADY OF BEASTS
RELATIONSHIP

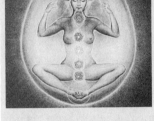

SHAKTI
ENERGY

FREYA
SEXUALITY

HATHOR
PLEASURE

◆ South. Hathor was the Egyptian goddess of love, mirth, and joy. Connect with what soothes you.

◆ West. Lady of the Beasts was a Sumerian goddess. On the card, she is depicted on a throne, attended by lions. Summon the strength of the bear and sovereignty of the lion when you meditate on his card.

◆ Center. Shakti was the Hindu goddess who, through her union with Shiva, created the universe. She is the feminine aspect of the Hindu god. She reminds us that to find the Great Spirit in the center, the creator of the universe, we must embrace all aspects of ourselves, masculine and feminine.

Purpose and Presence

So, as you can see, you can create your own readings for any purpose. Define a general purpose: love, career, health. Choose an oracle deck with which you click. And set up positions so that each card's meaning has an application to your life.

The key step is to get clear on your purpose—whether it's to open yourself to the greater good or understand a direction for your life—then use the cards in a way that supports that purpose.

The Least You Need to Know

◆ When choosing from the many oracle decks out there, choose imagery or archetypes that resonate for you.

◆ You may want to draw upon the writings of contemporary personal-growth authors for oracle decks. Many of them have distilled the key tenets of their books into neat little decks of cards.

◆ A quick, one-card oracle reading can provide daily insight and serve as an anchor of knowledge throughout the day.

◆ Oracle decks can be used for meditation and contemplation, or they may be used for readings.

◆ Oracle readings are structured with two meanings: the meaning of the card and the meaning of the position.

Instant Oracle Wisdom: Answers, Right *Now!*

In This Chapter

- ◆ Portable wisdom
- ◆ Talismans, treasures, and nature's amulets
- ◆ Words from the Hall of Wisdom
- ◆ Royal robes

Sometimes you need answers on the go. A conflict flares up between you and a loved one. Your boss calls a surprise meeting. Or maybe you need an extra measure of patience with your children or with heavy traffic. No matter. Whether it's the office, the golf course, or a busy airport, you can get oracle wisdom here and now.

It's just a matter of making your oracle wisdom portable. With the hands-on tips that follow, you can get answers whenever and wherever you need them. So let's take oracle wisdom on the road.

Wise Words—Anywhere and Everywhere

Oracle messages can come in many forms, as you know by now. But it's not so much a matter of finding the messages as it is being in the right state of mind. That, you have control over!

So seek first the wisdom of your Higher Being, and the messages will follow. Believe me, being a Higher Being and all, He'll know how to find you, no matter where you are. Keep the conduit open to your intuition, and you'll recognize the messages (and messengers) when they come. They may even make sense in an instant, crystal-clear way. The more you practice using your intuition, the faster it will become clearer.

The most vital step you can take, if you want access to answers on the go, is to cultivate that state of receptivity. That means making the most of the oracle wisdom you have already received by keeping it paramount in your mind.

Make a point of beginning each day in communion with your Higher Being. Just have a daily conversation. That may mean spending some time in meditation, prayer, or journaling before your day begins. But spend time giving your inner thoughts to your Higher Being and listening, just listening.

This continual Source of wisdom is your best friend. Your spouse may not want to know it *all*—but He (or She) does! If you know you are facing a lot of challenges in the day ahead, you can ask for special wisdom. And you can even be specific: Ask for it to show up in ways that will get through to you. Acts of kindness, angels, words, music, allies, even superheroes ... if these get your attention, then by all means, say so!

Honor the messages you have received by taking steps to keep them in the forefront of your mind. Starting off your day in meditation is the first step. But carry the wisdom forward by distilling a reading or meditation into one simple sentence:

Today I offer my gift of insight to others.

Today I am open to receiving all the fruits of my labor.

Today I walk through the day letting the light of the Divine shine through me.

Today my heart is open, overflowing with compassion.

Today I will listen to my inner voice.

Today I heed the higher calling for my life.

Or you may have received a flood of insights and want to distill it down to one simple word or phrase that triggers them:

- *Soar*
- *Flourish*
- *Give birth*
- *Plant seeds*
- *Trust*

- *Believe*
- *Know*
- *Be here now*
- *Imagine*

Take a reminder with you so that you will have this idea in front of you many times during the day. Put a Post-it Note where you will see it: on the bathroom mirror, on your computer screen, on your dashboard. Or, take one card from an oracle deck reading and place it where you will think about it from time to time during the day: at the coffee pot, clipped to your wallet.

After you do an oracle reading, like some of the ones we suggested in Chapter 19, you may want to create a visual reminder for yourself, such as a collage. This is especially vital for readings that are on the epiphany level. An *epiphany* is a profound, lasting realization that sparks change in your thinking or your life. If a recent reading was setting off all sorts of light bulbs, if it produced a quantum change in your outlook, you want to keep that wisdom active.

One way to do that is to make a collage, using photos of scenes or objects that have meaning, overlaying some of the messages you received. If there is a contemporary or historical figure who provides oracle wisdom to you or who exemplifies the vision and wisdom that work for you, you may want to include a photo of that person in the collage. You may want to include quotes from this person that resonate for you. Or, by another turn, if there are images that evoke your image of the Divine, such as angels, include those. Or simply include images that produce in you the feeling you had when you received the oracle: peace, compassion, joy.

Wise Words

An **epiphany** is a sudden, significant new understanding. This profound realization often results in the experience of dramatic inner and outer changes. Author Caroline Myss defines an epiphany as "a sudden illumination of our intimate union with the Divine." The Roman Catholic Church celebrates Epiphany on January 6, as the day the wise men arrived to honor the birth of Christ child.

This act of carrying your oracle wisdom forward into your day is all quite necessary, because as the Greeks knew, oracles like a show of gratitude. It shows you are really listening. Take your message to heart.

Talismans and Treasures

A talisman is an emblem of wisdom. The English word derives from the Greek word *telein*, which means "to initiate." The word originates from a religious rite. It also can mean "to complete." So a talisman was an emblem of having completed a religious rite, of having been initiated into wisdom. Generally, it's a ring or stone, and it may have inscriptions or bear engraved figures that symbolize the beliefs of the bearer. In common usage, it's a magical object that wards off evil spirits.

A talisman is something you carry or something you place in your field of vision to keep you touch with the wisdom you have acquired. An amulet is an emblem you wear, a precious stone or a symbol such as a cross.

Small emblematic objects have been used since time immemorial to remind people of the sacred meaning of life. The power behind these objects is the faith of the bearer, no matter what the cultural or religious origin of the object itself. Irish author James Joyce once said, "Any object, intensely regarded, may be a gate of access to the incorruptible eon of the gods." The object may be a shell from a walk on the beach, a Roman Catholic saint, a Zuni bear fetish, a little Buddha statue, or a precious stone. Let your faith define it.

Stones of Life

The placement of stones was one of the earliest human attempts to connect with the Divine. The origin of this natural impulse to seek a connection is probably in the belief that the earth itself was the body of the goddess-creator. Rocks and stones were believed to be the bones of the goddess. Stonehenge, of course, is the most magnificent of these ancient wonders, but there are countless little stone monuments scattered throughout the British Isles and Europe. The menhirs (tall, upright stones) at Carnac, in Brittany, France, are several thousand—yes, thousand—gigantic uncut stones arranged in 11 orderly rows. How gigantic? Some are estimated to weigh as much as 250,000 pounds.

Another area of fascination is the *living stones*—enormous boulders poised on the point of another rock. The slightest bit of pressure will sway the boulder, but if you pushed hard with all your might, you could not budge it. One of the most notable living stones is the Gygorian stone in the Strait of Gibraltar, known as the Rock of Gibraltar.

In India, *lingam* and *sakti* stones are held sacred. Lingam stones are polished stones from the Narmada River, and you may know them from *Indiana Jones and the Temple of Doom*, because that's what they were all looking for. The lingam is the symbol of the Hindu god Shiva. Because it is a phallic symbol, it is associated with regenerative power and it signifies a point of creation and enlightenment. Where you find the lingam, you'll find the yoni, the symbol of the female genitals. In Amarnath in the western Himalayans, a lingam is formed every winter by dripping water that freezes, drawing many pilgrims.

There even may be a reference to a lingam ceremony in the Bible. In Genesis, the Hebrew patriarch Jacob performs a ritual of pouring milk or oil on a stone with sacrificial intent. Jacob woke in the morning, took the stone he had used for his pillow, set it up as a pillar, and poured oil over it. He set the pillar in the place where God had spoken to him and named the place Bethel.

Allusions to the sacredness of stones pop up everywhere in the Christian faith: the rock of refuge, the rock upon which the church of Christ was built, Jesus as the cornerstone, David's five smooth stones, the rock Moriah upon which the altar of King Solomon's temple was built, the white stone of Revelation. Then there are the tablets on which the Ten Commandments were inscribed, the original of which were believed to have been traced by the very finger of God.

The Greeks and Romans also placed great significance on stones. They often would acknowledge the sanctity of stones by placing their hands on a stone pillar when taking an oath. And they used stones for divination. Helen of Troy is said to have predicted the destruction of Troy by reading the stones.

Because stones are unchanging, immovable, and eternal, they made an appropriate emblem of the Divine. How can you make use of them? One, by carrying with you a stone that has deep meaning for you, perhaps because of where you found it or because of qualities it possesses. Another is by visiting stone monuments and gardens. Or build your own stone monument in your yard, on your balcony, or on your personal altar. Take a few moments to explore their personal meaning for you, examining how the stone defines your concept of Supreme Creator.

Gems and Other Precious Objects

Gems, minerals, and precious metals also connect us with sacred wisdom. The Egyptians believed they were vital in sending the dead off to the spiritual realm, and they adorned their mummies with gold, jewels, and amulets to invite good spirits and ward off evil ones.

Zuni fetishes are animal figures carved into semiprecious stone. They are hand-carved, and they represent the spirits of animals or forces of nature. The Zunis are a Southwestern Indian pueblo tribe, and the tradition originated from discovering naturally formed stones that resembled people or animals. They were believed to be the forms of ancient animals or people turned to stone. The fetishes have a spirit force that can help or hurt the bearer, if treated properly. The six most common animals represent the four directions, the upper world, and the under world: mountain lion, north; bear, west; badger, south; eagle, sky; mole, underground; wolf, east.

Tell It Like It Is

Zuni fetishes have a spirit force that guards the bearer, and they are used in Native American kiva ceremonies. Fetishes often carry an arrowhead or a bundle of coral or turquoise tied to the back of the animal. These are offerings. Some fetishes have an inlay of coral or turquoise heartline that runs from the mouth to the center of the body. This heartline represents the lightning bolt of the Great Spirit.

Rings in particular were believed to have magical powers. Plato describes a ring in the second book of his *Republic* that could make you invisible if you turned the stone setting inward. Other magical rings were believed to give you good health. In one legend, Apollonius of Tyana extended his life to more than 130 years because he had seven magical rings given to him by an East Indian prince. The Pythagorean signet ring bears a five-pointed star and is a symbol of health. Disciples of Pythagoras wore this ring, with the inscription in Greek of YTEIA or in Latin of Salus, both of which mean health. In many cultures, when a king wanted to make sure his messenger was recognized as an official representative, he sent the messenger with his signet ring, which was engraved with special inscriptions or emblems.

Then there are good, old-fashioned charms. Carolyn's daughter received a kit to make charm bracelets for her sixth birthday. The charms were all kinds of symbols to cheer a little girl's heart: angels, kittens, bows, puppies, butterflies, and shoes. Sometimes your daily reminders can be just this simple: a few of your favorite things.

Lance Armstrong "Live Strong" bracelets—those sunflower gold rubber bracelets—abounded the year he won his seventh Tour de France and retired (maybe!). It's the perfect example of a contemporary amulet. It reminds us that we are in a fight against cancer, and because Gary works with many people facing illness, it keeps him mindful of why he does the work he does. Armstrong is a powerful, wise man who confronted his illness and triumphed over it, not letting it steal his dreams. By wearing a Live Strong bracelet, Gary remembers to have the same optimistic, can-do attitude.

Even rabbit's-foot charms, which were popular in the 1950s, were amulets. So were fuzzy dice that hung from rearview mirrors, or troll dolls in the 1960s or mood rings in the 1970s. And do you remember pet rocks?

Buddhist teacher Thich Nhat Hanh suggests carrying a pebble in your pocket. Each time a thought about suffering enters your mind, he says, reach into your pocket. Cup the pebble in the palm of your hand. Say, "I am angry. I suffer." Then: "I am doing my best." Finally: "Please help me."

Many religious traditions use beads to focus their prayers. Tibetan Buddhists use mala beads, with each bead drawing a mantra or affirmation. Christians, particularly Episcopal and Orthodox, use the rosary with 33 beads; Muslims use a strand of 99 beads, reciting all the names of God.

Tell It Like It Is

If you're hesitant to use amulets and talismans because you reject the idea that we are subjects to the whims of fate or susceptible to the wrath of evil spirits unless we ward them off, then we can't blame you for not wanting to jump in. But another way of looking at amulets is that they keep the most important thoughts prominent in our minds—our highest and most empowering thoughts. They can become more like affirmations of what we *do* believe and what we *do* embrace. They can close the gap between aspiration and belief.

Bast: Bejeweled Wisdom

Bast is the Egyptian cat goddess, and she ruled fruitfulness, playfulness, music, and dance. She is often depicted as a cat, and sometimes wearing jewelry. Like fuzzy dice, flamingoes on the front lawn, or mood rings, she reminds us to be playful.

BAST
PLAY

Bast reminds you to take a mini vacation. It might mean a brief trip to the ice cream shop in the middle of the afternoon, or it might mean a quick call to a friend to tell a joke. She reminds us to give ourselves a mental break from the day-to-day intensity of life, to give yourself a moment that is just for fun, or just for you. Bast nudges us to go away for the weekend. Gary is allergic to cats, so he admires Bast from afar.

Egyptians and Their Amulets

Perhaps no other culture has left us with as many clues about their beliefs and practices as the ancient Egyptians. By equipping their mummies with amulets with which to pass into the afterlife, they told us a lot about them. Here's a quick summary, compiled from sacredtexts.com, much of which came from *The Egyptian Book of the Dead:*

♦ **The heart.** The heart was the seat of the power of life, but it was also the conscience. The Egyptians guarded it after death with special care, mummifying it separately and replacing it with an amulet. (If you'll remember from the goddess Maat in Chapter 16, hearts had to be weighed in the Hall of Justice.) Many heart amulets were made of carnelian; some were made of lapis lazuli.

♦ **The scarab.** Heart amulets were not enough; that just got the deceased back to zero by keeping away the spirits that plundered hearts. So the Egyptians also put stone scarabs with their mummies because of the scarab's remarkable powers. The scarab gave new life and existence to the bearer.

♦ **The buckle.** The buckle was from the belt of Isis, and it was usually made of carnelian, red jasper, or another red stone. This amulet brought the protection of the blood of Isis, who raised her husband Osiris from the dead.

♦ **The vulture.** This amulet brought the protection of Isis. In each talon, the vulture held the ankh, the symbol of life.

♦ **The collar of gold.** This amulet gave the deceased the power to free himself from his swathings.

♦ **The papyrus scepter.** Made of mother-of-emerald, or a light green or blue porcelain, this amulet restored the bearer to strength and vigor, healing the wounds he received in life.

♦ **The soul.** This was a hawk with a human head, and it was usually inlaid with gold and precious stones.

♦ **The eye of Horus.** This amulet is one of the most common. It was made of gold, silver, granite, hematite, carnelian, lapis lazuli, porcelain, or wood. The eye of Horus brought strength and health.

♦ **The ankh.** As discussed in Chapter 13, this was the symbol of life.

♦ **The shen.** This amulet represented the sun's orbit, and it represented eternity.

Blodellwedd and Sedna: What's Holding You Back?

Of course, the time when we need wisdom on the go the most urgently is when we have made a mistake or suffered a setback. For answers about how to handle that, let's turn to two goddesses in the Goddess Oracle Deck, Blodellwedd and Sedna.

Blodellwedd is a Welsh goddess who was married to Llew, but she had her eye on Gronw Pebyr. She divulged the secret to Gronw Pebyr of how Llew could be killed. Her father, Gwydion, sentenced her to death and turned her into an owl.

BLODELLWEDD
BETRAYAL

SEDNA
VICTIM

Sedna was an Eskimo goddess who was the mother of all sea creatures. One of many legends says that she fell in love with a bird spirit, then spurned him. Her father attempted to rescue her from the spirit, but he got frightened and threw her overboard from a boat. She tried to climb back in, but her father cut off all her fingers, and those became all the sea creatures.

One shaman ritual with Sedna is about taboos. When a taboo is broken, she takes the women's sewing materials and casts them over the seals so they can't be hunted. A shaman is called in to perform a ritual that brings her forth. When she possesses the shaman, all the other men hold on to him tightly. During the moments she possesses him, it is safe for all the men to confess their breaking of taboos. After this is complete, her hair turns silky and smooth, and she returns to the sea. The light returns to her eyes, all sea storms subside, and after four days, it's okay to hunt again.

Blodellwedd is the betrayal; Sedna is the victim. Most of us have played both roles in life, and Gary finds they are common themes in relationship therapy. Clients may feel that others betray them, or they may feel guilty that they have betrayed others. This is not always betrayal in the traditional love relationship sense, but betrayal in terms of, for example, a mother facing illness feeling that she is betraying her children by breaking her promise of being there for them.

And the victim role is so predominant in our society that it has probably achieved its own archetype status. We live in a society in which crying victim has a lot of associated rewards. If we are a victim, we don't have to be responsible for ourselves. We can sue in the courts and get big bucks. We can cover our own bad behavior by crying victim first.

At Your Peril

Just because you can find oracle wisdom anywhere and everywhere doesn't mean that it is. If you find yourself decoding license plates for oracle messages, maybe you have gone too far. As always, the test for oracle wisdom is to keep your eyes focused on your Higher Being and listen to your intuition. When you do that, the right sources of wisdom come to you at the right time.

To be the victim is to give up personal responsibility, which is disempowering. This is what Gary emphasizes with clients, whether they are having relationship problems, facing illness, or having problems at work.

A victim requires a betrayer. If betrayal is your worldview, you give everyone around you a degree that they may not deserve, or even want. And if we seek to betray others, we bring betrayal to ourselves. Karma is a boomerang.

If victim and betrayer are themes for you, then this is an opportunity to look at yourself, your relationships, your worldview. It is an invitation for change. Heed their mistakes, and let those be words of wisdom: How might you not be living up to your word? To your true values? To your highest purpose?

The Robes of Success

In high school, Gary had a coach who wore the same sweater to every game. He joked that it was his lucky sweater, because he had worn it on the day of a big game, and the team had won. Many of us have clothes that make us feel more powerful, more in our element. Maybe they make us feel more professional, or sexier. When we want to feel that way, we don these clothes. The 1980s were the decade of the power tie, but we weren't the first people to know that to swing things your way, you had to dress the part of success.

When Carolyn was forging her way ahead in the mostly male newspaper world, she and a female colleague would use the expression "putting on the war paint" to describe the ritual of putting on makeup and getting dressed for work. They were sharing tips about how to manage their bosses and present their work at meetings and get heard, and the war paint—how they appeared—was a vital element of how they came across. The expression refers to the warrior brave going into battle, but it could just as easily refer to the Broadway actor or opera singer.

Prophets and seers, kings and knights—all of them had their rituals of getting ready to receive wisdom. The conditions had to be just right. The ritual of communion in the Catholic Church is a ritual about preparation—preparing one's heart to receive God's wisdom.

... and into the Beyond

We have just barely scratched the surface, but you get the idea. Come up with your own ideas about what anchors you and calms you—or gets you in the warrior frame of mind. Yoga's warrior poses bring forth your power. Mountain pose brings forth your strength. Mandalas can be a great resource for mini meditations. Music can have a calming effect, with chants or drums. And sometimes, a simple candle can light the way.

The Least You Need to Know

- ◆ Stay each day in a sense of communion with your Higher Being, and your oracle wisdom will be instant and on the go.

- ◆ When you receive an epiphany, keep the wisdom active by making a collage or recording it in your journal.

◆ Carry a talisman or set up a shrine in your field of vision to keep in touch with wisdom you have inquired.

◆ Ancient stones are awe-inspiring examples of the ancient people's desire for wisdom.

◆ The Egyptians used amulets to guide the passage of the dead into the afterlife.

◆ Robes and garments—the clothes you wear, the look you accomplish—prepare you for wisdom by putting you in the right frame of mind.

Chapter 21

Loving Oracles

In This Chapter

- Attracting love
- Choosing someone just right for you
- Navigating conflicts
- Grieving for a relationship that must end

Love is one of life's great and magnificent mysteries. It's the little emotion that takes root in the soft soil of forgiveness, that blooms with the sunlight of gratitude. It requires sunshine and sustenance, and in return, it provides us with the same. This complex emotion defines much of who we are. Many of us identify ourselves as husband or wife, father or mother, son or daughter. We are defined by *who* we love, and the *way* we love shapes our unique imprint on the world.

Still, love as we might, we don't always understand love. We may be concerned with attracting a soul mate or selecting someone who is just right for us. Or we may need help in rejuvenating a relationship, navigating a conflict, or healing a broken relationship. When it comes to love, we need all the wisdom we can get.

Love and Life

For this chapter, we have developed a series of hands-on oracle readings that you can use to ask your most vital questions about love. But you will find that you can easily adapt these exercises for just about any area of your Nine Wise Ways. Many of the techniques for attracting love are the same for attracting health or wealth. Many of them apply to being authentic and purposeful and making good choices. So after you develop a structure for a reading, you may want to apply them to other areas of your life.

Your State of Mind

As you know, the most important element that shapes a reading is your own state of mind. We have discussed that in previous chapters, but here is a quick checklist that you can run through before developing a reading for yourself.

- Clarify your intention.

- Clear your heart and mind. Empty yourself of distractions.

- Examine your reasons for asking.

- Summon gratitude for the wisdom you are about to receive.

- Honor yourself wholly—strengths, weaknesses, and all those little quirks.

- Honor your Source. Spend a few minutes acknowledging the kindness and wisdom of the Divine.

- State your willingness to be open.

- State your willingness to let go of old thoughts and old ways.

- State your willingness to let go of dictating the outcome.

The best way to ferret out any impurity in your preparation is to start by brainstorming your question. Spend 10 minutes doing a free-write in your Oracle Journal about your question. Let yourself go deeper and deeper into the question. Write without questioning or judging or evaluating. Ask yourself why you need this or want this. Ask yourself whether it's a need, want, or desire. Go ahead and let yourself prescribe the solution. ("If only such and such would happen, then I would be happy ….") Then ask yourself *why* that would make you happy. The only way you can let go of the outcome being just exactly that is if you understand you have the attachment. Many people find that their original question only got them halfway there—that they needed to shoot higher, ask for what they really wanted.

At Your Peril

Be wary of "stacking the deck" when you set up an oracle reading. If you *really* want your relationship to work and you'll do anything to make it work, you may set up a reading that will perpetuate your personal mythology that the relationship is meant to work, if only you try harder. By the same token, if you have already decided you're outta there, your reading may be skewed to confirm that decision. If so, then reframe your request: "Because I have decided to leave this relationship, please show me how to do it respectfully and gracefully."

Structuring Your Reading

Although there are a thousand and one ways to structure a reading, two key elements define one: the positional meaning of the spread and the style of the oracle deck you use, which we discussed in Chapter 19.

We have identified a few major styles of spreads that you might use for love oracles or any other area of your life, but it's really easy to come up with your own customized readings. Define the positions, or meanings, for each card in the spread.

- **About you.** Design a spread that gives you insight into developing qualities in you.

- **About you and someone else.** Design a parallel spread of cards that sheds light on the qualities in you, comparing and contrasting them with someone else. This shows you how the two of you interact.

- **About your desired goal.** This helps you analyze an existing situation or define an ambition.

- **A quick read on the situation.** Use a three-card past, present, and future reading to get a snapshot of a current situation.

- **A full analysis of a situation.** Examine yourself, the key players in a situation, and the unfolding of events in a comprehensive way. Usually this involves 7 to 12 cards.

- **A progression.** This kind of reading maps out the steps to success with your goal. It's a chronology of the journey ahead.

- **About the issues.** Name the issues for your situation. Each card represents insight about that issue.

Your Soul Mate: Three Miles Ahead

If only the signs were so obvious … If only your soul mate could stand, like those people greeting business associates at the airport, holding a sign that said, "Over here! I'm your soul mate." Or, even better, if you could mapquest the location of your soul mate—3.2 miles north, 1.3 miles east, one block past the library ….

But it's not so easy, and that's what these readings and exercises are all about. Here, we focus on what to do to attract a soul mate, but these exercises also work for rejuvenating a long-term relationship.

It's all about attraction. Whether you have yet to meet your soul mate or whether you have a soul mate but you feel like you are off his or her radar screen, it's about lighting up the screen. It's a cliché to say that to find love, we must first love ourselves, but it is true.

Gary has seen so many people try to be a person they believe other people will love. Or, he has seen people meet someone, then try to live for them. Often, when he discusses this issue with clients, he will use the analogy of taking a photograph. Some people look their best in a photograph when they are not posing but just being themselves. You are much more attractive when you are just living your life and being who you are. If someone is worth being involved with, you want them to love the real you, not the pose you take for them.

That said, love doesn't just come knocking on your door. It does take effort, including the work on yourself to really come into your own. You have to work to complete yourself first, to establish your life's direction, instead of waiting for someone else to complete you. Find your path, and you will find someone whose path converges with yours.

So our first reading looks at how complete you are in your Nine Wise Ways. If you are like most people, you are a work in progress. You may be mostly complete in one area but still have some incomplete patches. It might be useful to remember experiences you have had where you were complete, or incomplete. By complete, we mean: Is it clear what your purpose is? Do you absolutely, positively know what your path is? You may want to use your Oracle Journal to write about this little dialogue with yourself. From there, set an intention for your reading. Make some notes about what each card tells you about your path in this area.

Love _____

_____

_____

_____

Prosperity _____

_____

_____

_____

Career/Calling _____

_____

_____

_____

Family and Community _____

_____

_____

_____

Home and Hearth _____

_____

_____

_____

Well-Being _____

_____

_____

_____

Creativity _____

_____

_____

_____

Learning/Self-Actualization _____

_____

_____

_____

Spirituality _____

_____

_____

_____

Inspected by No. 37

This reading assesses the qualities in you that are attractive to a soul mate. Brainstorm a list of your qualities that make you supremely qualified to be someone's soul mate. Kindness and honesty come up a lot, but be specific about your own brand of kindness. Write in your Oracle Journal about it. How do you define kindness? How have you recognized it in others who have loved you? How have you failed to recognize it in others?

Narrow your list down to five attributes you have that would be attractive to a mate. Then identify two challenges you face before you are truly ready to meet him or her. Deal out five cards vertically on the left, two cards vertically on the right. Contemplate each card and meditate on how it applies to your life. What surprised you? What intrigued you?

Aphrodite: Radiating Love

APHRODITE
LOVE

Aphrodite, from the Goddess Oracle Deck, is a good card to contemplate when you are at this juncture—whether it be to attract a soul mate or stir up a new attitude in an old soul mate. As the Greek goddess of love, she exudes love. She was irresistibly beautiful, and she was filled with passion for life. She wasn't afraid to show her *radiance*. She held nothing back. This goddess wasn't worried about boundaries. She lost nothing by giving it all away, because she was so abundantly full of love. Her love and passion exceeded the bounds. It was overflowing.

Wise Words

Radiance is the quality of being bright or brilliant, sending out rays of light. It can also mean showing pleasure, love, or a sense of well-being. Radiance issues from a source of light. When we talk about being radiant in relationships, we mean letting the light of the Divine shine through you.

Call upon Aphrodite for radiance. When you are radiating an openness to love, you, too, are irresistible. And don't worry: radiating like this is not indiscriminate. Yes, you'll attract a lot of interest, but the truth is, those who are not functioning authentically and with integrity will not sustain their interest. Being real, being full of beauty, being committed to a higher path—it's dazzling; but if it's not what they are looking for, if it's more than they can handle, they will move on. Radiating, then, is sort of a spiritual game of adverse selection. Radiate your highest self, and those who are not there yet will not stay in range.

Aphrodite inspires us to make a point of practicing gratitude and generosity. Make gratitude a daily practice. Be thankful for your gifts and for the joy of life. There is nothing more attractive than a person who is generous with his or her money, time, or life spirit. When we are focused on giving, we take the focus off of ourselves and place it on others. We worry less about what we are going to get—in this case love, or maybe just a few dates—and instead we focus on making the world around us a better place. Being giving can replace the anxiety of not having a lover. Instead, what flourishes in your heart is a sense of oneness with the world.

Tell It Like It Is

Sometimes Gary recommends volunteer work to his clients because it takes them out of themselves. Gary has seen it make a dramatic difference in their happiness and their inward focus. One caveat, though: if you choose volunteer work with the goal of meeting people to date, that puts you right back on the hunt. Instead, find something meaningful to you, something that makes the most of your skills. Choose the cause you are most concerned with and focus on that.

When you are at ease with yourself and the world, you vibrate differently. You begin to attract people who are vibrating the same way, who are also centered. And isn't that what you want?

Mr. (or Mrs.) Right

Carolyn's father had a favorite line he used whenever anyone complimented him on his four daughters (and as a deacon in the church and financial adviser who taught workshops, he often had audiences for his one-liners). Over the years, he got used to people coming up to him and exclaiming how lucky he was that his daughters were so beautiful. He was quick to laugh that he had nothing to do with it, making fun of his lack of hair or lack of thinness, and he was quick to give away his secret: Easy. Just marry the pretty girl.

It's all in the selection. When you are looking for someone to share your life with, do you know what you want? Do you want someone who will bring out the best in you? Do you want someone, as did Carolyn's father, who will have strengths (beauty) in areas that you don't? Or maybe you just want someone with good relationship skills. And then again, consider what role this person will play in your life. Are you looking for a friend, lover, partner—or all of the above?

When you are choosing a relationship, there are two prime considerations: who he or she is and how the two of you are together. Ah, the chemistry question ....

Our first reading is about *who* your person is. Brainstorm a list of qualities you'd like to find in a potential soul mate. Distill it down to the most essential seven. Do seven cards for each of these qualities.

Our second reading is about how compatible you are with your soul mate. It examines how each of you perform in the roles you play in the relationship. The five roles are Friendship, Partnership, Lovers, Skills, and Leadership. The first column of five cards is about you, evaluating the way you perform in that role. The second column of five is about the object of your desire.

Navigating the Rough Spots

Everyone's incompatible, or so says a minister Carolyn once knew. What he meant by that is we all have rough edges, and those come out when we are in a relationship with someone. And no matter how compatible we think we are with someone, we will inevitably find those jagged places that don't quite fit, and we will have to find a way to bridge the divide. That, the minister said, is the spiritual assignment: to find a way to come together even when you see more differences than similarities.

When you hit a conflict in a relationship, it can feel like you have fallen into a void. You might feel empty, or abandoned. You might feel a little bit crazy. Or you might feel lost—the thought of not having this person in your life might make you feel displaced. Major conflicts in a vital relationship can feel as though the foundation of your life is crumbling.

This is a time when you need all the wisdom you can get. Instead of a reading, we suggest you go within. It's time to dig deep. You might try one of the techniques we have suggested in previous chapters—a technique that touches your soul like going for a nature walk or drumming. Conflicts in a relationship can be healed when we examine our most vulnerable parts, and some of the techniques we have mentioned allow you the contemplation and introspection that get you there.

> ## Oracle Advice
>
> Try designing and/or coloring a mandala as you contemplate your relationship. Begin by giving this relationship to your Higher Being. As you work, contemplate questions such as these: What is this situation trying to teach me? What would bring greater joy to this relationship? What part am I playing in this challenge? What quality would most prepare me for working this out? What or who would support me in being more loving to my partner? What do I need to be more aware of when we talk it out? What should I consider before making a final decision?

Drumming or chanting have a way of letting wisdom in sideways. You are not going straight on toward the goal of wisdom. Instead, you slow down, and just let the wisdom come to you as it comes.

Many couples institute regular, loosely structured ways to stay connected. Date night is one idea, where you just go out on the town, but another variation on that is a walk-and-talk, where the couple commit to setting aside time just to walk together, talk, and listen. Another is the full-moon dinner—which involves going out for dinner every full moon, knowing that on that night you have a commitment to really be present to each other. Make this a carved-in-stone commitment. Set up ground rules that you won't invite other friends and you will make sure you have a baby-sitter for the kids. It's comforting to know that your "someone else" considers the relationship so important that he or she will give you undivided attention. Actually, it's quite exhilarating. That's what dating is, really, and why it's so exciting: you know that someone is waiting and wanting to spend time with you.

When you do this, you build up relationship points. You stock the reservoir with love and trust. If something does come up and you have to cancel, or if you bump into friends at the restaurant and you invite them to your table … it doesn't matter so much because most of the time—11 full moons out of 12—you have spent time with just each other.

Knowing that you have your partner's attention at a specified, known time—knowing that you have that commitment—can come in quite handy when you need to navigate a conflict. Buddhist monk Thich Nhat Hanh, in his book *Anger* (see Appendix B), suggests coming together on Friday evenings to heal conflicts. Let's say something comes up on Tuesday. It feels fatal to the relationship. Your partner may respond angrily, and he or she may not even seem to hear your feelings. But you both agree that you will talk about it on Friday evening.

This commitment has an amazing effect. One, you can stop stewing about it. (True, not necessarily right away. You may have to stew about it all through Wednesday.) But sooner or later, you will let yourself soften. You will remember that there are a lot of love points in the reservoir. You may even remember kinder things your lover has said in the past, and those may counterbalance the angry words. Two, you can be assured that your lover has committed to hearing your feelings—and to working it out. Three, there is comfort in knowing there is a process. There are rules. This is how we deal with things.

Healing with Family, Community

Acknowledging that you have different styles can be one of the first steps toward healing, whether it's with your lover, your family, your family of origin, your co-workers, or your community. When it comes to family of origin, differences in styles can be magnified to such a degree that family members stumble again and again over issues. That's because our family members want to see us in the same way they saw us growing up. It's not about wanting to hold you back. It actually comes from a very loving place. They are afraid that if you change, you will grow away from them.

Harriet Lerner points out in her many practical self-help books about relationships (*The Dance of Anger, The Dance of Intimacy*; see Appendix B) that many of the patterns that develop within families are about protecting family members from the knowledge that we have changed. It's threatening to think that someone we love might be different. Maybe, we think, we will lose them.

Or if you are the one who has changed, and other family members are telling you this is unsettling through subtle or overt ways, then you may feel the pressure to crawl back into the mold so that they will love you the way they always have. You may only be subconsciously aware of the grave emotional risk you take if you announce to your family that you are different. But then again, what if you took the leap of faith and did say, with a loving heart, "I'm different from you, but I still love you."

Part of the discomfort and distance you feel when family members, co-workers, or community members subtly convey pressure to conform so you will be loved is their fear that you are judging them because you have chosen a different ethic for your life.

What if you let them know that while you might be a little unconventional, you absolutely love their preservationist values? Or what if you let them know that while you follow the straight and narrow, you kind of admire their free-spiritedness? For about 99 percent of the people on this planet, this information will be a relief! *You mean you don't judge me! You mean you* like *me!*

When you need healing with a family member, co-worker, or community, you might try an oracle reading that helps you understand the other person's motivations. Make a list of five qualities in the other person or the group that you find baffling. If the person has come across as judgmental, noncommunicative, combative, inflexible … whatever, add it to the list. Then distill your list down to five qualities.

Now, take the oracle deck of your choosing and deal out the cards in two parallel vertical rows of five. The first column is the person or group you are dealing with. The second column is you. Each card within the column represents one of those qualities. Your question may be how you understand that quality in the other or practical roll-up-your-sleeves skills for dealing with it. By examining the second column, you will get a look in the mirror. What qualities of judgment or inflexibility exist in you? What is your reflex when you encounter combativeness or shutting down in another person? Believe it or not, it's different for different people. Some people see combativeness in another, and it fires them up. Others see combativeness and wisely run for cover.

Grieving: When a Relationship Must End

Sometimes a relationship must end. The hard part, sometimes, is knowing what we already know. Carolyn remembers praying fervently for her marriage *not* to end. She poured this intention into every prayer and meditation available to her, including prayer cards at her church that she diligently filled out every week, knowing that it meant someone else would pray for the exact same thing, just as she had requested.

One night she was talking with her sister, and she just couldn't understand why God (her name of choice) wasn't giving her a clear answer. Her sister (who perhaps is quite near to qualifying as an angel oracle herself) said that God loved her too much to leave her in the dark like that. Maybe you already have the answer, her sister suggested. Her sister asked her to search her heart. Right after Carolyn did, she found an answer, an answer that she didn't want to know: *I can't change him. I can't live with him the way it is.* Carolyn was in the emergency room with unexplained abdominal pain when she heard this voice. The oracle message came to her clearly as if the elevator doors of the hospital opened and God himself was standing right in front of her speaking the words. (We love it when it's this clear!)

It's important to take the time to let yourself grieve the end of your relationship. Go ahead and indulge yourself. Let yourself be sad. Let yourself be angry. Let yourself have fantasies about what it should have been. It's only when you let yourself acknowledge your hopes and dreams for the relationship, painful as they might be, that you can heal.

Take complete analysis of the relationship with an oracle reading that is based on tarot's Celtic Cross similar to the one we introduced in Chapter 19.

Oshun: Love and Comfort

OSHUN
SENSUALITY

Oshun, one of the goddesses in the Oracle Deck, is known as the Queen of the Sweet Water among the Yoruba people of Africa. She sometimes is known as the Lady of Charity. Oshun is the one to whom you turn when you have loved and lost, or simply when you are struggling through a conflicted relationship. She is the conduit for comfort. She provides what is needed, and she makes the way a little easier.

Oya: Cry Me a River

OYA
CHANGE

Oya, also a Yoruba goddess, rules violent rainstorms. Her husband disappeared. Later she learned he committed suicide, and she was so aggrieved she sent a tumult. She cried and cried until she became the River Niger.

Oya reminds us that grief is about transformation. Transformation? Change? You may say, *I don't want this. I didn't ask for this.* Neither did Oya. She did not say, *gosh, it would be so nice to become a river. I would feel so much better. All the pain of losing my husband would go away if only I could become a river that nourishes the earth. That is what I have always wanted to be.* Oya, we can assure you, did not have any other aspirations other than restoring the life she knew. But she let herself feel the sadness, and in allowing it, she became something new.

The Power of the Third

Author and spiritual teacher Marianne Williamson often talks about the power of the third—a third entity that brings a wiser sense of love and compassion to relationships. Every relationship needs this mystical third entity to guide forgiveness and healing. This mystical third person—the Divine—helps us transcend our limitations. Oracle wisdom is the threshold for communicating with the mystic third entity.

The Least You Need to Know

- The factors that determine the nature of a reading are the positional meaning of the cards and the meaning of the cards themselves.

- Your state of mind, more than the positions you choose or the deck you use, determines the quality of your loving oracle reading.

- Oracle readings about relationships can be about you, about your loved one, or about the situation.

- Use oracle techniques such as drumming, chanting, journaling, or nature walking to gain perspective and insight about your relationship.

- Use parallel oracle readings to understand how your style differs from your soul mate's.

- Use extensive oracle readings to examine the end of a relationship so that you deepen your understanding of it.

Chapter 22

The Future of Oracles

In This Chapter

- ◆ The end of oracles?
- ◆ The marriage of science and spirituality
- ◆ Know thyself: why oracles are still relevant
- ◆ Vision for the future

Will we ever get too smart for oracles? After all, even the Greeks retired their booming enterprise at Delphi after a few centuries. At one point, Plutarch, who served as a priest at Delphi, argued in *The Obsolescence of Oracles* that the gods had abandoned the oracles.

Is it possible that someday science can explain all this, and there will be no more mysteries to explore? Will we ever get over the desire to find patterns of meaning in everyday life? Will we ever relinquish the thirst to know the future? Or is it possible science alone cannot satisfy us? In this chapter, we examine what the future has to offer.

The Man (or Woman) Who Knew Too Much

In *Paradise Lost*, John Milton wrote that the oracles were "struck dumb" upon the birth of Christ. Instead of mysterious pronouncements, puzzles, symbols, dreams, and visions, the world had a clear, true voice. No more ambiguity. No more leaving a little to guesswork.

And then in the twentieth century, with the rise of science, we came to expect that all phenomena could be explained with verifiable scientific proof. In the twentieth century, humans invented airplanes, cars, movies, computer chips, and nuclear bombs, to name just a few. Contemporary theoretical physicist Stephen W. Hawking once said that we are near the end of the search for the ultimate laws of nature.

Then again, there is what we don't know. As we have often said, we don't know what we don't know. Sir Isaac Newton was aware that he only discovered a fraction of the vast ocean of knowledge. He said, "I do not know what I may appear to the world; but to myself I seem to have been only like a boy playing on the seashore, and diverting myself in now and then finding a smoother pebble or prettier shell than ordinary, whilst the great ocean of truth lay all undiscovered before me."

Toward the end of the century, scientists began to develop the chaos theory, which seeks to explain what's happening when dynamic systems don't behave in a linear, logical way—when what's occurring appears to be occurring at random. Chaos theory says that one initial, seemingly insignificant effect may determine the way a system unfolds. This is called the butterfly effect, in which the flutter of a butterfly's wings may affect the atmosphere. Suddenly, this theory demanded that science explain more complex mysteries. What it reminded us was that science has yet to explain everything.

Now, scientists are working to prove string theory, which says that the building blocks of the universe are one-dimensional extended objects, rather than particles. String theory is hoped to be the theory of everything, which fully explains and links together all known physical phenomena. Many believe that proving the theory of everything will prove the existence of God, a sovereign intelligence that designed such an elegant universe.

Can religion and science explain everything? The way Michael Wood puts it in *The Road to Delphi: The Life and Afterlife of Oracles* (see Appendix B) is "the gods appear whenever we think we know more than a human creature ordinarily could." Meaning: just when we think we have all the answers, the gods appear to say there is so much more. By that reasoning, certainly, we still need oracles! Oracles are still around because, at least occasionally, we recognize that we don't know everything—and we can't.

Jungian author Dianne Skafte has another theory in *Listening to the Oracle* (see Appendix B). She reminds us that the oracles, such as the one at Delphi, were always a little squirrelly. You couldn't just ask direct questions, and you couldn't get direct answers. So you couldn't just ask what would happen in the future. And you couldn't just ask,

"Should I marry this person?" or "Will I win the battle?" This was considered impertinent. When you consider that visiting the Oracle at Delphi was a major life event—just having the money and wherewithal to get there was a feat—you definitely had to get it right. Skafte points out the main focus of a pilgrim to an oracle site was in making a proper tribute to the deity. It was all about being in proper alignment with the Divine. So she says the pilgrimage to an oracle was more about the experience of enlightenment—contact with the Divine.

That numinous experience of the Divine may be what drives our quest for knowledge. And it may be that very soon we will see the convergence of science and spirituality in a qualitative understanding of the Divine. Or not. Perhaps the intelligence is so vast and so elegant that it will always elude capture. But the quest will always be there.

The Marriage of Science and Spirituality

Joseph Campbell argued that it's not science that has cut us off from knowing the Divine. When Bill Moyers interviewed Campbell in 1985 and 1986 for the PBS series *The Power of Myth*, Campbell told Moyers that new discoveries of science actually reunite us with the ancients, and the way they knew the universe. Campbell said we are starting to recognize in the wholeness of the universe "a reflection magnified of our own most inward nature; so that we are indeed its ears, its eyes, its thinking, and its speech—or in theological terms, God's ears, God's eyes, God's thinking, and God's Word."

Take the big bang theory, for example, which says that the universe originated 20 billion years ago with one violent explosion. This theory is accepted by most astronomers today, and most of the world's religions have accepted it as scientific proof of a creation event—when the Divine created the universe. Count among them liberal Christians, the Roman Catholic church, modern Islamic scholars, Kabbalistic Judaism, and certain branches of Hinduism.

Emerging theories such as big bang are spurring some scientists to merge spirituality and science in ways that explain spiritual truths more clearly. More and more scientists, such as those affiliated with the movie *What the (Bleep) Do You Know?* (www.whatthebleep.com), are exploring the limitations of our perceptions, the way our perceptions form our reality and the hidden dimensions beyond our personal reality. Recognizing the limits of our perceptions and the way they shape what we see is a step to *enlightenment*. It's as we have said often: we don't know what we don't know unless we allow ourselves to know it.

Wise Words

Enlightenment is the state of becoming aware of truth, to be free of ignorance, prejudice, superstition, or limited perception. True enlightenment, says Eastern teacher Maharishi Mahesh Yogi, is based on full development of consciousness. He said, "Knowledge is not the basis of enlightenment; enlightenment is the basis of knowledge."

When we seek enlightenment, we open ourselves to new dimensions of knowledge. As German poet Rainer Maria Rilke wrote in his novel *The Notebooks of Malte Laurids Brigge* (Vintage International, 1990), "I am learning to see. I don't know why it is, but everything penetrates more deeply into me and does not stop at the place where until now it always used to finish."

The Mythic Journey

Many of the oracles we have used in this book stem from ancient myths—the goddess oracle, the Greek myths and the Oracle at Delphi, Egyptian mythic gods and their oracles. But modern myths exist and play a strong role in uniting our global culture. Just look at the lines of people waiting for the next *Star Wars* movie or Harry Potter book. Consider the appeal of *The Lord of the Rings*. It's because our technology, our gadgets, are not enough. Our computers will not save us. Our intuition is what serves us. Our intuition tells us there is something more. Even with all of our getting of scientific knowledge, we need myths to explain what technology cannot explain.

And myths are the universal stories, the song of the universe, as Campbell put it. They are the stories that record the human experience. In myths we find the clues to our potentiality. Will that desire to find our highest potential ever go away? We don't think so.

As we move ahead in the twenty-first century, we face many challenges: preserving the environment for our children, grappling with overpopulation and global warming, continuing to modify our energy consumption, living and working and getting along with each other in a global village, the epidemics of cancer and AIDS, embracing diversity of ethnicity and belief systems. We face many personal challenges, too: in the United States, nearly 50 percent of marriages fail. In many other countries, too many children die because they don't receive adequate health care. Even with 6 billion people on the planet, many people face loneliness or a sense of a lack of purpose. Oracles, through myths, present the opportunity to understand and surmount these challenges, as individuals and as a global community.

Intuition: Coexistence, and Now Convergence

In the twenty-first century, we don't rely on prophets to tell us when we must go to war or plant crops. We have elaborate bureaucratic structures—the State Department and the Agriculture Department, respectively—that study various phenomena and collect data to make interpretations about dangerous enemies or calamitous weather.

But even that data must be interpreted, and so intuition still plays a role. Intuition plays a role in all scientific, rational thought, as the origin of creative thought. Intuition is the thing that propels us forward with a theory. In science, there is a principle known as Occam's Razor, which means starting with the simplest explanation. When you see a charred tree, do you think it was burned by the fumes of an alien spaceship or struck by lightning? Go with the lightning. It's the same idea taught in medical school: when you hear hoofbeats, think horses—not zebras.

Intuition nudges us to act on the theory that the hoofbeats we hear are horses. And intuition reins us back in if some other evidence is present that doesn't quite explain that the hoofbeats are horses. Intuition is the nagging doubt that sends us back to the lab, to try the experiment one more time, to explain chaotic, random events that don't fit into a neat order.

Intuition is often described as knowing something without really knowing how you know. But another way of explaining intuition is that it brings forth *all* sensory information from the environment.

Intuition has coexisted with rationalism for ages, a sinuous current just below the surface, but now the two currents are converging, as we are able to explain more and more all levels of information. The more we understand randomness and chaos, the more we understand intuition.

Oracles are the convergence of our desire to seek meaning, the Divine's desire to commune with us, and our openness to all levels of sensory information.

Being the Wisdom

Let us remember the words above the portal to the temple at Delphi: Know thyself. These words greeted pilgrims who had traveled dusty roads from afar, perhaps saving for many years and traveling for many months. And it may be that, just like the mythic hero's journey, the journey itself is the education, and the words above the threshold are the purpose of the journey written in stone. It's possible that the pilgrimage itself to the oracle is the journey of self-knowledge—and that's what it's really about.

We live in a time of unprecedented self-exploration. The goal of self-knowledge is awareness—by being mindful of oneself, one can achieve a state of wholeness. This means embracing all parts of yourself—good, bad, and ugly.

The ancient Christian philosopher Irenaeus wrote that "the glory of God is a life fully lived." That means achieving a state of wholeness, of being complete. To be complete means you are comfortable living in your skin, just being who you are. You accept the aspects of yourself that might be considered faults. You see yourself in the context of a larger sense of life. You are aware of your talents and your unique contributions to the world. You know your true purpose.

Will we ever outgrow the need for that? Jung called this the process of individuation. He said we each have a personal unconscious and a collective unconscious. The personal unconscious contains all of the things we don't want to think about. It is a dumping ground for repressed memories. The collective unconscious belongs to all of us, passed on from one generation to the next. It contains archetypes we have discussed in this book, including the shadow.

The shadow is your dark side, aspects of yourself that you have disowned. For instance, if your family told you it was not okay to be an artist, that side of yourself may reside in your shadow. Individuation is getting in touch with our true selves. Jung thought that we spend the first half of life developing a personality and adapting to the outer world—education, family, children, relationships. During the second half, we focus on the life of the spirit. This is about achieving individuation.

The first act of courage, according to Jung, is to come to terms with our own shadow by acknowledging that it exists. We have to learn to accept that side of ourselves. These aspects of ourselves can be frightening and shameful.

Individuating means accepting your masculine side if you are a woman, your feminine side if you are a man. When we see older men becoming softer or older women becoming more aggressive, this is a sign of individuation. In a world where gender-specific behavior is so important, where we are judged by others as to how masculine we are as men, or feminine as women, it is no wonder that these aspects of ourselves are often not recognized until we are older. At that point, acceptance from others may not be so important. There is a freedom that comes with getting older.

> **Oracle Advice**
>
> During individuation, it's good to have a therapist or a close friend help you. That's because looking at repressed thoughts and desires and memories can be terrifying. We need to be able to acknowledge all of this, over time, without letting it define us. We need to be able to accept that each one of us has a shadow but the shadow is a part of us and not all of us. This is a slow process.

Being individuated means understanding and accepting our true life's purpose. It may be a time of simply accepting who we are and what we have accomplished, but it can also be a time of wanting change, such as a midlife career change. When you understand that individuation is unfolding, it is no longer surprising that middle-aged men want to get more involved with their children and grandchildren or want to leave the corporate world to do something that makes a contribution to society. And it also makes sense that some women want to start new careers or start their own businesses.

Individuation can happen any time in life, not just at midlife. Gary thinks some children are lucky enough to grow up in families where they are encouraged to be themselves and to be open and exploratory. In those families, individuation comes earlier. And it can continue all your life.

At Your Peril

Is individuation another word for self-absorption? Is it a luxury we can ill afford in our security-minded times? Does it detract from a sense of community? Joseph Campbell saw value in the rugged individualism that Western culture—particularly American culture—is known for. The Western emphasis on the individual was quite necessary for the expansion of our collective consciousness, he said. Individualism places a value on the sanctity of every human life—the right to pursue love, liberty, and happiness. With empowered individuals, the collective consciousness grows wiser and stronger.

Oracles and Harmony

Campbell defines sin as getting out of touch with harmony. He believed that the seasonal rituals of religions were vital to keeping us in touch with an eternal core of truth. These rituals reenact the cycle of a Christ figure who comes into the world, teaches us, dies, is resurrected, and returns to heaven. He says we need these ceremonies to keep us in tune with the cycle of time. And throughout time, the human urge to do so is unmistakable. We need to connect with this cycle and understand it, technology and science aside.

It seems unlikely that we will ever outgrow the need for connecting to this cycle of life. When we don't, we are out of balance. Oracles are the script for this cycle, the original manuscript that reminds us of our place in it. When we tap into oracle wisdom, we are retrieving the lines from this script of life—a timeless script that draws on wisdom more vast than the surface of our daily lives.

Who am I, and where am I supposed to go? We don't want to get our operating instructions from the top layer of thinking in our culture. We want an operating system that reveals the timeless mysteries of life. We want a software that gives us a series of clear, logical signals. Campbell described the inner workings of a computer as "a whole hierarchy of angels—all on slats." Isn't that lovely?

Ix Chel: Keep It Flowing

IX CHEL
CREATIVITY

When we continue to seek out oracles, we keep the conduit open to creativity and wisdom. We keep the connection open. We say we want to learn and grow.

Let's turn to Ix Chel from your Goddess Oracle Deck. She was the Mayan goddess of creativity and childbirth. It was her job to protect and nurture the fecundity of women. She presided over weaving, magic, health and healing, sexuality, water, and childbirth. She keeps the waters of creativity ever flowing, and she is often depicted holding the sacred womb jar upside down, from which the waters of creativity flow.

Use Ix Chel when you need to connect with your creative flow. You can meditate on her image when you need to remember to connect with something outside of yourself, to awaken your awareness to the presence of the Divine in your everyday life. If you have been feeling disconnected, you may have lost sight of the need for oracle wisdom. You may have just been skimming the surface of your own wisdom, and you need to go deeper within. We often lose sight of a perspective on the whole of our own lives—that we are not the role we are playing at a particular moment in time—father or mother, supervisor or employee. Our roles change. Our interests change. Our opportunities, potentialities, and possibilities shift as people move in and out of our lives.

Then again, you may be feeling self-sufficient, as though all the knowledge you need is contained within yourself or within the bounds of rationalism and logic. When her card comes up in a reading, she is reminding you to take in information from all sensory levels.

Ix Chel's symbol is the dragonfly, delicate and iridescent. She reminds us that our connection to oracle wisdom is sometimes just as delicate, but also exquisite, when we only let it capture our attention.

Acknowledgment: The Two-Way Street

According to Plutarch, there was another inscription at Delphi: "Thou art." This was the response to the god Apollo's greeting, "Know thyself." It was what the pilgrims uttered in return, acknowledging that God was God. It was like saying, "Amen." It was like saying, "you are who you are, and I recognize you."

To connect to deeper awareness, we must always acknowledge the identity of the Divine. In this book, we have used a term—Divine—that isn't associated with one particular brand of religion. That's deliberate. We want you to identify that for yourself. We wanted to leave room for you to define that. But once you do, acknowledge the force when you encounter it.

Vila: Calling Forth Your Power

VILA
SHAPE-SHIFTING

Vila, from the Goddess Oracle Deck, was a shape-shifting Slavic goddess who was eternally youthful. She ruled the forests, the clouds, and the mountains, and as such, she was able to call forth whirlwinds, hailstorms, and rain. She had long, beautiful hair, and she had wings.

She reminds us of the magnificent power of nature—and of youth. She is the magician who can transform. Whirling winds and swirling rain are her trademarks.

Let's take note of her symbols of power:

- ◆ **Beauty.** She was said to be so beautiful, she left those who encountered her transfixed. Although Vila is about physical beauty, what we are really talking about here is the power to capture the attention of others. In what ways do you do that? Through your talents? Through your gift for words, or for music?

Through the grace with which you live your life? Perhaps your beauty is subtle, an aesthetic that you bring to the way you treat others. Honor the unique ways in which you contribute to the world.

♦ **Wings.** Her powerful wings could transport her through the forests and the clouds—to anywhere she wanted to go. She had complete mobility. What gives you the ability to go places—places not everyone can go? Another way of asking the question is, what are your resources? Maybe you make a good salary so that you can be generous to causes or be generous in your thoughts and actions. Be thankful for your abilities.

♦ **Eternal youth.** She had fresh, enthusiastic energy, untainted by limitations that come with the hard knocks of life. Are there areas of life to which you still bring an innocent, trusting energy? What do you just love? Whatever brings you bliss has the power to transform those things that other people call obstacles.

♦ **A transforming force.** Vila harnessed the power of nature, not for destruction but for renewal and transformation. In what way do you use your personal power? Is it for the purpose of uplifting yourself and others?

A Vision for the Future

Hermes is the founder of Egyptian learning, founder of the healing arts, the author of the arts and sciences and the author of the mystical immortal Emerald. He is often identified with many of the early sages and prophets—an oracle, if you will. According to an account in Brian Brown's *The Wisdom of the Egyptians* (see Appendix B), Hermes had a vision in which the Egyptian god Osiris appeared to him. Osiris introduced himself as "the sovereign intelligence who is able to unveil all things."

Imagine what you would say if presented such a vision. Hermes replied that his desire was "to behold the source of beings, O divine Osiris, and to know God." Immediately, Hermes was plunged into a "delicious light." Then he experienced the presence of all beings. After that, he was encircled in darkness and plunged into "a humid chaos, filled with smoke and a heavy, rumbling sound." From the abyss, a voice rose, a cry of light. A flame shot from the depths, rising to the heavens. A force of order began clearing the chaos, and "choruses on constellations" spread over his head. The voice of light filled infinity.

Osiris asked Hermes if he had understood what he had just seen. He said he did not. Osiris told him the light he first saw was divine intelligence, containing the potential of all things. The darkness was the material world, the world of the flesh, where humans live. But the flame rising from the depths was the divine word. Osiris said, "God is the Father, the Word is the son, and their union is Life."

Hermes was in awe. He was a changed man. He said, "I no longer see with the eyes of the body, but with those of the spirit."

This story from the history of ancient Egypt illustrates that our desire to meet up with the "sovereign intelligence" goes way back. Humans of all forms and all cultures, from all times, past, present, and future, want to encounter that force that unveils all things. That quest is primal. It is eternal. We will always want to know.

Tell It Like It Is

The seven spheres in Hermes' vision compare to the seven devas of India, the seven amshapands of Persia, the seven great angels of Chaldea, the seven sephiroths of the Kabbalah, the seven archangels of the Christian apocalypse. They also relate to the seven colors of the rainbow, the seven chakras, and the seven notes of the scale.

Hermes asked how it was possible that he could see this vision, and Osiris told him it was because "the Word is in thee." Then Hermes asked that he might see the "light of the worlds, the path of souls from which man comes and to which he returns."

Hermes looked up to see the starry heavens, stretched through infinite space, and he was enveloped in seven luminous spheres. Osiris told Hermes that they were the seven spheres of all life. The spheres represented wisdom, love, justice, beauty, splendor, knowledge, and immortality. When someone comes to the upper sphere, Osiris told him, he recovers a vision of divine things and becomes luminous himself, "for they possess the divine in themselves and radiate it in all their acts."

Oracles will always be with us. The desire to know all things is deep within us, burning like an eternal flame.

Hermes never forgot this vision. The memory of that night at the temple of Amen-Ra, under the stars and in the shadows of the pyramids, was a constant and loyal companion. The wisdom he gained there was a consistent strain of inner music to his life. A voice spoke to him, saying, "The soul is a veiled light. When neglected, it flickers and dies out, but when it is fed with the holy oil of love, it shines forth like an immortal lamp."

In looking at the Great Pyramids of Egypt, theologians and scientists have tried to explain how they were built and why they were built. Though they examine the engineering for clues into the Egyptian society and the brilliant minds that created the pyramids, the real question is what urge inspired such a monumental feat.

In *The Secret Teachings of All Ages* (see Appendix B), Manly P. Hall suggests there is only one urge in the soul of humans capable of fueling such a supreme effort: the desire to know and understand the Divine, the desire to exchange the narrow limits of human mortality with the greater breadth and scope for divine enlightenment. In other words, we want to know the Divine. We want to experience the Divine. He defines the pyramids—the place where Hermes dreamed—as the gateway to the eternal.

That same impulse is the essence of the quest for oracles, to find that sacred threshold that unites the mortal with the Divine, to dwell in that space of enlightenment. That's why the future of oracles is limitless. That urge to reach eternity will always be with us.

The Flame of Wisdom

Never let the getting of wisdom flicker out. Always nurture your desire for wisdom—on many levels, through many conduits—with devotion. Seek the wisdom that transcends time and culture. Seek the wisdom that, as King Solomon said, gains understanding. Seek the wisdom that is eternal. And keep the flame burning.

The Least You Need to Know

- Religion and science don't explain everything, and that's why oracles will remain integral to the human experience.

- The urge behind seeking oracle wisdom is to achieve that numinous experience of encountering the Divine.

- As spirituality and science converge, we are gaining an understanding of *how* we experience oracle wisdom.

- One purpose of oracle wisdom is to promote greater self-knowledge and help the seeker achieve individuation.

- To keep the flow of oracle wisdom coming, it's important to acknowledge, with gratitude, the Source.

- Our quest to know and understand a sovereign intelligence will never die.

Oracle Finder

Here's a guide to just about anything oracles—oracle sites, oracle decks, oracle pilgrimages, and even oracles for fun. With a few clicks of the mouse, you could be on your way to more oracle wisdom.

Oracles of the World

Oracle of Delphi. Located in Delphi, Greece. One of the most famous and long-lasting oracles. This was an oracle of Apollo, and the priestess who served as messengers there were called Pythia. Tours are available to the present-day site.

Oracle of Didyma. Located in modern-day Turkey, this city once was part of Greece. This was another oracle of Apollo.

Oracle of Dodona. Located near the small city of Iannina, in northwestern Greece. This was an oracle of Zeus. About.com describes it as the "unforgettable forgotten oracle."

Oracle of Siwa Oasis. About 300 miles (500 kilometers) west of Memphis (modern-day Cairo), the ancient capital of Egypt. This oracle was the home of Amun-Ra, one of the most powerful Egyptian gods.

www.archaeonia.com. An interactive journey through the era of ancient Greek civilization.

www.ancientgreece.org. A comprehensive guide to ancient Greece, including extensive background on the Oracle at Delphi.

news.nationalgeographic.com/news/2001/08/0814_delphioracle.html and www.sciam.com/article.cfm?articleID=0009BD34-398C-1F0A-97AE80A84189EEDF. At these two sites, you'll find out about the scientific explanation for the Oracle of Delphi.

www.isidore-of-seville.com/oracles/12-3.html. This site offers a collection of images from oracle sites all over the world.

www.realmagick.com. A resource and library focused on sharing knowledge in areas outside the purview of standard science, including the priestess oracles.

Pilgrimage Sites

www.nationalgeographic.com. The website of the well-known magazine; sacred sites of ancient oracles and modern-day oracles are often featured.

www.sacredsites.com. A website focused on sacred sites around the world, as well as a wide range of links to related resources.

www.206tours.com/pilgrimages. This site offers pilgrimages and sacred journeys, including trips to Lourdes, France; Medjugorje; Egypt; Italy; and Ireland (to walk the steps of St. Patrick).

www.glorytours.com. This travel agency specializes in overseas tours for Catholics and Christians.

www.1heart.com/pilgrimage.html. This St. Louis-based company specializes in pilgrimages to sacred sites in France, including cathedrals and ancient stones.

www.bodymindspiritjourneys.com/perujun201905.htm. Body Mind Spirit Journeys offers tours to sacred sites around the world for spiritual transformation and personal growth. Trips include Mayan sites, Ireland, France, and Greece. They also offer trips for women only.

www.purplemountaintours.com. These tours are offered by the Purple Mountain Healing Center in Vermont, promising sacred journeys, goddess tours, and soulful travels.

Oracle Decks

For a more detailed guide to tarot decks, go to the American Tarot Association website at ata-tarot.com. Or go to www.usgamesinc.com/newstore/home.php, the source for many styles of tarot decks, as well as crystal oracles and dog wisdom decks. Seriously, this maker of classic tarot cards offers many styles of self-help cards.

Here's where to find some of the oracle decks mentioned in Chapter 19.

Celtic Tree Oracle by Colin Murray and Liz Collins. New York: St. Martin's Press, 1988.

The Phoenix Cards. Reading and Interpreting Past-Life Influences with the Phoenix Deck by Susan Sheppard. Rochester, VT: Destiny Books, 1990.

Angel Medicine: How to Heal the Body and Mind with the Help of the Angels by Doreen Virtue, Ph.D. Santa Monica, CA: Hay House, 1999.

Healing with the Fairies by Doreen Virtue, Ph.D. Santa Monica, CA: Hay House, 2001.

Archetype Cards by Caroline Myss. Santa Monica, CA: Hay House, 2003.

Cards of Alchemy by Raymond Buckland. St. Paul, MN: Llewellyn Publications, 2003.

The Druid Animal Oracle by Philip Carr-Gomm. New York: Fireside, 1995.

Lord of the Rings by Terry Donaldson. Tolkien Enterprises, Inc.

Moon Oracle by Caroline Smith and John Astrop. U.S. Games Systems 2003 (see the U.S. Games website at the beginning of this section).

For sources for the oracle decks from self-help authors, check Appendix B for publishers.

About Archetypes

Archetypes figure prominently in oracles. Find out more about the Jungian teachings on archetypes by checking out these Jungian institutes in the United States:

Los Angeles: www.junginla.org

San Francisco: www.sfjung.org

Chicago: www.jungchicago.org

Boston: www.jungboston.org

About Spirituality

Throughout this book, we touched on teachings from different spiritual belief systems. If you'd like to find out more, here are a few selected sites to get you started:

www.sacred-texts.com. An archive of sacred texts that includes many of those referenced in this book

www.beliefnet.com. A website focused on spiritual issues from a range of belief systems and perspectives

www.zenguide.com. A comprehensive online resource for practitioners of Zen and Buddhism

www.jcf.org. The official website of the Joseph Campbell Foundation

www.godserver.com. A website with extensive links to a wide range of spiritual organizations

www.acim.org. The official website of A Course in Miracles, a spiritual self-study system

Oracles for Fun

www.buttafly.com/starbucks/index.php. Tell this oracle about your favorite Starbucks drink, and this surly oracle will reveal more about your personality than you wanted to know.

www.cs.virginia.edu/oracle. This is the famed Oracle of Kevin Bacon, in which you can link the ubiquitous movie star to any other movie star in just a few degrees of separation.

Appendix B

Resources

Akhtar, Dr. Salman. *Objects of Our Desire: Exploring Our Intimate Connections with the Things Around Us.* New York: Harmony, 2005.

Anderson, Sherry Ruth, and Patricia Hopkins. *The Feminine Face of God: The Unfolding of the Sacred in Women.* New York: Bantam, 1992.

Arrien, Angeles. *The Tarot Handbook: Practical Applications of Ancient Visual Symbols.* New York: Jeremy P. Tarcher/Putnam, 1997.

Berkowitz, Rita, and Deborah S. Romaine. *Empowering Your Life with Angels.* Indianapolis: Alpha Books, 2004.

Bolen, Jean Shinoda. *Crossing to Avalon: A Woman's Midlife Pilgrimage.* San Francisco: HarperSanFrancisco, 1994.

Brehony, Kathleen A. *Awakening at Midlife: A Guide to Reviving Your Spirit, Recreating Your Life, and Returning to Your Truest Self.* New York: Riverhead Books, 1997.

Brown, Brian. *The Wisdom of the Egyptians.* New York: Brentano's, 1923.

Brown, Dan. *The Da Vinci Code.* New York: Doubleday, 2003.

Buxton, Richard. *The Complete World of Greek Mythology.* London, England: Thames and Hudson, 2004.

Cameron, Julia. *The Artist's Way: A Spiritual Path to Higher Creativity.* New York: Jeremy P. Tarcher/Perigee, 1992.

Campbell, Joseph, *The Hero with a Thousand Faces, Second Edition*. Princeton, NJ: Princeton University Press, 1968.

Campbell, Joseph, with Bill Moyers. *The Power of Myth*. New York: Anchor Books, a division of Random House, 1991.

Davis, Jeff. *Journey from the Center to the Page: Yoga Philosophies and Practices as Muse for Authentic Writing*. New York: Gotham Books, 2004.

De Avila, St. Teresa. *The Collected Works of St. Teresa*. Icn Pubcns, 1976.

———. *Interior Castle*. Des Plaines, IL: Image, 1972.

Dyer, Wayne W. *The Power of Intention: Learning to Co-Create Your World Your Way*. Santa Monica, CA: Hay House, 2004.

Flynn, Carolyn, and Arlene Tognetti. *The Intuitive Arts on Health: Using Astrology, Tarot, and Psychic Intuition to See Your Future*. Indianapolis: Alpha Books, 2003.

Flynn, Carolyn, and Erica Tismer. *Empowering Your Life with Massage*. Indianapolis: Alpha Books, 2004.

Flynn, Carolyn, and Shari Just, Ph.D. *The Complete Idiot's Guide to Creative Visualization*. Indianapolis: Alpha Books, 2005.

Foundation of Inner Peace. *A Course in Miracles*. Mill Valley, CA: 1975.

Fox, Matthew. *Creativity: Where the Divine and Human Meet*. New York: Tarcher Putnam, 2002.

Frankl, Viktor E. *Man's Search for Meaning*. New York: Pocket, 1997.

Friedman, Robert Lawrence. *The Healing Power of the Drum*. Northampton, MA: White Cliffs Media, 2000.

Gawain, Shakti. *Creative Visualization: Use the Power of Your Imagination to Create What You Want in Your Life*. Novato, CA: New World Library, 2002.

Gerwick-Brodeur, Madeline, and Lisa Lenard. *The Complete Idiot's Guide to Astrology, Third Edition*. Indianapolis: Alpha Books, 2003.

Gibran, Kahlil. *The Prophet*. New York: Knopf, 1923.

Gilovich, Thomas. *How We Know What Isn't So: The Fallibility of Human Reason in Everyday Life*. New York: Free Press, 1993.

Gleason, Katherine A., and Arlene Tognetti. *The Intuitive Arts on Money: Using Astrology, Tarot, and Psychic Intuition to See Your Future*. Indianapolis: Alpha Books, 2003.

Goldberg, Natalie. *Writing Down the Bones*. Boston and London: Shambhala Press, 1986.

Goldman, Karen. *Angel Voices: The Advanced Handbook for Aspiring Angels*. New York: Simon & Schuster, 1993.

Gould, Joan. *Spinning Straw into Gold: What Fairy Tales Reveal About the Transformations in a Woman's Life*. New York: Random House, 2005.

Hall, Manly P. *The Secret Teachings of All Ages, Reader's Edition*. New York: Jeremy P. Tarcher/Penguin, 2003.

Hanh, Thich Nhat. *Anger: Wisdom for Cooling the Flames*. New York: Riverhead Books, 2002.

Harvey, Andrew, and Anne Baring. *The Divine Feminine: Exploring the Feminine Face of God Around the World*. Berkley, CA: Conari Press, 1996.

Hay, Louise L. *You Can Heal Your Life*. Santa Monica, CA: Hay House, 1984.

Hope, Jane. *The Secret Language of the Soul: A Visual Key to the Spiritual World*. San Francisco: Chronicle Books, 1997.

Jewell, Cathy, and Arlene Tognetti. *The Intuitive Arts on Family: Using Astrology, Tarot, and Psychic Intuition to See Your Future*. Indianapolis: Alpha Books, 2003.

Küstenmacher, Marion, and Werner Küstenmacher. *Mandalas for Power and Energy*. New York: Sterling Publishing, 2003.

Lefkowitz, Mary. *Greek Gods, Human Lives: What We Can Learn from Myths*. New Haven, CT, and London: Yale University Press, 2003.

Lenard, Lisa, and Arlene Tognetti. *The Intuitive Arts on Love: Using Astrology, Tarot, and Psychic Intuition to See Your Future*. Indianapolis: Alpha Books, 2003.

Lerner, Harriet. *The Dance of Anger: A Woman's Guide to Changing the Patterns of Intimate Relationships*. New York: HarperCollins, 2005.

———. *The Dance of Connection: How to Talk to Someone When You're Mad, Hurt, Scared, Frustrated, Insulted, Betrayed, or Desperate.* New York: HarperCollins, 2002.

———. *The Dance of Intimacy: A Woman's Guide to Courageous Acts of Change in Key Relationships.* New York: HarperCollins, 1990.

London, Eileen, and Belinda Recio. *Sacred Rituals: Connecting with Spirit through Labyrinths, Sand Paintings and Other Traditional Arts.* Gloucester, MA: Fair Winds Press, 2004.

Marashinsky, Amy Sophia. *The Goddess Oracle.* London: Element Books, 1997.

McClain, Gary, Ph.D., and Eve Adamson. *Empowering Your Life with Joy.* Indianapolis: Alpha Books, 2003.

———. *The Complete Idiot's Guide to Breaking Bad Habits.* Indianapolis: Alpha Books, 2003.

———. *The Complete Idiot's Guide to Zen Living.* Indianapolis: Alpha Books, 2004.

Myss, Caroline. *Anatomy of the Spirit: The Seven Stages of Power and Healing.* New York: Three Rivers Press, 1996.

———. *Invisible Acts of Power: Personal Choices That Create Miracles.* New York: Free Press, 2004.

———. *Sacred Contracts: Awakening Your Divine Potential.* New York: Harmony Books, 2001.

———. *Why People Don't Heal and How They Can.* New York: Three Rivers Press, 1998.

Piver, Susan. *Joyful Mind.* New York: Rodale, 2002.

Pliskin, Marci, CSW, ACSW, and Shari L. Just, Ph.D. *The Complete Idiot's Guide to Interpreting Your Dreams, Second Edition.* Indianapolis: Alpha Books, 2003.

Plutarch, *Plutarch's Lives, Volumes 1 and 2.* New York: Modern Library Classics, 2001.

Reeves, Judy. *The Writer's Retreat Kit.* Novato, CA: New World Library, 2005.

Richardson, Cheryl. *Life Makeovers: 52 Practical & Inspiring Ways to Improve Your Life One Week at a Time.* New York: Broadway, 2002.

———. *Take Time for Your Life.* New York: Broadway, 1999.

Romaine, Deborah S., and Arlene Tognetti. *The Intuitive Arts on Work: Using Astrology, Tarot, and Psychic Intuition to See Your Future.* Indianapolis: Alpha Books, 2003.

Ruiz, Don Miguel. *The Four Agreements: A Practical Guide to Personal Freedom.* San Rafael, CA: Amber-Allen Publishing, 1997.

———. *The Mastery of Love: A Practical Guide to the Art of Relationship, a Toltec Wisdom Book.* San Rafael, CA: Amber-Allen Publishing, 1999.

Shaughnessy, Susan. *Walking on Alligators: A Book of Meditations for Writers.* San Francisco: Harper SanFrancisco, 1992.

Sher, Barbara. *Wishcraft: How to Get What You Really Want.* New York: Ballantine Books, 1979.

Skafte, Dianne. *Listening to the Oracle: The Ancient Art of Finding Guidance in the Signs and Symbols All Around Us.* San Francisco: HarperSanFrancisco, 1997.

Sontag, Susan. *AIDS and Its Metaphors.* New York: Picador, 2001.

Thibodeau, Lauren, Ph.D. *Natural-Born Intuition: How to Awaken and Develop Your Inner Wisdom.* Franklin Lakes, NJ: New Page Books, 2005.

Tognetti, Arlene, and Lisa Lenard. *The Complete Idiot's Guide to Tarot.* Indianapolis: Alpha Books, 2003.

Tolle, Eckhart. *The Power of Now: A Gateway to Spiritual Enlightenment.* Novato, CA: New World Library, 1999.

———. *Stillness Speaks.* Novato, CA: New World Library, 2003.

Turner, Patricia, and Charles Russell Coulter. *Dictionary of Ancient Deities.* Oxford and New York: Oxford University Press, 2000.

Virtue, Doreen. *Angel Medicine: How to Heal the Body and Mind with the Help of Angels.* Santa Monica, CA: Hay House, 2004.

———. *Healing with Angels: How the Angels Can Assist You in Every Area of Your Life.* Santa Monica, CA: Hay House, 1999.

———. *Messages from Your Angels: What Your Angels Want You to Know.* Santa Monica, CA: Hay House, 2002.

Welch, Suzy, and Jack Welch. *Winning*. New York: HarperCollins, 2005

Williamson, Marianne. *A Return to Love*. New York: HarperCollins, 1996.

————. *Everyday Grace: Having Hope, Finding Forgiveness and Making Miracles*. New York: Riverhead Books, 2002.

Wood, Michael. *The Road to Delphi: The Life and Afterlife of Oracles*. New York: Picador, 2004.

Glossary

ankh   An ancient Egyptian symbol often found in mummy cases and temples. They are the symbol of life, and they are believed to be a precursor to the Christian symbol of the cross.

archetypes   Universal personalities that are common to human experience. Archetypes such as the wise old man show up in myths and in our dreams. Swiss psychologist Carl Jung believed that these symbols were the subconscious mind summoning us to heal our psyches.

centered   A psychological state of remaining calm amid the interchange of your needs, wants, and desires with others' needs, wants, and desires. When you are centered, you choose how much you let external influences change your thoughts and actions.

clairsentience   A state of heightened awareness in which all five senses are operating at their optimum. It means "clear-feeling." This heightened sensory awareness stirs the imagination and activates creativity.

collective consciousness   The thinking layer of human knowledge. It represents the result of the innate wisdom in all of us, the highest and best thinking of all humans.

enlightenment   The state in which we reach the fullest development of our consciousness. In enlightenment, we are freed from the limits of our perceptions and our prejudices.

epiphany   A profound, lasting realization that sparks change in your thinking or your life. It is a sudden, significant new understanding. This profound realization often results in the experience of dramatic inner and outer changes.

hamadryad   The belief in the ancient Gaia mythology that the earth was the mother goddess, that nature and spirit are intertwined. A nature spirit's life is linked to a feature of nature—a tree, a river—and when she dies, the tree dies with her.

integrity   The quality or state of being complete. It means to be unimpaired. When you live with integrity, you live in harmony with all facets of yourself.

intuition   Direct knowing that comes without conscious reasoning. Intuition comes in the form of impressions, inklings, and little glimmers of insight. Some people describe it as instinct, a gut reaction, or a hunch.

metaphor   A figure of speech that makes an implied comparison between a symbol and a situation. Metaphor has the power to illumine a situation in a way that direct language does not.

mindfulness   The state of keeping your mind on what you are experiencing in the present moment. Mindfulness is experiencing life with full awareness, engaging all the senses. With mindfulness, you do not let the thoughts of the past and the future cloud your experience of the here and now.

najt   The Mayan word for spiral. Mayan time is not linear like Western time, with a beginning, middle and distinct end. Mayan time moves in cycles.

oracle   A divine message. An oracle can be the message itself, the person who embodies or delivers the message, or the place where the message is received. An oracle can have one, two, or all three of these aspects.

pilgrimage   A journey made to a shrine or holy place to deepen wisdom. The journey requires preparation of the heart and usually in and of itself provides lasting insight.

radiance   The quality of emanating light. It can also mean showing pleasure, love, or a sense of well-being.

sacred contract   An agreement that defines your overall relationship to your personal power and your spiritual power. You have made agreements with certain beliefs, and those define your energy and how and where you use it.

sacrifice   An act of offering something of value for a higher, more-rewarding calling. An offering of the life of a person or an animal to a deity is a sacrifice. Sacrifice, though, is not defined by deprivation or loss, but rather a barometer of your intention to submit to a higher good.

sanctuary   A place set aside to allow you to focus your heart and mind on the Divine. It can be a refuge, where you seek protection or just quiet, shutting out the dangers and worries of the world. It is a place in which to commune with a higher presence.

selective thinking   A process of selecting out favorable evidence and only remembering that. Unfavorable evidence is ignored to bolster a belief you already have.

shaman   A priest, magician, medicine man, or spiritual healer who has the capacity to influence the spirits of the spirit world. Shamans have the ability to go to the spiritual realm, as well as to change into other beings and take other forms.

skepticism   A philosophy that you must always question the validity of all knowledge. A skeptic is engaged in a constant state of inquiry. A skeptic questions all assumptions.

suffering   A state of experiencing undue pain and struggling against it. Buddhist monk Thich Nhat Hanh describes suffering as the agent of beauty that makes love possible and life meaningful. When you practice *karuna*, or compassion, it helps you suffer less. It transforms the suffering. *Suffering* is like compost, and *karuna* is like the flower. If you know how to make use of suffering, the compost, you can bring about the flower and the beauty.

synchronicity   The phenomenon of two unrelated, disconnected events that occur at the same time, but are interconnected. A synchronicity creates a transcendent truth.

transformation   The ongoing process of psychological and spiritual growth—the challenges as well as the triumphs. It is the challenges of life—the curveballs—that provoke us enough to change.

Zen koans   Paradoxical stories that conclude with a question that a Zen student must ponder. The most famous Zen koan is "What's the sound of one hand clapping?"

Index

Joyce, James, 182
Judaism, biblical oracles, 20
Julian the Theurgist, 19
Jung, Carl, 36, 57, 59, 88, 116, 178, 188, 236, 296
Juquila Virgin shrine, 87
Just, Shari, 95

K

Kabbalah, 19
Kali card, 48-49
karma, 127
    perceptions, 130
Khvarenanh, 19
kindness, importance of, 160
King, Martin Luther, 58, 61, 105, 162
knowledge economy, 63-64
Kuan Yin card, 150
kuten, 18

L

labyrinths, 191-192
Lady of the Beasts card, 261
Lakshmi card, 83-84
Lao Tsu, 92, 159, 163
Lennon, John, 58, 60
Leonardo da Vinci, 60
Lerner, Harriet, 285
Librarian of Basra, The, 63
Life Makeovers, 252
Lilith card, 193
Lincoln, Abraham, 58
lingam stones, 267
Listening to the Oracle, 292
literature, sacred texts, 217-219
living stones, 266
Long Count calendar, 225

Lord of the Rings, The, 294
Lord of the Rings Deck, 250
Lourdes, France, 25, 87
love
    importance of, 275-277
    relationships, ending, 286-287, 289
    soul mates, finding, 278, 280-286
Lovers in the Lilacs, 270

M

Maat card, 216-217
Macbeth, 177
Maeve card, 161-162
Man's Search for Meaning, 105
mandalas, 188-189
Mandela, Nelson, 101, 105-106, 157
Mann, Thomas, 182
Marashinsky, Amy Sophia, 10
Martin, Steve, 16
Marx, Karl, 63
Mary of Nazareth, 20, 25
Matrix, The, 13
Maya, rituals associated with, 35-36
Mayan calendar, 17, 224-225
meditation, importance of, 31-32, 142-143
Medjugorge, Bosnia and Herzegovina, 25
Merchant of Venice, The, 211
messages (oracle), forms, 264-266
messengers (oracle)
    finding, 98-103, 105
    personalization, 108-109
    qualifications, 105-108
    questions, asking, 114-121
metaphor, 217-218
Michelangelo, 88
milagritos, 87
Milton, John, 291
mindfulness
    importance of, 33, 89, 143-144
    practicing, 159

T